A HISTORY OF THE TRADING STANDARDS INSTITUTE

Sponsored by the College of Fellows
Trading Standards Institute

Michael Jeffs
Jim Humble

A HISTORY OF THE TRADING STANDARDS INSTITUTE

Sponsored by the College of Fellows
Trading Standards Institute

Michael Jeffs
Jim Humble

A HISTORY OF THE TRADING STANDARDS INSTITUTE
Sponsored by the College of Fellows
Trading Standards Institute

by Michael Jeffs & Jim Humble

Copyright © 2014
The College of Fellows
Trading Standards Institute
Sylvan Court
Basildon SS15 6TH

ISBN 978-0-901340-78-8

Layout by Cockasnook Books
www.cockasnook.co.uk

Printed by The Russell Press,
Russell House, Bulwell Lane, Nottingham NG6 0BT
www.russellpress.com

Cover illustration:
'The Leet Jury, or Ward Inquest'
George Cruikshank (1792 – 1878)

Contents

House of Lords

Introduction by The Right Hon. Lord Howe of Aberavon CH QC who held the posts of Solicitor General, Minister of State Trade and Industry, Foreign Secretary, Chancellor of the Exchequer, Deputy Prime Minister and Leader of the House of Commons.

I welcome this well-researched record of the history and organisation of weights and measures and trading standards over the past 150 years. It's an equally long time since Anthony Trollope started a novel claiming *"All the English world knows, or knows of, that branch of the Civil Service which is popularly called the Weights and Measures"*. I am not sure it is quite that well known today, but this History will certainly help to show how a relatively small group of local government officers have become the ambassadors of fair trading and consumer protection.

I particularly commend the Institute for its pioneering work in seeking a single system of measurement in the UK – the metric system. And despite an unceasing flow of regulation from Westminster and Europe, I admire the way in which they have been able to adopt and adapt a widening range of comprehensive duties with energy and skill.

They should be proud of their achievements.

I wish them well.

Geoffrey Howe

House of Lords, London SW1A 0PW
Telephone: 020 7219 6986   Fax: 020 7219 0587
howeg@parliament.uk

College of Fellows

The College is delighted to sponsor this History of the Institute reflecting its growth and development over the past 130 years. The College was formed 60 years ago and is a registered charity supporting welfare, educational and research activities of behalf of the membership.
Fellowships are awarded to persons who have made original or exceptional contributions or who have rendered outstanding or distinguished service. The College is supported by donations from branches of the Institute, gift-aided contributions from Fellows and bequests from former colleagues.
The list of contributors to this history is well recognised in the Appendices. However many may not be named or recognised in the text. To those the College apologises. No matter how comprehensive, it can only be a snapshot of key events which have shaped the Service over the years. To those unsung volunteers, whether working day to day to deliver branch activities, sharing expertise on training courses or supporting members as officers or Institute staff, this document stands as a record of their achievement in delivery of a Service of which all can be proud.

Bob Wright FTSI
Chairman College of Fellows 2008 – present

Foreword

The Trading Standards Institute celebrated over 130 years of professional and public service at its Conference and Exhibition in 2013. The annual showpiece now attracts over 1,000 delegates, members and visitors to listen to ministers, politicians, consumers and speakers from business, across an international spectrum. The range of issues dealt with by the modern trading standards service is extraordinary. Its beginnings were in weights and measures, but it now spans an astonishingly broad canvas, from public health and well-being to eCrime, scams and global internet shopping; consumer safety to personal finance and debt; animal health and food fraud to counterfeiting and metrology: a truly comprehensive service which protects consumers and honest business alike.
I am delighted that the College of Fellows commissioned this History because it is a fascinating record of the manner in which the ambitions of early colleagues in 1881 were realised in the modern Institute. We are particularly indebted to Michael Jeffs for his research, many of the Institute records having been destroyed on two previous occasions, by the bombing of the office of our Honorary Secretary in London 1941 and then by the flooding of the Institute Library in 2000, when many valuable documents, records and papers were turned to papier mâché.
This book charts a story of constant development and evolution, but 1968 with the Trade Descriptions Act was probably the time of a great leap forward. Suddenly a quiet, responsible, hardworking, unassuming inspectorate was propelled into the consumer and media spotlight. Complaints originally dealt with in single figures were received by trading

standards departments in their thousands. Advice services blossomed, and trading standards showed it was possible to help consumers with their problems and also give sound and helpful advice to fair and honest trade. The cheats, the sharks, the cowboys were the scallywags.

I am proud the Service was able to gain the trust of consumers, business and government. Report after report praised the diligence and dedication of TSOs, and as a result they were asked to take on more and more functions: on credit laws, on product safety, unsolicited goods, food and drugs, animal health, bargain offers, misleading advertisements, underage sales, explosives, anti-counterfeiting and an unending flow of new legislation from Europe. The downside was that ministers, local authority employers and probably society as a whole expected the service to take on duty after duty with scarcely any increase in resources. The fact that the service was able to cope and bloom is a great tribute to its capacity for innovation: innovation in management, in technology, in enforcement techniques and in uniformity and cooperation.

In parallel with the growth in legislation, the Institute had to forge relationships with many new partners: the Office of Fair Trading, the National Consumer Council, the Food Standards Agency, the Audit Commission, LACOTS, the National Measurement Office, Consumer Focus, the Better Regulation Executive and a plethora of government ministries and their ministers. All this against a backcloth of constant local government change and reorganisation. Some might wish we could return to the economical and effective trading standards services in the big metropolitan authorities in the mid-80s, at which time our consumer protection infrastructure was the envy of the world.

In Europe, the Institute and its members have been a catalyst for greater cross-border understanding and cooperation. The comprehensive nature of trading standards has enabled the service to relate to specialist enforcement services in almost every other European member state. This has led to dedicated Euro-wide market surveillance cooperatives on product safety, food law and metrology – to the benefit of citizens and commerce.

Now Trading Standards needs to chart a new way forward. Public funding cuts are decimating local services, and the Institute is urging government to look at the dire consequences for consumers and business. Trading Standards has a critical role. Nowadays we have a modern confident Institute partnering its members and the new National Trading Standards Board in battling market abuse and consumer fraud. The new TSI is fulfilling roles once performed by government domestically and in Europe. TSI-approved consumer codes now replace those once delivered by OFT.

TSI is now a £3m 'not for profit' social enterprise with a modern membership spanning the private, public and third sectors. As it moves towards a Royal Charter, it continues to demonstrate the ingenuity and inventiveness with which the trading standards service has survived. This History, charting as it does the good times and the bad, gives a most valuable perspective.

Ron Gainsford OBE
FTSI Vice President, Chief Executive TSI 2002-2013

Author's note

Writing the biography of an organisation was a strange undertaking for me. There are no parents to be credited (or blamed) for the achievements (or failures). The organisation was homeless for 90 years but, like many humans, has moved frequently since then, with all the emotion and upheaval of a house-move.

Unlike many people the organisation has had constant principles, aims and objectives since the day of its birth.

After the first two chapters the format follows a fairly standard pattern. The first part of each chapter describes the external factors which were having an impact on the Institute. The second part of the chapter looks at the decisions that the Institute took to further its principles and aims and to provide a service for the community.

It has been a privilege to delve into the stories of trading standards and to meet some of the present day Fellows. Despite various setbacks I hope it is a story faithful to the truth.

Mick Jeffs MTSI

Acknowledgements

To the legions of members, past and present who became actively involved in Institute business and made this history happen. To College Chairman Bob Wright and Registrar Phil Bottomley for responding to the ideas of Chris Armstrong and Jules Golbey, the TSI Librarian. Together, they initiated the creation of this comprehensive and invaluable record.

To Mick Jeffs who wrote the first longer draft of the book. For his painstaking study of agendas and minutes of committees, reports, magazines, journals and diaries covering 130 years of enforcement history – more than eight million words. Mick was Assistant Chief within Warwickshire County Council for twenty-five years; is an enthusiastic local historian and vice-chairman of the patient forum of local hospitals.

To Jim Humble OBE for editing the process and bringing it to fruition. Also for adding his experiences of time spent as CTSO Croydon, the Office of Fair Trading, the Metrication Board, LACOTS, NMCU, NCC; the Methven Committee, the Eden Committee and the Institute Council, covering a period of almost five decades.

To other members of the commissioning team including Tom Philpott, Ron Gainsford OBE, Chris Armstrong and Sandy Driskell (TSI Information Officer), and to other Institute members including Steve Jarvis (Pump Maintenance School) and Peter Nelson (the Association of Inspectors of Weights and Measures). Thanks also to the staff at TSI Headquarters, including Karin Layton, Phil Owen, Bob Shepherd and Jackie Fisher, and to Noel Hunter OBE for his encouragement and advice.

Anthony Trollope (1815-1882) wrote in his book *The Three Clerks*:

"All material intercourse between man and man must be regulated, either justly or unjustly, by weights and measures"

"Weights and measures is a well-conducted public office... that it may be said to stand alone as a high model for all other public offices whatever."

"...so high a level is required at weights and measures, a scale of salary equally exalted has been found necessary."

CHAPTER ONE – Before 1880

Genesis of Trading Standards

Before the Beginning: This chapter reviews some episodes from the history of consumer protection and trading standards. It describes the names and duties of many officials who carried out similar roles to those performed by Weights and Measures and Trading Standards Officers (TSOs) today. There was no formal organisation of inspectors before 1881, although some individuals did give evidence to government commissions in the 19th century. Inspectors were first appointed under the Weights and Measures Act 1835 but did not organise themselves until after the Weights and Measures Act 1878. They were descended from many groups of people who performed analogous roles under different names and within different organisations. However, the origins of the Institute were firmly based in the desire to see justice and fair play between traders and their customers.

In this book reference to the Institute sometimes includes bodies with earlier names: the British Association of Inspectors of Weights and Measures, the Incorporated Society of Inspectors of Weights and Measures, the Institute of Weights and Measures Administration, the Institute of Trading Standards Administration and, of course, the Trading Standards Institute.

The Need for Standards: In early times people shared what they could afford to give away in what is known as a 'gift economy'. In many places the gift economy evolved into a system where people exchanged goods and services in a process we call 'bartering'. In bartering both parties try to negotiate a deal which gives them optimum satisfaction. Satisfaction with the deal depends on the quality and quantity of the goods or services exchanged.

The next stage was for some goods or services to be given to another person where the other party paid money. Very soon trading extended beyond small settlements and commerce between communities began. In Britain the Celts did not have money before 106 AD, but the Romans had used money during the occupation of much of Britain from 43 to 410 AD.

In bartering and trading it was very useful to have a way of measuring the quantity or size of goods and the amount of services. In the case of goods, a means was developed for measuring the weight, volume or dimensions. In the case of services, there may have been a measurement of the size of a field that was going to be ploughed. This measurement was initially carried out on a local basis using units invented locally. When trading took place over a wider area the state and the law began to be involved. Economists recognise that uniformity in the use of weights and measures for trade was second only in importance to a stable currency. Currency was itself often defined by its weight.

Quotations: The importance of accurate and fair measurement was recognised by most civilisations. It is useful to review some of the quotations passed down through the ages.

In the Book of Proverbs in the King James Bible (at 20:10), generally accepted to have been written between the 10th century and the 6th century BC, there is the statement:
> *"Divers weights, and divers measures, both of them are alike abomination to the Lord."*

In the Koran (Sura 21:48), it is said that:
> *"Just balances will be set for the day of resurrection."*

In Britain, the Magna Carta, a decree sealed under oath by King John in 1215, includes the words:
> *"Let there be one measure of wine throughout our kingdom and one measure of ale and one measure of corn, namely the London quarter, and one width of cloth whether dyed, russet or halberjet, namely two ells within the selvedges. Let this be the same with weight as for measure."*

A plaque in Truro in Cornwall erected in 1615 is engraved:
> *"Who seeks to find eternal treasure shall use no guile in weight or measure."*

A much-quoted report given by John Quincy Adams to the Senate of the USA on 22nd February 1821 contains the statement:
> *"Weights and measures may be ranked among the necessaries of life, to every individual of human society."*

As a counterbalance to these enthusiastic statements of support a Bristol newspaper of 2nd November 1878 claimed:
> *"An Act of Parliament comes into force on the first of January (1879) which may take many by surprise and cause no little consternation among the trading classes. If strictly carried out the provisions of the Weights and Measures Act (1878) will make it one of the hardest and most vexatious statutes that has ever harassed the commercial life of England."*

Units and Definitions: A central tenet in the history of measurement is the honesty of descriptions of goods and services, and these depend on sufficiently precise definitions. A logical place to start is by looking at some of the units of weights and measures that have been used. There are many books on this subject including *Metrical Miscellanea*

12

and Muddle by Robert Grice, published by the College of Fellows of the Institute in 2010. The earliest units of measurement of length were derived from the human body: feet to measure distances, hands to reckon height, the forearm for length, and a thumb's width for smaller objects. But these were crude and variable units. Units of weight and capacity measure were even more arbitrary. A unit of weight may be a stone that is comfortable in the hand, with many different systems of measurement developing throughout the world. Some of the earliest were in Ancient Egypt and Ancient Greece.

Units in Britain were a complex mixture of those used by the Romans and the Anglo-Saxons. The pound was brought to Britain by the Romans who called it *libra*, hence the abbreviation lb. The subdivision of this pound was the *uncia* in Latin or *onza* in old Italian (hence the abbreviation oz). 12 of these made a pound. This evolved into the Troy system which was one of a number of systems used in Britain.

A foundation of our system for many centuries was the grain. This was initially defined by the weight of a grain of barley (the grain of wheat is typically about 25% less). We all know that grains vary in weight both from individual plants and because of variation in moisture content. However, this was a basis of our weights and had also played a similar role in other civilisations.

The common everyday unit was the pound, but the question was "what is a pound?" Many were different. There was the Troy pound, the Apothecaries pound that was the same weight but divided into different smaller weights. The pound Avoirdupois became the pound normally in use and this was defined as 7,000 grains in 1824. To add further confusion there was also a Tower pound and a Mercantile pound. The difference between the lightest and heaviest pounds was about 33 percent. Some trades habitually bought goods using one pound which was heavy and sold using another which was lighter.

Units of length were subject to even more dispute and legend. The inch was defined as the length of three barleycorns – the difference in men's shoe sizes even today. The Palm of four inches was in use until around 1820. The foot of 12 inches is actually longer than most human feet. One story is that the yard was the distance from the chest-bone to the fingertips of King Edward I.

The Saxon eln or elne was equal to the length of the arm. The ell was used to measure the width of woven cloth and two ells was about 47 inches. The mile has had many different definitions. A memorable rhyme is that "George the Third said with a smile, Seventeen-sixty yards in a mile". Capacity measurement was usually carried out in units of pints, quarts, gallons and bushels. The pint was roughly a pound of water but, as we have seen, the pound varied in definition.

Standards: The confusion about units and the accuracy of weights, scales and measures led to advantages for devious and crooked dealers. This provoked petitions of protest to a series of kings. Various monarchs repeatedly issued decrees to standardise the units. Edicts were ignored because of the lack of inspection and enforcement.

One of the earliest edicts was made by Alfred the Great, who declared in 876 that the measure of Winchester was to be the standard. King Edgar, King Ethelred and Canute all enacted similar laws.

The Anglo-Saxon laws that required the official stamping of weights and measures remained in force after the Norman Conquest in 1066. Under the new regime of William the Conqueror, it was decreed "that the measures and weights shall be true and stamped in all parts of the Kingdom". Soon after 1066, he commanded that all weights and measures throughout the realm be uniform and marked with his royal seal to authenticate them. He also transferred the standards from Winchester, the administrative capital, to the commercial capital, the Tower of London.

Richard I, the Lionheart, continued these laws. In 1197 he provided standards for every county. However this valiant attempt at standardisation failed due to the strength of local customs.

Magna Carta: The next major trigger point was Clause 35 of Magna Carta, sealed by King John in 1215. As we have already seen, it declared that throughout the realm there should be one measure of wine, one for ale, and another for corn. The London quarter or Saxon seam or pack-load was to be the unit for corn, equal to 8 bushels. There should also be a standard width of dyed cloth, russet, and halberjet, namely two ells within the selvedges. And it should be the same with weight as for measure.

These edicts from Magna Carta were repeated at least ten times in subsequent legislation. From 1266 there were periodic local Assizes of Bread and Ale to fix the quantity and quality of these essentials to daily life. The Assizes regulated the weight of the Farthing Loaf and the quantity of a Penny of Ale. Bread had to be weighed by the King's Standard pound. Bakers or brewers who gave short measure could be fined, put in the pillory or flogged. Around 1300, Edward I declared that standards of bushels, gallons and ells should bear the Iron Seal of "Our Lord the King".

In 1496, Henry VII distributed standards of weights and measures to 43 English county towns. In 1526 Henry VIII outlawed the Tower pound and the Mercantile pound. New standards were made at Winchester, and when the metal for the Winchester bushel was being poured Shakespeare was writing Julius Caesar. The Tower pound had to be outlawed again by Queen Elizabeth. She distributed the standard weights to 57 towns in England and Wales, and these standards were successfully used until 1824 – a period of over 230 years.

The Act of Union 1707 forbade certain of the customary weights and measures in Scotland. There was a Parliamentary Report on Standards in 1758, but no firm action was taken until 1824 when definitions of units were confirmed and new standards were made.

In addition to the distribution of standards of weights and measures, it was necessary to compare them with those which were being used by traders. There developed the practice of providing scales known as the King's Beam, or Trona, in important market towns and in ports to determine duties.

The King's Beams were operated by an official known as a Tronator. The Beam was probably a statera or steelyard rather than an equal-armed beam as we know it today. There was a King's Beam at Truro surviving in 1795.

In 1813, a letter to a grocers' magazine drew attention to the inclusion of the wrapper in the weight of 1 lb of sugar which cost 1s 2d. This was an early example of a practice which was to lead to a long-running campaign by the Institute. The Bread Act 1836 established the only short weight offence in English law. There was no standard weight prescribed for loaves of bread until the First World War.

The Weights and Measures Act 1824 followed the report of a commission in 1821. It was a major milestone, but there was still great confusion and "manifest frauds" because of a lack of local uniformity and enforcement. The preamble to this act set out the need for better legislation in these words:

"Notwithstanding it is provided in the Great Charter that there shall be but one measure and one weight throughout the realm, and by the Treaty of Union between England and Scotland, yet different weights and measures, some larger and some less, are still in use, and the true measure of the present standards is not verily known, which is the cause of great confusion and manifest frauds."

New sets of standards were made following the Act of 1824.

One set of the standards was kept at the Houses of Parliament, but this was destroyed in the fire in 1834 which razed the Palace of Westminster to the ground. Strangely, the standards were not remade until the passing of the Weights and Measures Act 1855. In 1866, maintenance of the primary national standards and verification of local standards was transferred from the Exchequer to the Board of Trade under the management of the Warden of Standards.

New Commissions: A Commission on Weights and Measures in 1838 heard evidence from a number of inspectors including those from Bristol, Clerkenwell and Southwark. It was notable that Inspector Gingell of Bristol was allowed ample time to make criticisms of the law, scale-makers and other inspectors. A total of five Weights and Measures Acts were superseded by the Weights and Measures Act

1835 and this Act was again amended in 1859. Amongst new provisions the 1835 Act outlawed the use of heaped measures and directed that measures of capacity should be stricken or level. The 1859 Act required market owners to provide scales and balances and weights and measures. It also empowered clerks of markets to check the weights of goods.

In 1866 maintenance of the primary national standards and verification of local standards was transferred from the Exchequer to the Board of Trade under the management of a Warden of Standards. In 1867 a Royal Commission on Weights and Measures was appointed. It issued five lengthy reports, concluding in 1870. These eventually led to the Weights and Measures Act 1878 which consolidated many previous Acts and stipulated that Inspectors of Weights and Measures must be appointed by local authorities. This was a comprehensive statute which remained in force until 1963. The Commission also recognised the need to have effective administration of other legislation such as the Petroleum Act 1868 and the Sale of Food and Drugs Act 1875.

Weights and Measures 1878: The 1878 Act was largely a consolidation measure but it contained some new provisions. The early sections deal with lawful units of weight and measure. The 1878 Act defined metric units by reference to Imperial units, for example -

1 metre = 1.0936143 yards (i.e. 1 yard = 0.91439916 metres)
(in 1963 this became 0.9144 metres exactly)
1 kilogram = 2.2046223 pound, lb (i.e. 1 pound = 0.45359243
kilogram) (in 1963 this became 0.45359237 exactly)

Inspectors were required to use the local standards for testing traders' weights, measures and equipment. It was not until 1889 that working standards were allowed to be made and used. The Act dealt with unjust weights and measures but did not create offences of giving short weight or measure. The Act went on to deal with stamping and the verification of new equipment. Local authorities had to appoint a sufficient number of inspectors and each inspector had to enter a recognisance to the Crown in the sum of £200.

The inspectors were given various powers which included entering specified premises and inspecting and testing equipment. There was also a power to seize unjust equipment. An inspector could require weights, measures and equipment to be brought to a specified place at a specified time for testing.

A court was allowed to award a part of a fine to an informer. This included an inspector until an amendment in 1904. The Act also set out the roles of the Board of Trade and local authorities. The Act extended to Scotland with some minor amendments and also to Ireland until 1920.

Standards of Quality: A parallel concern was about the true quality of goods or services. The assessment of quality in early bartering and trading depended on the knowledge and skill of the two parties. The fairness of the bargain was often compromised by the ability of one party to persuade the other to accept his (or her) biased assessment. Some of the first legal controls were on everyday foods that were frequently adulterated or of unacceptable quality. Often quoted is the Assize of Bread and Ale (Assisa Panis et Cervisiae), a decree of 1266 by Henry III. This was a major turning point. The decree gave a specific responsibility for enforcement that will be looked at later. Another early example was the history of hallmarking of precious metals which dates from a statute of Edward I in 1300.

An assize dating 1671 stated that all bakers must have undergone an apprenticeship, that all their bread had to be marked with an individual sign, that they had to produce 13d of bread for 12d (the 'baker's dozen'), and that a 'foreign' baker's bread had to weigh more than that produced by the native bakers of a town. The Adulteration of Food and Drink Act 1860 gave local authorities the right to appoint an analyst (later known as the Public Analyst) to test the descriptions of foods in particular.

Price Control: The selling price of bread was controlled from the twelfth century until 1815. The price was dependent on the price of wheat and that in turn depended on the weather and success of harvests. Under the Weights and Measures Charter of Henry VII in 1497, the prices of 21 products were controlled.

Metrication: Creeping up on all the variety of imperial and customary units of weights and measures in Britain was the metric system. It is generally accepted that the system was first proposed in 1670 by Gabriel Mouton, the vicar of St. Paul's Church in Lyons, France. He suggested a decimal system of measurement based on the length of one minute of arc of a great circle of the Earth (now called a nautical mile, 1852 metres). The first official step was when France set up a commission in 1791 to look at metrication during the French Revolution. In this official system the metre was defined differently as one ten-millionth of the distance from the equator to the North Pole at the Paris meridian, otherwise referred to as a quadrant of the globe. The first French law on metrication was passed in 1799. Many in France did not accept the metric system. For example, Napoleon hated the metric system saying:

"Nothing is more contrary to the organisation of the mind, memory and imagination. The new system will be a stumbling-block and source of difficulties for generations to come. It is just tormenting the people with trivia."

In 1812 Napoleon introduced an alternative system using the names of the old units which were redefined in terms of metric units. For

17

example the metric pound was 500 grams. Other countries adopted similar units. However, the full metric system was restored in France in 1837. An International Metric Commission first met in 1870 and gradually the system began to spread around the world. A Metrication Convention was signed by 20 countries, including 15 in Europe, in 1875. We will see how the metric system fared in Britain in the next chapter and most succeeding chapters of this book.

Scales and Weights: Weights had to be used with some type of weighing machine. The simplest was the equal-armed beam scale and illustrations exist of some of the early examples in Egypt.

Weighing equipment in use in Britain in the Middle Ages included the Balancia, an equal-armed balance, and the Auncel. One definition of the Auncel states it was a scale with many pans, and the word auncel became used as the name for a deceitful merchant. The Desemer and the Bismar also had a moveable fulcrum and a fixed weight, and were forms of Auncel. The Auncel was outlawed in Britain in 1351 (and again in 1359 and 1429) because it was too easy for sellers to mislead or deceive customers. The Libra, an equal-armed balance (see the astrological sign of the same name) has no relation to the scale company of the same name. Trutina was also an equal-armed balance. The Trona was a weighing machine set up in a market place, which was probably the King's Beam mentioned earlier.

An alternative method of weighing without using heavy weights or smaller weights which could easily be lost, was the Steelyard, or Statera, with a fixed fulcrum and with a pan for goods and on the longer end either a pan for poises, which are equivalent in weight to the quantity, or a sliding weight which rests in notches to determine the quantity. It is said to have been named in 1320 from the Yard in Upper Thames Street in London where steel was traded. This is now the site of Cannon Street Station.

The following six inventors are noteworthy because their inventions were keys to the development of more complex weighing machines. Leonardo da Vinci (1452-1519) is credited with the invention of the first self-indicating scale that had unequally spaced graduations. Jean Charles Borda (1733-1799) realised that use of the substitution method overcame errors in the lengths of arms of beam scales. Carl Friedrich Gauss (1777-1855) suggested weighing twice by swapping goods and weights on a beam scale to overcome length of arm errors. Gilles Personne de Roberval (1602-1675, France) designed the Roberval machine that has the goods pans above the equal-armed beam. It was termed a counter machine. Later the inverted Roberval machine was designed. Another style of counter machine was designed by Beranger. John Wyatt (1700-1766) of Birmingham invented the compound lever-weighing machine in1741, and this led to the development of weighbridges and platform machines.

Petroleum: One of the first records of the existence of petroleum was made by Herodotus in 450 BC when a flammable layer was noticed floating on water. The modern industry of extraction and use of petroleum began in the USA in 1859. It very soon became necessary to understand the dangers of petroleum with reference to its flashpoint and various methods of measuring the flashpoint were developed.

The first act to control the storage and supply of petroleum in Britain was the Act for the Safe Keeping of Petroleum in 1862. Further dangers were recognised and a select committee report in 1867 was followed by the Petroleum Act 1871. The Act of 1871 was renewed annually by Parliament until made permanent in 1879.

The main control of petroleum was (and is) by licensing by the local authority with conditions attached to the licence which could be adapted to local circumstances. Inspectors were appointed to enforce the Acts and they had powers of entry and sampling. Over 100 authorities authorised enforcement by Inspectors of Weights and Measures.

Explosives: When the Explosives Act 1875 was enacted, various substances were included in the definition of explosive, including gunpowder and dynamite. The first measure of control was the requirement to register and pay a fee of 1s 0d. This fee stayed the same for over 100 years. It was then necessary to store the explosives and use them in a proper way. Inspectors had powers to inspect storage arrangements.

Measurement and Inspection: We have seen that many monarchs in Britain issued edicts in an attempt to standardise units of measurement. They met with limited success. This was due to the lack of will of local officials, failure to make proper provision for enforcement and/or the action of devious and dishonest traders. At various times different groups and individuals in the community were given, or assumed, roles of inspection and enforcement.

From Anglo-Saxon times, i.e. before 1066, national legislation and local byelaws invested overall responsibility for weights and measures in mayors or lords of the manor or manor courts. In different parts of the country these later became known as Hundred Courts or Courts Moot or Courts Leet. They usually delegated the enforcement duties to a Bailiff, a Constable or a Sheriff. From the 10th century in some counties, the Manor Courts appointed Sheriffs to carry out the duty to require weights and measures to be stamped with their value.

An official, called the Aulnager (or Alnager), was created by Richard I in 1197. This title appears to be related to the name of the unit of measure of the width of cloth which was the Ell. The task of this official was to measure the width of woollen cloth and to fix a lead seal to each roll if it was the correct size. The post was abolished by William III in 1699.

An Ordinance for Bakers, made law in 1250, stated:

> *"No measure is to be made unless it is sealed with the seal of the corporation of the town and inspected by the mayor and bailiffs. ... All measures and yards are to be inspected and carefully examined twice every year. The standard bushels, gallons and yards and the seals are to be kept by mayors and bailiffs and six legally sworn citizens."*

A similar law by Henry III in 1266 ordained that six lawful men should gather all the measures of each town to be checked. Juries carried out inspection under the Act of 1266, and another statute was needed in 1325 to deal with the appointment of juries. Local Stamping (Verification) Courts, which were linked with Courts Leet, were responsible for local weights and measures from about 1325. This function later passed to county commissioners and then to justices of the peace. In 1340, Edward III also tried to improve the situation and enacted that "Standards are to be sent to every county. There shall be appointed two good and suitable persons, or more, to inspect and see that the measures and weights agree with the standards. They shall have authority to punish all persons found in default." This is believed to be the first time that the word "inspect" was used in a statute in connection with weighing and measuring.

The great majority of sales from early times up until the 18th century took place in markets. The system of granting charters to markets involved the appointment of clerks to the markets, and they often also took responsibility for the accuracy of weights and measures. The first recorded Clerks of Markets were appointed under Edward III in 1340. They were known as King's Officers.

In the Midlands many Chief Inspectors of Weights and Measures had responsibility for the conduct of markets right up to local government reorganisation 1974. In 1795, the powers of Sheriffs were passed to Justices of the Peace, or Commissioners of the Peace They were required to appoint Examiners who were the first full-time equivalents of Inspectors of Weights and Measures, although not yet under that name. The movement towards modernisation of control began in the second half of the 18th century when the Assize of Bread procedure was revised in 1795. Under this Assize, Justices of the Peace were required to see that accurate local standards were provided and that Examiners were appointed to supervise weights and measures within their jurisdiction.

From 1815, many corporate towns had taken over the powers of the Justices of the Peace to appoint Examiners. In the Municipal Reform Act of 1835, town councils were elected by ratepayers. The Weights and Measures Acts in 1834 and 1835 required the appointment of Inspectors of Weights and Measures in counties as well as in cities and boroughs. In the following year a new Bread Act finally abolished the old Assize of Bread and replaced it with a general requirement that loaves should be of standard quality and be sold by weight. It is interesting to note that even in the 20th century some inspectors still favoured the title of Assizer.

Curiously, there appears to have been an overlap of enforcement powers, because the jurisdiction of manorial courts was not generally abolished until 1865, when control passed to the newly established local authorities. In fact the Weights and Measures Act 1878 specifically states that it does not "abridge the power of the leet jury etc." Despite these reforms, administration was again found to be deficient, mainly because police or untrained part-time officers were appointed as inspectors instead of specially trained staff.

Livery Companies: In London and a few other large cities, there was a different system of controls dating back to 1196 in which a Jury, or Ward Inquest, was appointed to inspect the weights and measures of traders. This system continued in some parts of London well into the 19th century. Also in London there was a reliance on what we now call self-regulation. The powerful Guild Companies supervised the trading standards of their members.

For example, the Founders Company had a special role in weights and measures within three miles around London. It was established by a charter from King James in 1614. They had the right to stamp and adjust all small brass avoirdupois weights and this power lasted until 1899 when the Board of Trade took over.

Quality: Some of the earliest officials involved with the quality of food were the Ale Conners. They were first appointed under Henry III's decree of 1266, the Assize of Bread and Ale (Assisa Panis et Cervisiae) by local assizes or manorial courts. The decree dealt with quality and price and later with weights and measures. The Ale Conner tested the quality of ale by pouring some on a wooden bench and sitting on it for half an hour in leather trousers. If the trousers stuck to the bench then the ale was adulterated. Failure to comply with requirements of the Assize could lead to the punishment of offenders including fining, flogging, pillory or tumbrel. Bakers could even be burnt in their own ovens. Ale Conners were often paid half of the fines which were imposed on offenders, and they existed in some areas until early in the nineteenth century. John Shakespeare, the father of William the playwright, was an ale conner in Stratford-upon-Avon in 1556. The Adulteration of Food and Drugs Act 1872 created the position of Food Sampling Officers. Significant improvements were made by the Sale of Food and Drugs Acts of 1875 and 1879.

Commerce: Before 1500, the only premises that we might recognise as shops in Britain were those selling bread, ale or meat. It was not until the 19th century that large chains of shops began to grow. One of the oldest is Debenhams, founded in 1813, with Harrods established in 1824. The oldest department store was Kendal's, established in

Manchester in 1836, and this was the nucleus around which House of Fraser chain grew. The John Lewis empire began in 1864. International Stores began as the International Tea Company in 1878 in Brentford. Catalogue shopping started with the Fattorini Watch Club in about 1855, which developed into the Empire Stores. John Ruskin (1819-1900), the academic, artist and author, was earning a living as a grocer in Notting Hill in 1874.

Cooperatives were important in reforming the supply of goods and services. One of the earliest cooperatives was the Shore Porters Society in Aberdeen in 1498. The first consumer cooperative was formed in 1769, again in Scotland. However, the Cooperative movement as we know it today started in Lancashire with the Rochdale Pioneers at Toad Lane, Rochdale in 1844.

On the Lighter Side...

All the chapters in this book deal with weighty matters, often in more than one sense. Each chapter will end with a section called *On the Lighter Side...* As a start, Publius Cornelius Tacitus (56 to 117 AD) said:

> *"In a state where corruption abounds, laws must be very numerous."*

Perhaps this explains why we now have so many laws (red tape).

It is said that the definition of one unit of length in China around 2700 BC was the distance between the two knots on a piece of bamboo that made a particular sound.

The Board of Trade was founded in 1786, and its many members included the Lord Chancellor, the Speaker and the Archbishop of Canterbury. It never met, and its duties were performed by the President of the Board and the officials. The Board was subject to some ridicule. At the time of the Napoleonic Wars the following ditty appeared:

> *"This highly paid official, Is greatly overpaid. There never was a Board, and now there is no trade".*

The 4th Report of the Commissioners of Weights and Measures in 1870 included the following results on the accuracy of inspectors' balances in a number of boroughs:

- *"the veriest trifle can be detected"* Droitwich
- *"a feather will turn the scale"* Middlesbrough
- *"a very small amount which cannot be detected will turn the scale"* Warwick
- *"a pin would turn the scale"* Montrose
- *"an infinitesimal amount will turn the scale"* Inverness.

CHAPTER TWO – 1880 to 1899

Earliest Days of the Institute

Introduction: These were the formative decades of the Institute. Modern consumer protection probably began with the Weights and Measures Act 1878. This Act was significant because it replaced all previous laws and regulations on weights and measures and appeared to provide a structure for the uniformity of inspection and enforcement. The Warden of Standards had moved from the Exchequer to the Board of Trade in 1866, and the Board was expected to be able to guide local authorities

Despite the Warden's guidance, there were wide differences in local application. This lack of uniformity was the main incentive for inspectors to join together in some form of organisation. However, there were conflicting views on appropriate membership, and initially two rival organisations emerged: the British Association, which wished to include scale-makers, and the Incorporated Society, which did not. The early conflicts were resolved in 1894 when most inspectors realised that a unified national organisation would foster uniformity, create a more professional approach and become an effective tool for gaining improvements in the legislation.

This was the time when married women were given the right to acquire their own property (under the Married Women's Property Acts of 1870 and 1882). Technology was advancing, and in 1881 Sir William Armstrong's home at Cragside was the first to use electric lights. The gramophone was invented in 1887, and in 1897 Marconi was given the patent for radio communication.

We now see how the first weights and measures organisation was established and the kinds of issues with which they were confronted.

British Association of Inspectors of Weights and Measures: It is very likely there were conversations between inspectors working for different authorities, but there is no evidence to show inspectors worked to improve uniformity prior to 1881. Nevertheless, a number of the inspectors appointed under the 1878 Act must have realised some form of national association would be of advantage. Initial progress was made in the North of England.

In 1880, Tom Wimhurst, the Chief Inspector of Weights and Measures in Manchester, proposed a form of cooperation, the primary aim being to facilitate an exchange of information and ideas among appointed inspectors. Tom probably discussed the idea around Victorian office tables or with a (full) pint of something appropriate in hand. Clearly the omens were good, and in July 1980 he sent out the following letter:

Weights and Measures Office,
Bloom Street, Manchester,
July 1880

Sir,
It has been suggested to me that it would be desirable to form an Association of Inspectors of Weights and Measures, similar to the Gas Managers' Association, &C.
Considering the importance of the positions occupied by Inspectors of Weights and Measures, especially since the Act of 1878 came into force, it is thought that much good would be done if an Association of Inspectors of Weights and Measures was formed, the rules for governing which should be framed at a Meeting to be hereafter convened. The Association would be able to give valuable information to its members, and it would be the means of securing greater uniformity in the working of the Weights and Measures Act, by the reading of Papers at its Annual Meetings, &C.
Should you be willing to join the Association please let me know, and also state when would be the most convenient time for you to attend a Preliminary Meeting in August or September
Yours truly,
Tom Wimhurst.

Encouraging replies must have been received because, along with two colleagues, he issued a further letter two months later:

Weights and Measures Office,
Bloom Street, Manchester,
14 September 1880

Sir,
Proposed Association of Inspectors of Weights and Measures

In reference to the circular sent in July by Mr. Wimhurst, we beg to inform you that a PRELIMINARY MEETING of Inspectors of Weights and Measures will be held at the above office, on MONDAY, the 27th. inst., at 3 o'clock in the Afternoon, when we shall be very glad to meet you and any other Inspector you may know. Trusting you may be present,
We are, yours truly,
Tom Wimhurst, Manchester;
James Johnson, Salford;
J W. Robinson, Stockport.
PS. We shall be glad to meet you, if convenient, at 10 o'clock in the Morning, at the above Office, when we will

*show you as many places of interest in Manchester and
Salford as time will permit.*

Following this initial get-together in September 1880, Tom
Wimhurst invited twenty inspectors and a small number of scale
manufacturers to the inaugural meeting of the British Association of
Inspectors of Weights and Measures. This took place in the Mayor's
Parlour, City Hall, Manchester on 9th and 10th of May 1881. There
was an exhibition of equipment at the meeting and two formal
papers. Tom Wimhurst spoke about his *Experiences as an Inspector*
and Mr Hare of Birmingham explained the *Principles and
Construction of the Counter Machine.* An exhortation made by Mr
Hare was that inspectors should not just test scales when they were
empty but should put weights in the pans and shift the positions of
the weights to see if there were errors. Wise counsel indeed!
At this inaugural meeting, Mr Wimhurst said, *"Some local
authorities neglect the Weights and Measures Act because it is not
a paying one. One inspector will have the scales oscillate; another
will have them vibrate; one to start from the level; another will
allow anything. I have known scales condemned which I have found
accurate. In other districts we find inspectors allowing anything. As
measures of length you will find brass nails driven into the counter,
at just what distance apart suits the proprietor."*
When reading the details of early meetings one must admire the
determination, unity of purpose and dedication. Supporters made
the best of difficulties and persevered for a dozen years. Sadly,
their leader, the founding father of the Institute, Tom Wimhurst,
died suddenly in 1885 and did not see history nurture his child.

The **Inaugural Meeting** clearly took place following hours of
diligent research because it agreed a comprehensive collection of
34 rules. The founder members were 29 "Ordinary Members" who
were Inspectors, 16 "Extraordinary Members", who were
manufacturers of weighing and measuring equipment, and eight
"Honorary Members" including HJ Chaney, the Warden of Standards
at the Board of Trade. Membership of the British Association had
increased to 124 by 1891. The initial subscription rate is unknown,
but in June 1893 the subscription to the British Association was
increased to 10/6 for inspectors receiving less than £200 per year
and 21/- (£1.05) for those earning over £200.
Scale-makers were accepted as Extraordinary Members of the
British Association with full voting rights. However the admission of
'trade' members was not universally accepted. Inspectors,
particularly those in the London and the South-East, were aware of
different political and commercial pressures.
They were anxious to secure recognition in a climate that looked
askance at links with trade and industry. The British Association

sought to ease the position for dissident inspectors by providing the special category of extraordinary membership for the people from trade and industry. This was designed to allow them to contribute their technical knowledge and expertise, which would be of great advantage of the Inspectorate as a whole.

The Record: The magazine of the British Association was named *The Record*, and the first edition was dated October 1882. It was planned to publish the periodical three times each year. The first edition of *The Record* opened with words in the loquacious style of the times: *"In obedience to the resolution of the last Annual Meeting we make our humble bow, and trust that the leaflet we now present to you may soon be found too small for the important work we have undertaken."*

It was intended that *The Record* would have two or three articles in each issue, a selection of reports of appeals heard at Quarter Sessions, full reports of all appeals to High Courts and letters (anonymously if requested). The British Association of Inspectors of Weights and Measures soon gained respect from the Board of Trade and was influential in the promotion of new legislation. This is dealt with later.

Incorporated Society of Weights and Measures: We now turn to the origins and actions of the splinter group that refused to support the British Association. They were all inspectors who refused to accept scale-makers as members of an *inspectors'* organisation.

The following circular was issued by Messrs Cliffe, Houghton and Martin (Inspectors for the County of Surrey) and Smith (Inspector for the County Borough of Croydon).

> *Sirs*
> *Following positive responses a Conference of inspectors was held in Anderton's Hotel, Fleet Street, London on January 12th 1892. This meeting discussed the desirability of forming an organisation to take joint and uniform action under the Weights and Measures Acts. The claims of the existing British Association of Inspectors of Weights and Measures were fully considered.*
> *The inspectors present came to the unanimous conclusion that the British Association did not satisfactorily fulfil the objects for which it was established, but needed some necessary reforms. The three main reforms considered absolutely necessary were the elimination of the scale-making element, the establishment of a headquarters in London, and more frequent conferences.*

In the event of these not being agreed at the next annual meeting of the British Association immediate steps should be taken to form a new organisation.

The next action was to appoint a committee consisting of Messrs Cliffe, T Kyle, Mattinson, Houghton, Morgan, Tomlin, Wright, Smith and Martin to give effect to the resolutions of the meeting. They set to work at once and wrote to the Committee of the British Association asking if it would be willing to receive a deputation. The Secretary of the British Association agreed to receive a deputation in Manchester on 31st March 1892. The deputation arrived and urged the claims of their supporters. After much discussion, the Committee of the British Association conceded scale-makers could not take office but they absolutely refused to ask them to withdraw from membership. The deputation regarded this decision as unfortunate, but the British Association Committee said no further action could be taken until the meeting of the new association in June 1892.

A meeting of 40 dissidents was held on April 7th 1892. A discussion took place upon "the want of uniformity and its results". It was agreed that there was a need for an incorporated society whose object should be uniformity and whose constitution was in no way connected with the scale-makers. They canvassed all inspectors present to use their influence to persuade other members of the British Association to agree.

A sub-committee of 'dissidents' was appointed and they drafted constitutional amendments and forwarded them to the British Association. They also decided that some of their group should join the British Association and attend their meetings in order to present alternative views. Two 'dissident' inspectors joined the British Association along with five others already in membership. The proposed amendments were moved but were unsuccessful even though a number of the scale-makers had generously offered to withdraw. After the vote, Mr. Kyle, speaking for the dissidents, said that he regretted the decision. His group had done everything in their power to bring about unity. They would therefore lay the matter before their supporters with a view to forming a new organisation.

Note: It was reported that a member of the dissident group accepted office under the British Association and then altered his most pronounced opinions for the sake of office. Readers will appreciate this caused considerable notoriety at the time.

Arguments continued. It was claimed that the membership of scale-makers was an anomaly which diminished the influence, and prejudiced the impartiality, of inspectors. The 'dissidents' said it lowered the status of the British Association in the eyes of the

27

public and created suspicion in the minds of local authorities. The London County Council endorsed this view.

A new society needed to be formed. Circular letters were sent to inspectors all over Great Britain inviting them to become members of a new society. It was claimed the new society would be established for purity, independence, the acquisition of knowledge and the general interchange of ideas; to promote uniformity of action and the fostering of friendly feeling by social intercourse. Inspectors joined from as far north as Inverness and as far south as Cornwall. A number of noblemen and gentlemen were invited to accept nominations for vice-presidency.

Society's First AGM 1892: There was a fever of meetings, discussions, arguments and negotiations during 1892. For example, there were 22 meetings of the committee of the British Association and 12 meetings of supporters of the new society. The impasse over members from the trade remained.

On 9th November 1892, the first Annual General Meeting of a new Society of Inspectors of Weights and Measures was held at Anderton's Hotel in London. The British Association regarding this as an unconstitutional breakaway group. However this meeting agreed that a society should be established for:

- *"The advancement of scientific and practical knowledge of, and the attainment of force and unity in the practice of testing weights, measures, weighing and measuring instruments*
- *The promotion of the interchange of ideas amongst inspectors under the Weights and Measures, Food and Drugs, Petroleum and Explosives Acts;*
- *The doing of all such other lawful things as are incidental or conducive to the attainment of the above objects."*

The first chairman of the Society was Thomas Kyle of Buckinghamshire. To explain a source of some confusion, there were three members named Kyle during the period 1892 to 1895: James Kyle in London, Talbot Kyle who moved from Wakefield to Dorking and Thomas Kyle in Aylesbury, Buckinghamshire. Thomas was the Chairman until 1898 when he resigned and the post of Past Chairman was created. This procedure was agreed to stabilise the establishment of the 'new' Society. Tribute was paid to his "untiring energy and zeal, apart from the sacrifice of both time and money". This statement is probably one that could be applied to many who served the Institute in subsequent years.

First Executive Council: This consisted of six honorary officers and thirteen council members from as far as Portsmouth and Nairn. At the AGM in November 1892, a category of Honorary Membership was agreed. These should be gentlemen who took an interest in the carrying out of the Weights and Measures Acts. However this was quickly amended to exclude scale-makers – a decision which met with great applause.

The apparent antagonism to scale-makers should not be misunderstood. They were respected tradesmen who did a great deal to make and maintain accurate equipment. However, they were thought not to have the same status as inspectors in achieving uniformity of enforcement and campaigning for improved legislation. In addition they had their own trade association.

The total membership of the Society at the time of the first AGM was 103, including 17 Vice-Presidents and one Honorary Member. The annual subscription for their journal the *Monthly Review* was 6s. On a lighter note it was recorded that the first meeting ended with a "friendly and social meat tea".

This new organisation was initially known as the British Society of Inspectors of Weights and Measures, but the word British was later discarded. The Society was not initially an incorporated body but was an institution under the Literary and Scientific Institutions Act 1854. It was recognised by the Board of Trade and was granted a charter of incorporation on 2nd May 1893. It then became the Incorporated Society of Inspectors of Weights and Measures, a title which survived for nearly half a century. The achievement of incorporation was probably an important factor in the eventual merger with the British Association.

The first provincial meeting of the Incorporated Society was on 28th April 1893 when Thomas Kyle of Buckinghamshire read a paper on *The Coal Act* and AJ Street of London spoke on the subject of *Weights*. The periodical published was the *Monthly Review*,No.1 of Volume 1, dated December 1st 1892.

The Editorial stated: *"When it is remembered that twelve months ago there was no such society in existence and that we have had to contend against an Association of some years' growth, it must be a congratulation to all of us when we are able to announce a total membership, including 17 Vice-Presidents, of 103."*

It is pleasing that the *Monthly Review* has been maintained at a high standard under successive voluntary editors and titles. The title page of the first edition of the *Monthly Review* declared that it was *"A record of proceedings and matters of interest under the Weights and Measures, Food and Drugs, Petroleum and Explosives Acts."*

It was also headlined as *The Official Organ of the Society of Inspectors of Weights and Measures*. Unfortunately, it was very soon found that the accounts books of the Incorporated Society did not balance. In 1895, it was agreed to make subscription to the *Review* available to non-members at 12/- (60p) per annum. In August 1897, it was reported that the income raised was still insufficient.

Second AGM 1893: The second AGM of the Incorporated Society was held on 10th and 11th August 1893. Papers were read about *Larger Weighing Instruments* and *The Food and Drugs Act*. It is noteworthy that even at this early stage a paper was presented on what came to be known as 'ancillary' legislation. The first set of rules of the Incorporated Society was also confirmed, and the Executive Council appointed committees for Finance, Weights and Measures, Food and Drugs, Petroleum and Explosives and Parliamentary Matters. These were to remain in place for many decades with only minor changes to their names and scope.

A key feature of the Institute has been the district or branch organization. This began with establishing divisions when Talbot Kyle of Wakefield was appointed Chief Consul. This post survived until the AGM in 1894 when the post was renamed Chief Corresponding Member. The idea was that each division should have a Consul to deal with local issues and to collect and distribute information. These Consuls later also became Corresponding Members. Consuls were appointed in 12 divisions with instructions

- to keep in touch with members in their divisions
- to note any irregularity or cause of dissatisfaction
- to make themselves acquainted with their divisions
- to collect information relating to legislation
- to collect general information of value to the Society
- to make reports to the Chief Consul by 15th of each month
- for the Chief Consul to report to each meeting of the Executive Council.

The **Chairman of London County Council** was always invited to meetings (and always attended) and became the President of the Incorporated Society until the 1950s. Sir John Hutton, the first President, was very active and an asset to the Society in being a journalist and able to help with the initial design and style of the *Monthly Review*.

As an early contribution to the uniformity of enforcement in April 1893 the Executive Council responded to three queries from members that were about spring balances, coal and bread.

From the start, the Incorporated Society lived up to its title and its aims. It was able to influence the Board of Trade's regulations. There was no talk in those days of 'consumer protection', but the Society was clearly intending to lay down and enforce rules to protect shoppers from short weight and general chicanery. These early inspectors showed they were keen to promote ethical trading practices and build their profession's reputation with high standards of conduct and strict qualifications for entry

Amalgamation: In March 1893, the Vice-President Mr Morris, a County Inspector, gave a paper to a Special General Meeting of the

British Association which included the following stout defence of their view on scale-maker membership:

> "*Scale-makers became members of the British Association because they gave much valuable information, greatly needed in those early days, when many Inspectors had no knowledge whatever of the mechanical construction of any except the simplest form of scales.*
>
> "*Inspectors were few in number and their means less, therefore the manufacturers themselves, being anxious to see better education universal, agreed to assist in the formation of the Association. They had no wish to dictate or interfere, in any way. They would not join as members but gave their names as extra-ordinary members, with subscription one guinea.*
>
> "*From that day to this no manufacturer has ever made use of his voting powers upon any trade question, but all have given whatever advice and assistance that lay in their power to any and every inspector.*"

It was noted that the supporters of the 'splinter group' advocating the elimination of the scale-maker membership spoke glibly of the need for "purity and independence". But in ironic tone the Editor of *The Record* questioned the "purity and independence" of the new Society which had already invited local councillors, the employers, to become Vice-Presidents.

It was reported that the British Association had 60 Board of Trade qualified members whilst the Society had 72. Some members queried the whereabouts of another 130 qualified inspectors who were missing.

A Special General Meeting of the British Association held in March 1893 had issued invitations to every inspector north of the River Trent. The rules of the British Association were changed at this meeting so that there were just two membership categories, Ordinary and Honorary Members. The scale-makers resigned from the defunct Extraordinary Membership category and applied to be Honorary members instead.

Joint Meetings: There was quite rapid progress. At a British Association meeting at Norwich on 29th and 30th June 1893 a resolution was passed "*that some steps be taken by this Association to bring about an amalgamation of the two Societies, in the interests of peace, unity and uniformity in our profession as Inspectors of Weights and Measures.*"

It was agreed to leave the negotiations on amalgamation to four chosen members and the Executive Council, but progress was not easy. At a subsequent meeting of the British Association on 10th August 1893, a motion to merge the two societies was put forward, but failed to gain a majority. There was yet another meeting for the

31

British Association to discuss amalgamation on 15th December 1893, followed by a joint meeting of the Special Committees of the Incorporated Society and the British Association at the Guildhall, London, on 22nd February 1894, at which each organisation was represented by seven members in an endeavour to seek an amicable solution.

Colonel Howard Vincent MP, by unanimous request, presided over a successful outcome. The *Monthly Review* of the Incorporated Society praised Colonel Vincent with the following words: *"We are bound to testify not only to the tact and discretion which the Colonel showed throughout the meeting, but to the fertility of resource in meeting all the difficulties which presented themselves before him. It is no reflection on the gentlemen who formed the committee to say that the successful result was largely due to the Chairman's own personal efforts."*

The British Association also praised the chairmanship of Colonel Vincent. The report in the March-April 1894 edition of *The Record* of the British Association set out the amalgamation scheme in momentous terms. It said that *"the dividing line between the organisations had been narrow. Each Society evidently had identical aims and objects in view. Considerable forbearance was shown by both sides when dealing with minor points or details which were not matters of principle."*

The Amalgamation Committee reported that the name of the society would be the Incorporated British Society of Inspectors of Weights and Measures. A meeting of the Executive Council of the Society took place on 9th March 1894 at the Society's new meeting place at the First Avenue Hotel, Holborn, London.

The British Association met on 6th April 1894, confirming that it also agreed with amalgamation. Amalgamation was finally accomplished with goodwill on all sides at a Grand United Meeting on 7th June 1894 in the County Hall of London County Council. Membership of each organisation had reached a little over a hundred with some inspectors having dual membership.

Note: It is interesting that Mr Whitehead, the Chief Inspector of Leeds, had resigned his appointment. He was a prominent member of the Executive Council of the British Association and was the leader of the section seeking to prevent the elimination of scale-makers. It was observed that *"over this question, he almost irretrievably led some of his colleagues astray"*. Mr Whitehead subsequently accepted a "responsible position" in the firm of Messrs W & T Avery, Scale Manufacturers in Birmingham.

The first AGM of the united organisation took place on 11th and 12th July 1894. Members were exhorted to make a special effort to be present. Two papers were read about weights and measures by leading inspectors, one from the North and one from the South. An excursion was also arranged, although most of the time was taken up with procedural matters. One problem was deciding the constitution of the Executive Council. One faction wanted representation on a geographical basis, whereas others wanted equal allocation to the constituent bodies. The second option was adopted for the first year. Other decisions which were made included the appointment of officers and fixing the dates for future meetings. The President, Sir John Hutton, congratulated members upon the amalgamation of the two societies and took care to point out there was much yet to be done before every inspector of weights and measures in the kingdom was a member. This would probably take time. It was very desirable that everything should be done to follow the course indicated and to secure, if not everyone, at least a representative number of those engaged in the profession.

Principles: Incorporated Society members quickly appreciated that the objectives of professional status and uniformity of practice could be advanced only by the development of other activities to extend the remit of the Incorporated Society's influence. Fundamental issues of concern included:
- the prohibition of short weight,
- the promotion of ethical trading practices and
- the up-rating of the qualification and status of the Inspector.

The autumn meeting in 1894 was held in Blackpool. At this meeting a proposal by the Hon Secretary, Allan Granger, to delete the word 'British' from the name of the Society was carried. The main reason was that use of the word British would exclude Irish inspectors. The name became the Incorporated Society of Inspectors of Weights and Measures. The membership list in 1894 included 144 ordinary members, one president, 34 vice-presidents and four honorary members. In 1897, local authority councillor delegates were invited to attend the AGM for the first time.

New Rules: In 1895 it was believed many poorly paid Inspectors could not afford to join. Discussions took place about a new category of Associate Membership. They would not have the right to vote but, for a small membership fee, perhaps 5s or 10s, they could receive the *Monthly Review*. A motion to have three categories of members, Members, Associates and Honorary Members was considered in January 1895 but, sadly, there was no agreement. Controversy continued about the membership of scale-makers. Despite the many years of acrimony, the Incorporated Society voted at the spring meeting in 1895 to permit traders (in the ordinary acceptance of the term) to be honorary members without voting powers. However, a special meeting was held in October 1895 to amend the rules again, when the category of Honorary Member was amended to exclude scale-makers.

The Prime Minister: In April 1894, Lord Rosebery, the Prime Minister, in his reply to the London County Council's 'Progressives' address, laid special stress upon the necessity for the careful and impartial carrying out of the Weights and Measures Acts. He said: *"We have seen the poor Londoner getting fair weight and measure when he purchased food, and also when he purchased coal, and I believe that in a hundred and a thousand homes there would at this moment be found to exist a spirit of gratitude that cannot be exceeded in exchange for this one bounty alone of the County Council."*

Diamond Jubilee: In spite of a commitment to hold more meetings of the Incorporated Society, there was a disappointing attendance at the autumn meeting of 1895. It was then decided to have just two general meetings each year instead of three. An exhibition on the subject of weights and measures was organised at the AGM to celebrate the Diamond Jubilee of Queen Victoria in 1897 at the Crystal Palace in Sydenham. This included a display of historical weighing and measuring equipment and demonstrations of how to detect fraudulent activities.

Expulsions: There were recurring instances from 1894 to 1899 of members being expelled by the Executive Council for non-payment of subscriptions. In 1897, the membership was about 170 together with 13 honorary members. In 1897 the annual subscription was increased to 16s 6d.

In 1898, the Executive Council agreed to encourage members to present papers to meetings by offering a financial reward for the best two papers presented. On a different topic, in May 1899 the Editor of the *Review* wrote about considerable support for renaming the Society as the Institute of Assizers, because it was uniquely descriptive and much shorter than the full title of the Incorporated Society. This was formally proposed but defeated. It is of interest to note that a proposal for a similar name change was put forward at the renaming nearly 50 years later and was again rejected.

Coat of Arms: The first version of the coat of arms assumed by the Incorporated Society appeared in the *Monthly Review* in April 1895. It was expected to meet with general approbation as a badge of honour and the means of perpetual recognition to the Incorporated Society. The Executive Council determined to adopt the crest and obtain official approval from the College of Arms. Application was made to the Earl Marshal, but the expense of £76 10s was deemed absolutely prohibitive. The 'Arms' were therefore assumed and never formally acquired. In this respect the Incorporated Society was not alone. The common seals of some of our principal towns and cities have no official origin, and some were

34

in existence even before the College of Arms was incorporated by Richard III. The design adopted included the crown to testify to the imperial connection, the scales as typifying the historic calling, and the swords symbolising justice. The spirit of the motto 'Addere legi justitiam decus' (it is an honour to combine justice and law) is unexceptionable, and, in the words of 1895, "*if the discharge of the public duties is evermore tempered by this spirit, it must greatly rebound to the prestige and honour of the Incorporated Society.*"

Conditions of Service: The British Association and the Incorporated Society both represented the profession on conditions of service. At various times they attempted to have salary scales unified across the country. They also campaigned to have a superannuation scheme set up for inspectors. The AGM of the Incorporated Society in July 1896 drew up a scheme which it hoped would be implemented by local authorities. In January 1897, a superannuation conference was arranged by the local authorities and a scheme was promoted by the municipal authorities. A little later a bill about superannuation was read in Parliament for the first time. This bill failed. Undaunted, the Institute's support for the campaign continued for many years.

Local Authorities: In 1884, it was remarkable that there were at least 14 manorial jurisdictions which could overrule the requirements of the Weights and Measures Act 1878. The Weights and Measures (Purchase) Act 1892 was intended to do away with the weights and measures powers of twenty manorial authorities or ancient Courts Leet. It allowed the local authorities to buy franchises from the ancient authorities which included Courts Leet for any hundred or manor, or any jury or ward inquest, or any lord or lady of the manor. In 1897, it was reported that the effect of the Act had been disappointing, as twelve of the courts still remained because some local authorities refused to allocate the funds. County councils were established in England in 1889 by the Local Government Act 1888. Boroughs with a population of less than 10,000 had to hand over their weights and measures functions to the relevant county council. In 1893, there were still 75 boroughs carrying out the functions, although some of them had an agreement with the county council to perform the function on their behalf.

Numbers of Inspectors: In 1893, it was reported that there were almost 600 inspectors in England, Scotland and Wales but only 256 held Board of Trade certificates (43%). By 1897 there were 434 inspectors in England and Wales and 87 in Scotland (total 521). In 1896, London County Council alone had 77 staff including 14 coal officers. Coal officers could be appointed under the 1889 Act, but there was no provision for training or qualification.

Other Organisations: Weights and Measures Inspectors were not the only profession who formed an organisation in this period. The Association of Public Sanitary Inspectors was founded in 1883 and became the present Chartered Institute of Environmental Health. The sciences of measurement were also advancing. In October 1898, a parliamentary committee recommended that a national physical laboratory should be established at Kew following receipt of evidence from experts who visited similar laboratories in Germany.

However, there was little public comment at this time on weights and measures matters from those whom we now call consumers, and therefore a speech in support of a new bill at the annual meeting of the Midland Federation of Women's Liberal Associations in November 1899 was unusual and very welcome.

Special Conference 1895: The Incorporated Society wasted no time in actively pursuing its aims. Within a year it invited the scale manufacturers to join a working committee to prepare proposals *"for removing the disabilities of the procedures observed under the weights and measures acts"*. A special conference was held jointly in Birmingham on 26th April 1895 at which 25 scale-makers attended along with 25 inspectors. Three resolutions were carried unanimously:

- The current weights and measures procedures lacked uniformity and were unsatisfactory
- Inspectors and manufacturers should make joint representation to the Board of Trade
- A committee of twelve should be established to agree the points to be discussed at another conference.

Another joint working party was convened on 6th May 1896. The Chairman was Jesse Collings MP, Under-Secretary at the Home Office. The Working Party produced a 64-page draft report which was debated by the Incorporated Society on 13th June 1896. Key recommendations were to achieve uniformity by placing responsibilities on the Board of Trade and harmonising local regulations. The Final Report had over 160 recommendations, some of which dealt with matters of detail. They included:

- New weights, measures and weighing machines to be tested and stamped
- Verification to be carried out by local authorities at least every 3 years
- No charge for an item submitted to an inspector's office
- Fees charged if items re-verified and re-stamped after repair
- An offence to forge, counterfeit or transpose a stamp

- Prescribed stamping fees must always be charged
- Standard of the examination for inspectors should be raised
- Detailed error allowances should be prescribed
- Legs and tails of counter machines to be of hardened metal
- No single beam balance should have greater capacity than 10lb
- Dial spring balances should have a soft metal plug for the stamp
- Machines must be provided with a balance box
- Corner testing to be carried out on sack machines

Board of Trade: A deputation of inspectors and scale-makers attended at the Board of Trade on 7th August 1896 to present the report to the President of the Board. However, there were political obstacles, and there was no response to the strong case for legislation at that time. This was one of the Incorporated Society's first experiences of ministerial delays on useful, if not necessary, legislation. There were many more similar experiences to come.

The Report was also sent to all local authorities, and in 1897, 90% of the 71 local authorities resolved to support the Incorporated Society's report. If ministers would not move, it was possible to promote a private member's bill. In1898, it was announced that a private member's bill was to be introduced in Parliament, and on 16th February 1898 the Bill had its first reading. In July it was learned the Bill had no hope of success. A bitter defeat. The Incorporated Society had to wait until 1904 before another friendly MP was successful in the ballot for bills. Most of the key provisions of the Conference Report were agreed and incorporated into the Weights and Measures Act 1904 (see next chapter).

One contentious consideration was the practice of some authorities to give rebates on verification fees for services rendered. A spokesman from the Board of Trade stated that this should be left to local discretion.

A J Balfour, who was later to be Prime Minister, was quoted as saying "*diversity is the very life-blood of local government and if uniformity was wished for they could only get it by centralisation*".

The AGM in 1895 agreed to make representations to the Board of Trade about stamping fees, and the perennial question about whether beer barrels should be stamped was discussed.

In some areas stamping offices were referred to as Courts of Verification or Verification Courts (VCs). Some of today's inspectors in 2012 may remember the physical efforts of setting up and staffing peripatetic VCs into the 1970s. In February 1895, the Editor felt it necessary to comment on criticisms of the inconsistencies and lack of diligence of the Inspectorate in the trade press including the *Hardware Trade Journal*. In April it was reported that the system in some local authorities where the inspector received a salary and also half of all fines paid was dying out. The system was in danger of encouraging unnecessary prosecutions when prevention rather than prosecution was more important.

Weighing and Measuring Equipment: One purpose of the 1878 Act was to ensure clarity and uniformity, but within two months the Board of Trade approved a 100 lb unit of weight, or cental, or 'new hundredweight'. The British Association wrote to protest at this inconsistency. However the cental survived as a legal unit. Again, in 1884, the British Association wrote to the Board of Trade urging that *"it did not consider it necessary, or desirable, that a new standard weight of 112 lbs should be legalised"*. It could only facilitate confusion and deception.

Following shortcomings in the Weights and Measures Act 1878, the British Association pressed for improved legislation. A leaflet issued with *The Record* in October 1888 stated that the British Association had written to the President of the Board of Trade criticising the Bill, urging inspectors to take steps to strengthen the hand of government against the "enemies of progress". The British Association was also disappointed the bill added significantly to the duties of inspectors but did little to make enforcement easier.

There were lengthy criticisms of the provisions relating to the verification of weighing instruments. On the other hand, there were numerous letters to the *Times* and other newspapers criticising the parts of the 1888 Bill dealing with the sale of bread, apparently drummed up by the bakery trade who felt itself beleaguered.

The Weights and Measures Act 1889 required that every weighing instrument used for trade had to be verified and stamped. The 1878 Act had only applied this requirement to weights and measures but not to equipment. The scale-makers wanted compulsory stamping. For the first time local authorities were permitted to provide working standards for the use of inspectors. The Model Regulations issued under the Weights and Measures Act 1889 did not have direct force in law but were enacted as byelaws in each local authority.

Despite detailed guidance on the Model Regulations by the Warden of the Standards Department, many divergent practices became established in different local authorities and by individual inspectors. The British Association welcomed the abolition of the abatement of verification fees in the 1889 Act but expressed disappointment about missed opportunities for change. The British Association would have preferred national regulations about stamping instead of leaving it to local bye-laws, claiming the increased penalties would be ignored by magistrates. They considered it would be better to make dry measures illegal, expressed concern about the power to hold local inquiries and thought Inspectors should not adjust weights.

Uniformity: Mr HJ Chaney, Warden of the Standards Department, held an inquiry in 1892 to decide whether earthenware measures should be stamped. He determined that they must be accepted for testing everywhere, and subsequently the Board of Trade instructed local authorities to amend local regulations to state that earthenware liquid measures were acceptable.

On a different tack, the first query reported in the *Monthly Review* in 1893 was about how to test an accelerating counter machine. There were often proposals for improvement in the law and in February 1893 a letter was published in the *Review* which proposed that weighing and measuring equipment should be stamped where it was to be used and not at the manufacturer's premises.

At the 1894 AGM a paper was read which proposed the following resolution: *"That it is desirable, in certain circumstances, to obliterate the verification stamp on a weight, measure, or weighing instrument."*

There was some support for this but also some reservations about putting forward a new regulation. No vote was taken at this time although this proposal was implemented later.

The quantity of scales, weights and measures in use at this time was impressive. For example the annual report for Birmingham in 1882 reported that 18,885 visits had been made, 286,771 weights examined and 3,083 weighing machines examined of which 254 were incorrect. 37 people were convicted of offences. Inspectors also stamped 188,657 weights, and 25,062 weights were adjusted. Some years later in 1896, it was reported that Inspectors for London County Council inspected more than 1.25 million weights and measures and rejected 20% of them. They examined 974,719 appliances and found 32,422 of them to be unjust.

The Coal Mines Regulation Act 1887 extended the provisions of the Weights and Measures Act 1878 to weights, measures and equipment used to determine the wages of miners.

Pattern Approval: From 1889 there were problems with decisions about the acceptability of novel weighing and measuring machines. There was no standard procedure for resolving differences. In 1894, Mr W Crabtree of Nottinghamshire moved that all new types of equipment should be considered by the Reference Committee of the Incorporated Society and that their decision should be binding until or unless it was rescinded. This was agreed, and the Committee was given the task of approving new machines and deciding if they were fit and proper to be stamped. The standing orders for the Committee appeared in the *Review* in February 1895. Rule number 12 was that *"twelve drawings to scale or photos of any appliances, to be sent for the opinion of this Committee, be forwarded to the Secretary fourteen days before the date of the meeting; that the appliances be forwarded, carriage paid, as* *instructed by the Secretary, and accompanied, when requested, by a representative, and if requisite, with the necessary testing equipment."*

The first submission to the Reference Committee was a steelyard known as the Bartlett's Globe Steelyard. After careful examination and testing, and after a few alterations in detail, it was decided that indeed it was a fit and proper instrument.

In 1898, the Dayton Money-weight Computing Balance was the subject of the first highly controversial decision. The Reference Committee and the Executive Council had doubts about its suitability, and the Society's solicitors agreed it was illegal. The matter was referred to the Board of Trade, and Mr Chaney of the Standards Department seemed to say that the decision rested with inspectors to interpret the regulations although he was personally inclined to accept the new price-calculating mechanism. Eventually, the Board of Trade ruled that an inspector would not be justified in stamping this scale. However, in 1904, it was later the subject of one of the first Certificates of Approval by the Board of Trade itself.

At the 1898 AGM there was considerable commotion because this same Dayton Money-weight scale was exhibited. This was thought by some to be inappropriate, but it transpired that it had been displayed with the prior agreement of the Society's Chairman.

Local Customary Measures: Despite clear legislation about what units of weights and measures were acceptable, inspectors struggled with the continued use of local measures. For example, the 'Scotch pint' of milk was, in fact, half a gallon. Inspectors must have been puzzled by the decision in 1883 in the 'Wee Gill and Half Munchkin Case' in Glasgow. On appeal the decision was that a publican may sell any quantity but must not falsely represent it as an imperial measure. Also, section 19 of the 1878 Act stated that no "local or customary measures" shall be lawful. The decision of the court appeared to be that the 'wee gill' and the 'half munchkin' were not customary measures. The 'wee gill' was six pennyworth of whisky, whilst an imperial gill was seven pence. At this time there was no requirement to sell spirits by measure.

In 1892, a deputation of licensed victuallers from Wales visited the Board of Trade in an attempt to have the measure called the 'blue mug' legalised. This was a measure of 2/3 pint commonly used for the sale of beer in a number of counties in South and Mid Wales. The President of the Board of Trade refused.

Weights and Measures Act 1889: This Act controlled the sale of coal, provided for model regulations and for the stamping of scales, as well as requiring appointed inspectors to satisfy the Board of Trade of their suitability by examination. This examination has had a number of names through the years but is generally referred to in this book as the 'statutory qualification (or examination)'. A major part of the 1889 Act related to the sale of coal and, basically, required that coal should be sold by weight. Detailed requirements applied to the delivery of weight tickets and the use of tare weights for vehicles, but the majority of offences related to the delivery of short weight. The prohibition of short weight in coal in the 1889 Act was unique and remained so for many years. Even in the sale of bread, under the Bread Act 1836, there was only a requirement to make the weight known – a system that encouraged wide variations in both weight and price. Inspectors were given additional powers and local authorities had powers to make byelaws relating to the sale of coal. In October 1889, the draft byelaws for the City of Manchester relating to coal were printed in *The Record*.

Law for Goods: In the agriculture sector, a Select Committee in 1893 recommended that corn should be sold by the hundredweight of 112 pounds and that the conversion factors from weight to bushel measures should be standardised. It took a further 28 years before the Corn Sales Act 1921 belatedly finalised this matter.

Shortcomings in weights and measures law encouraged inspectors to be alert to see whether cases of short weight or measure could be an offence under the Merchandise Marks Acts. The offence under the Merchandise Marks Act 1887 was *"that every person who applied a written false trade description to goods should be guilty of an offence unless he proved that he acted without intent to defraud."*

It should be noted that the burden of proof was on the accused and the prosecutor did not have to prove intent. A charge under the Merchandise Marks Act could only be brought if the statement of quantity was in writing. However the Act did not give anyone the power or duty of enforcement. In June 1894, it was confirmed by an appeal court that an invoice falsely stating 36 gallons accompanying a barrel of beer was a false trade description under the Merchandise Marks Act.

Net Weight: As early as October 1882, the British Association reported on the sale of tea by gross weight with unnecessarily heavy packaging. The same observation could also be applied to butter and sugar and other foods. In 1894, a number of cases alleging short weight of tea were instituted where the gross weight was correct but the net weight of tea was significantly short because of the weight of packaging. Some cases were successful and some were not. The *Record* reported that *"the practice of including the weight of paper in making up quantities of tea, tobacco, etc., seems to be gradually spreading throughout the country, as was to be feared after the decision in the case of Harris -v- Allwood."*

The point that influenced some judgements was that because the purchaser was aware that the paper was weighed with the goods no fraud was intended. However, in some cases the paper, instead of being placed openly in the scale, had been put under the scoop of the scale out of sight of the purchaser, thus rendering the scale itself unjust.

It was reported that the custom of Glasgow grocers was to weigh their tea without the paper, and that, although the other practice was growing, it had never been the practice of the trade in Scotland. The Glasgow court imposed a fine of two guineas upon the manager of the Home and Colonial Stores. It was reported in September 1899 that sale of tea by gross weight meant that people were robbed of £578,660 each year (equivalent to £50 million in 2012).

Short Weight: Inspectors struggled for years with the fact that there was no specific offence for giving short weight or measure, except for coal from 1889. One possibility was to charge for the offence of fraudulent use of equipment, but it was almost impossible to prove the offence if the equipment was itself accurate. This was a campaign which the Incorporated Society ran with for many years.

Metrication: A report on the advantages of the so-called 'Metrical System' of weights and measures appeared in *The Record* of the British Association in September 1893. Following this, the AGM of the Incorporated Society, held in July 1894, unanimously supported a call for the government to set up a Royal Commission to consider the desirability of adopting the metric system. In 1894 the Association of Chambers of Commerce also discussed the decimal system of coinage and weights and measures, and a resolution to press for the metric system of weights and measures was carried unanimously. The Incorporated Society was well represented at the meeting. A Select Committee on Weights and Measures was appointed by the House of Commons on 13th February 1895 "*to enquire whether any, and what, changes to the present system of weights and measures should be adopted.*"

In its first year of amalgamated membership, the Incorporated Society gave evidence to this Select Committee. Throughout 1897 there were reports in the *Monthly Review* on the progress of the bill to authorise metric units which eventually resulted in the Weights and Measures (Metric System) Act 1897.

The evidence to the Committee was only accepted in part, and the metric system was legalised but not made compulsory by the Act. The Board of Trade was authorised to make metric standards and an order in council in 1898 amended the table of metric equivalents in the 1878 Act. To celebrate the progress towards metrication in

1897, six members of the Incorporated Society went on an official visit to Paris as guests of the French government. It was noted that administration of weights and measures was centralised in France, and a report in September gave full details of the trip.

Other Matters: In August 1893, it was announced that an inspector in a "large town" had a financial interest in a patent spring weighing machine for weighing coal. In September 1893, a critical letter appeared in the *London Evening News* alleging that inspections by Inspectors of Weights and Measures were a "farce" because inspectors just looked at stamps on weights and measures and did not test them. A strong, but anonymous, reply was published ten days later. For many years the universal custom, except for Ireland, was to require local standards to be sent to the Board of Trade in London for re-verification. This system was relaxed, and in 1883 several sets were re-verified in Glasgow, and in 1884 sets were also verified in Manchester and in the south-western counties of England.

Food Quality: From its early years, the Incorporated Society was active in pressing for improvements in legislation other than weights and measures and submitted proposals for *"the removal of anomalies and inconsistencies in the sale of food and drugs legislation."* At the AGM in July 1894, the Chairman of the Incorporated Society claimed, *"owing to various decisions of the High Court, the Food and Drugs Acts are difficult to work, and adulteration is carried on to an ingenious extent"*. In October 1894, a substantial report by the Incorporated Society on the anomalies and inconsistencies in the food adulteration acts was received by a government select committee. They made the following points:

- It was unfair that the retailer should suffer for the act of a manufacturer when the retailer had no knowledge
- There was no provision for taking action against the manufacturer when the retailer was not at fault
- The label should be a protection where adulteration was in such quantity as to fraudulently increase the bulk of the food
- There was no provision for the circumstances where the amount of a sample was too small to subdivide into three parts
- There was no offence for hindering or obstructing an inspector
- Three sections of the Acts only applied to milk and not to food in general.

Food and Drugs Bill 1897 was introduced into Parliament although the Bill only addressed a few of the 23 of the Select Committee recommendations. Again there was frustration at government delays, and a new Food and Drugs Act wasn't published until 1899.

The outcome of a case reported in March 1897 was that a notice which stated "all spirits sold in this establishment are diluted" was not a sufficient disclaimer to avoid prosecution. Readers will notice the striking similarity to the deceitful disclaimers used on clocked cars in the 1970s.

In 1892, there were 29,028 analyses of food by local authorities and 12.0% of the samples were adulterated. In 1897, there was a case of the fraudulent use of the word "whisky" for other spirits. Local Medical Officers considered a proposal that there should be a standard for the composition of milk. The recommendation was that total solids should be 12% and the fat content 3.5%. This was agreed by the membership but with the fat content to be at least 3%. No action was taken by government.

Petroleum: The first petroleum prosecution published in The Record was in 1883. An engineer in Glasgow was fined 20/- (£1) for keeping five gallons of petroleum without a licence. New regulations were made in 1896 relating to the keeping and use of petroleum for powering light locomotives, which was the term used for early petrol-driven motor vehicles. Petroleum was defined as spirit with a flashpoint below 73 degrees Fahrenheit (23.8 degrees Celsius). A report of the Select Committee on Petroleum in September 1898 proposed to increase the dividing line between petroleum spirit and petroleum oil from 73 degrees to 100 degrees Fahrenheit (23.8 to 37.8 degrees Celsius).

Explosives: There were disturbing cases of ignorance and extreme carelessness in the use and storage of explosives. In 1897, an Airdrie man placed 10 pounds of gelatine dynamite in an oven next to a burning fire causing an explosion which killed his wife and sister. He was found guilty of culpable homicide but was dismissed with an admonition. Another man involved was fined £10 for storing 3,000 detonators and 600 lbs of gelatine dynamite in an unauthorised place. In 1897, there was a prosecution for storing one ton of dynamite and one ton of gelignite without a licence. The penalty was not published but the fine could have been as much as two shillings.

Merchandise Marks: The Merchandise Marks Acts were used by Inspectors to prosecute cases of false descriptions of quality as well as quantity. For example, in 1897, there was a case about arsenical soap which contained no arsenic! Many Weights and Measures Inspectors also enforced the Shops Acts. The Shops Act 1892 limited with the hours of work of young people in shops and warehouses. In 1895, a notice was required to be displayed about assistants' half-day holidays, the early closing days. An amendment in 1899 required seats in shops for female staff.

An Act which did not become of major importance for inspectors for nearly 100 years was the Sale of Goods Act 1893. This codified the common, civil, law which had been decided by the courts over many decades. It largely replaced the legal edict of the phrase "caveat emptor".

Prosecutions: Many cases of trade misconduct were reported in *The Record* and the *Monthly Review*. The first prosecution printed in 1882 was in Blackburn when a grocer was fined 20/- for having a pair of scales 6½ drams against the purchaser. The scales were forfeited. In 1884, a dealer was convicted in Manchester for selling unstamped drinking glasses which were marked half pint. Inspectors in Wiltshire were stamping subdivided milk churns. In 1894 in Kent it was confirmed that Post Office equipment was not covered by the 1878 Act and was therefore exempted from testing. There was a case in 1894 where soap had been applied to the bottom of the goods pan of a scale that caused the pan to stick to the counter when goods were dropped on to it. It falsely made the scale appear to be indicating good weight.
In 1888 one colliery owner had removed a 'Billy Fairplay'. This was a machine which weighed the undersize coal produced by a collier and the amount found was then subtracted from the weight he had produced during his shift. There was a report in 1894 about the Birmingham stamp of verification being fraudulently cut from old scales by a scale mechanic and being reused. In January 1896, there was a successful prosecution for using an unstamped beer barrel as a measure. In a strange case reported in February 1898 about the use of unstamped glasses, the verdict of Quarter Sessions was "Not Guilty, but don't do it again". In the very first edition of the *Monthly Review* in 1892 the first case reported was about a tramp who posed as an inspector and tried to charge a trader 3s 0d for an inspection. A number of such impostors were reported over the years and they were known as 'Wofflers'.

Exams and Qualifications: One key aim of the British Association was the education of inspectors to be able to deal properly with technical and legal issues. Inspectors wanted an examination, and this was achieved in the Weights and Measures Act 1889. It required that candidates possess "sufficient practical knowledge for the proper performance of their duties". The examination was initially for people already appointed as inspectors. An effect of the 1889 Act was to virtually abolish inspectors who were police officers, and newly qualified inspectors were appointed in many places.
The procedure for the first examination for the statutory qualification in 1890 was that the examination would last one day,

subjects 1, 2 and 6 in the morning and subjects 3, 4 and 5 in the afternoon. The subjects were:

1) Reading: Read 30 lines from the Model Regulations
2) Writing: Write 20 lines from the Model Regulations
3) Arithmetic (including decimals): 24 questions – 12 to be correct
4) Elementary Mechanics: 12 questions – 6 to be correct
5) Elementary Physics: 12 questions – 6 to be correct
6) Practical verification of weights and measures and weighing and measuring instruments

At the first sitting of the examination in London in 1890, 57 candidates passed and 20 failed. By the start of 1894, 292 inspectors had passed the examination. In February 1897, 31 inspectors passed. In March and April 1893, concern was expressed in the *Review* about some of the examination subjects. However, one letter expressed satisfaction at the recent addition of a paper on The Elements of English Law. It was generally agreed that it was important that standards of inspectors continued to be raised.

Comment: In January 1895 it was reported that *The County Council Times* had published the following sentence in a leading article: *"The question of Weights and Measures has assumed an importance which indeed properly belongs to it, but which it was never allowed to possess before."* There was hope that the star of the weights and measures profession was rising.

On the Lighter Side...

Tit Bits magazine in 1854 wrote about the earliest records of weighing. This included reference to Chapter 23 of Genesis, verses 15 and 16, when Abraham weighed out 400 shekels of silver. This reminds us of the equivalence of weight of precious metals with money value in many civilisations, including Britain. Continuing the biblical theme there is a reference to Job who prayed to be "weighed in an even balance" (Job 31:6) and Leviticus where "just balances and just weights" are demanded (Leviticus 19:36).

In 1897, the *Daily Mail* wrote about a visit made by a journalist to the Standards Department of the Board of Trade. Much fun was made at the expense of the staff. One of them was said to be watching the expansion of the standard measure of the Pole as the temperature increased.

The journalist was also told not to touch standard weights because he might knock a small fraction off them. There was amazement that standards of weights and measures in the USA were very slightly different to ours because of inaccuracies in the copies. The members of staff were described as being "mild-eyed" officials because of the suspicion that a "sharp" glare might exercise some negative effect on the weights.

There is an, hopefully, apocryphal story in the *Review* in 1899 about a driver of a coal lorry who received a large bonus from the boss because on every occasion his empty lorry was weighed he was not on the vehicle but he was always in it when it was weighed with the coal.

Some entertainment from 1888:

Puzzle: A man provided with a large boathook, and standing in one pan of a large pair of scales, is exactly balanced by a weight of 150 lbs in the other pan. If he now presses vigorously with the boathook against the arm of the scales, on his own side of the fulcrum, and near to the fulcrum, what will be the result? Will he rise, fall, or remain stationary?

Customer (to baker's boy): "Is your bread nice and light?"
Baker's boy (confidentially): "Yes, ma'am, it only weighs ten ounces to the pound."

When a learned judge was summing up for the jury in a case of burglary, one of the jury fainted. His lordship had just said, "In reaching your verdict you must give full weight to the testimony of the defence witnesses." At the words "must give full weight" the juryman fainted. He was a coal dealer.

CHAPTER THREE – 1900 to 1918

Regulations and War

Introduction: This chapter does not cover the full period of twenty years but ends when the War ends on 11th November 1918. In the streets of Britain, the first significant event in the period was the death of Queen Victoria on 22nd January 1901 after a reign of 63 years. This event was recognised in the February 1901 edition of the Incorporated Society's *Monthly Review* with black borders printed on every page.

Queen Victoria's reign was followed by the Edwardian era. It was the beginning of the decline of the landed gentry and of an improvement in the lot of the working classes. A distinctive style reflecting the art and fashions of continental Europe (sometimes known as 'Art Nouveau') influenced architecture, design, clothing, manners and shopping. The ranges of foods and other goods in the shops began to grow, as did many retailing companies with which we were to become familiar. In the range of offences detected by Inspectors, it was possible to see more devious and imaginative wrongdoing. However, it is impossible to judge whether the amount of unfair trading, or downright fraud, was really on the increase.

This was a very busy time in the life of the Incorporated Society. Membership increased in a gratifying way. Weights and measures laws were improved, and there was also attention to petroleum, explosives and food laws, as well as shopping hours. The main pieces of legislation were the Weights and Measures Act 1904 and the 1907 Weights and Measures Regulations.

Other notable events included a Lib-Lab pact in 1903, which gave the Labour Party its first ever taste of power, and the Entente Cordiale, which was signed with France in 1904. MPs were paid for the first time in 1911, and the Titanic sank in 1912. Sadly, a suffragette was killed by the King's racehorse in 1913, but the first votes for women were introduced in 1918.

War Times: The other main events for the nation in this period were, of course, the Second Boer War (1899 to 1902) and the First World War (1914 to 1918). It is appropriate to begin with the impact of these. A celebration in Glasgow was held in June 1901 to mark the return of William McLaren, an Inspector, from the front. The First World War had a more significant impact on the Incorporated Society. In 1916, it was confirmed that 30 members had joined the 'colours', eight of whom died in uniform. The first to die in service was James William Black of Edinburgh. The war ended with the Armistice at 11.00 am on 11th November 1918.

In December 1915, the post of Inspector of Weights and Measures was designated a reserved or 'starred' occupation, so that Inspectors were not liable to conscription. Under the Military Service Act 1916, all

British males were conscripted if they were aged between 18 and 41 and resident in Great Britain (excluding Ireland) and unmarried or a widower. Later in that year, conscription was extended to married men. In February 1916, it was confirmed that the post of Inspector of Weights and Measures remained a reserved occupation. In June 1916, there was a controversy about whether conscientious objectors should be employed in local government. There is no record of this dispute applying to any Inspector.

Wartime Orders: Numerous Food Control Orders were promulgated in wartime. For example, all spirits had to be reduced to 25 degrees under proof; there was a maximum price for jam and also controls on beer prices and descriptions. In April 1917, the Executive Council of the Incorporated Society demonstrated that Inspectors were ideally placed to enforce the Food Control Orders, and in 1918 Inspectors were given powers to enforce under the supervision of the local Food Control Committees. When the War ended in 1918, the Society helped to review many controls, which included cake and pastry, grain prices, flour and bread, rice, meat, cattle cake, bacon, ham and lard, milk, butter, cheese and margarine, potatoes and jam. In autumn 1918, an order required the net weight to be marked on canned meat. A comprehensive enforcement guide to Food Control Orders was published in the *Monthly Review* in January 1918.

There was also wartime control on the price of coal. This started with the Pit Price Order in 1915, followed by the Wholesale Price Order in 1917 and then the Retail Price Order in 1919. Towards the end of the War, the rationing of food was introduced. In autumn 1918, Inspectors were given powers to enforce rationing controls. There was a wartime prohibition on wasting food, and one unusual prosecution reported in a 1918 *Monthly Review* was for wasting food by throwing rice at a wedding.

Despite all the control orders, the law of supply and demand led to rising prices. In summer 1919, there was national unrest about the cost of living. As foods were gradually released from rationing, many traders and trade associations demanded the repeal of all the wartime controls and a return to the 'bad old days' of complete freedom. The Incorporated Society mounted strenuous opposition to this proposal and, along with more responsible trade associations, pressed for many of the emergency regulations to be made permanent.

Commerce: The development of large businesses has been referred to in previous chapters. A major landmark was the opening of what is generally acknowledged to be the first self-service store in Memphis, Tennessee, USA, by Clarence Saunders in 1916. It was called the Piggly Wiggly Store.

Women as Inspectors: There were occasional, and pointed, references to women being employed in inspection roles. In 1901, Wandsworth employed two women as food sampling officers. In July 1906, a female Food and Drugs Inspector was the prosecutrix in Dublin. In 1916, the City of Edinburgh came up with the 'novel' suggestion of employing women as Inspectors of Weights and Measures.

The initial response from the Board of Trade was that it was not a suitable job for women. Examples of unsuitable tasks included ascending a platform for the test of a crane weigher and carrying out "severe" interviews. However, the Board later said that it would not decline to examine a woman nominated by a local authority. In October 1916, a report on a case in Lanark indicated a female "inspector" had been obstructed by a retailer who refused to accept the third portion of a food sample. It has not been possible to find any specific policy of the Incorporated Society on this issue.

Weights and Measures Act 1904: In 1904, a new Weights and Measures Act was passed. It began as a private member's bill to implement the recommendations of the Conference of Inspectors and Scale-makers in 1895 and 1896. The Government took over the bill but dropped many provisions including those adding a short weight offence and provisions for inspectors' superannuation. It was not until 1926 that parts of the abandoned short weight clauses were to become law in the Sale of Food Act. The 1904 Act also amended the requirements for the qualification of inspectors.

The 1904 Act gave the Board of Trade the power to make regulations which would be mandatory on local authorities and their inspectors. They governed the testing, stamping and inspection of weighing and measuring equipment; the specification of tolerances and the power to grant certificates of suitability for the use of appliances. To draft these regulations, a departmental committee was set up in 1906 on which the Inspectors who had served on the Working Committee ten years earlier also served. One notable new regulation gave Inspectors the power to obliterate verification stamps with a stamp in the shape of a six-pointed star.

It is a tribute to the work of this committee that the 1907 Regulations stood the test of time. They remained effective right up to 1963 and formed the basis of regulations made under the 1963 Act. In total, 139 regulations and 63 instructions were issued to Inspectors. The power to issue instructions improved consistency. The regulations replaced the local byelaws and it was the responsibility of each local authority to see that Inspectors obeyed the new instructions. The Incorporated Society was extremely active for several years in guiding its members in their correct and fair interpretation. In 1908, regular articles were published in the *Monthly Review* about conflicting interpretations. One author was bold enough to claim that he was stating what he believed to be the view of 99% of the Inspectors. Advice from the Board of Trade came thick and fast. In 1911, the *Monthly Review* published 25 pieces of advice that had been given in the previous year alone.

Pattern Approval: At the start of the century, the Weights and Measures Reference Committee of the Incorporated Society continued with the task of examining new patterns of weighing and measuring equipment to see whether they facilitated the perpetration of fraud.

This task was taken on by the Board of Trade following the 1904 Act. Wilfrid Airy, M.I.C.E (1836-1925), who had written two books about ancient weights and measures, was appointed as Technical Adviser to the Board. Early decisions about pattern approvals were published in full in the *Monthly Review*. In 1905, Notice of Approval No 1 (Certificate No 3) was issued. It was for the Bartlett's Globe Steelyard, which had also been the first to be approved by the original Reference Committee. In 1910, over 90 patterns of equipment were examined and 57 were approved.

In 1902, the influential Glasgow Council proposed 17 amendments to the Weights and Measures Acts with which the Incorporated Society concurred. These included extending the law to Post Office scales; that it should be an offence to pretend to be an Inspector; that there should be a power to destroy unjust equipment, and that short weight in prepacked items should be an offence. At the AGM of the Incorporated Society in 1903, other improvements were suggested to recognise advances in the technology of weighing equipment.

In 1900, serious problems with the accuracy of weighing in retail shops in Cardiff were reported to the Society. The Grocers Association made five suggestions for improvement. These included a free annual check by Inspectors, allotted times for submitting equipment for test, use of police stations, allowing tests from other authorities and a prohibition on the local custom of requiring the repainting of scales after repair.

There was an undercurrent of concern about the continued use of 'accelerating' weighing machines. However, at the 1900 spring meeting of the Incorporated Society, a proposal that all lever weighing machines should be vibrating was defeated. In 1907, the regulations only allowed counter machines to be accelerating for a limited period, but in 1917 the Board made an order extending the time limit for accelerating counter machines to 12 months beyond the end of the War. Accelerating deadweight machines persisted well into the 20th century. In January 1913, there was a report about three remarkably large weighbridges able to weigh moving trains in Immingham.

Other Weighing Equipment: In 1904, a new memorandum from the Board of Trade was issued about Inspectors' standards and scale beams. One change was that the now familiar square or rectangular working standards of weight were permitted. In 1901, it was recommended that new weights and measures testing stations should be sited to avoid vibration from nearby tramways and underground railways. In 1907, the Postmaster-General confirmed yet again that Post Office scales and weights were exempted as Crown property. He claimed they were tested by Post Office staff and there were no problems.

A familiar challenge in the early years of the Incorporated Society was to express the theory of the beam in terms which members found most convincing. A typical example was in the *Monthly Review* of October 1901. A similar esoteric subject was discussion of the difference between a scale and a balance, which occupied correspondence columns in 1903. In 1902, an engineer wrote a paper for the *Monthly Review* about the new-fangled automatic weighing machines. In 1903, there was a letter mourning the passing of the 'Agate' scale and the rise of the spring balance. A lengthy article in 1905 referred to a widespread dislike of spring balances, but the author said that if they were properly made they were usually accurate. In August 1904, there was an illustrated article about "hook-tricks" which described at least nine ways in which the hooks and shackles on swan-neck beamscales could be manipulated to give short weight.

In 1901/2 there was advice about the inaccuracy of double weighing of large wagons and the use of the 'schooner' measure for beer in Glasgow. It was said to have originated in America and was about 2/3 pint. Subsequently, there was a successful prosecution for using a unit of measurement that was not permitted and the dismissal of a subsequent appeal in 1903. The first roadside petrol pump in the country was put into use at Beaulieu in Hampshire in 1913. The Reference Committee gave the opinion that the unit of the carat could not be used for the sale of diamonds because it was not in the list of Board of Trade standards. In 1913, The Board announced standards for the metric carat.

Taxi Meters and Gas Meters: In 1907 there was an unresolved controversy about the control of the accuracy of taximeters by the police and in 1911 Inspectors in Liverpool carried out exploratory road tests.

The Society found it curious that gas meters were not covered by weights and measures legislation. There had been separate provision for the testing of gas meters since the Gas Act 1859, and Weights and Measures Inspectors in some local authorities did carry out this duty. In 1914, a separate Association of Inspectors of Gas Meters was formed.

Net Weight Campaign: There was some overlap between concerns about short weight and the Incorporated Society's aim to ensure every sale to be by net weight. It was not only the Society, as many traders were embarrassed by the blemishes on their reputation from adverse publicity. The 1900 AGM focused on the continuing saga of sales of tea by gross weight. It was alleged in 1903 that extra heavy paper was being used for bags, especially with tea and sugar. In 1905, the Incorporated Society established a paper Sub-Committee. A report was published the following year and, together with the Law Committee of the Association of Municipal Councils, they made nine recommendations, including that:

- goods should be sold by net weight and in no other manner;
- goods weighed at the time of purchase must be weighed in the presence of the purchaser and
- goods delivered to the purchaser's house must be accompanied by a statement of quantity.

In 1916, it was acknowledged that the demand for legislation was partly met by the Report of the Select Committee in 1914. However, towards the end of 1916, the Board of Trade said that there was little prospect of enacting legislation to implement the Report so quickly.

Another special meeting of the Incorporated Society in Manchester in March 1918 agreed with applause a resolution with five parts:

- That, because of the war, the prevalence of short weight and measure had greatly increased
- That increases in prices and serious short weight had increased problems, especially for the poor
- That the Food Controller should require sales by net weight
- That a duty of enforcement should be placed upon Inspectors of Weights and Measures, and
- That the Executive Council should bring the resolution to the attention of the Minister of Food.

As we have seen the Incorporated Society was deeply concerned about the practice of including the wrapper in the weight of packets of tea and made numerous representations to the Board of Trade. In 1908, they estimated that £1 million was being paid for paper instead of tea. Some wrappers, made from lead foil, accounted for nearly one ounce (or 25%) of packets marked "4 oz including the weight of the wrapper". The same practice was rapidly being extended to other foods. Remedial clauses in a draft Weights and Measures Bill 1904 were withdrawn. In 1905, the Incorporated Society set up a Short Weight and Measure Committee demanding protective legislation. Resolutions of support for this came from local authorities and their associations. Petitions were sent to the Board of Trade.

It took 10 years, until 1914, before a Select Committee of the House of Commons was appointed to inquire into the subject. Although the Committee recommended a ban, the Government announced the time was still not convenient. The War eventually forced the Government to act. For rationing to be effective, it was necessary to equate weight and price, at least for essential foods such as bread and tea. The Tea

(Net Weight) Order and the Bread Order 1917 made sale by net weight compulsory. Bread was also to be sold in loaves of one pound or a multiple of one pound. Maximum price orders for many other foods enabled Inspectors to prosecute when the price charged did not agree with the quantity sold.

Short Weight: In November 1904, there was a review of the cases of short weight and measure which involved either the weighing of wrappers with food or the use of unstamped barrels, bottles, jars and churns. These had been issues of concern since 1881. In 1911, the Incorporated Society called for a private member's bill to make the delivery of short weight a specific offence. In 1913, there was a Short Weight Conference with representatives of 29 local authorities. Resolutions were agreed and a deputation went to the Board of Trade in April 1913. This resulted in the Parliamentary Select Committee on Short Weight, which published a report in 1914. The Committee Report included the following observations:

- Their main concern was to protect consumers and they had been much helped by the Association [sic] of Weights and Measures
- Local authorities should be able to prosecute under Merchandise Marks Acts
- There should be higher penalties
- Short weight should be an offence
- False oral statements should be an offence
- Some wrappers for tea were excessively heavy, but a limit on wrapper weight was impractical
- There should be defences for evaporation, mistake or the fraud of a servant
- A defendant may lay information against his servant.

Manchester City took the lead and wrote to the Board of Trade in 1915 to encourage the implementation of the recommendations of the Select Committee. However, it took a further 12 years, until 1926, for a short weight offence for food to be created and another 50 years for the first almost universal short weight provision. This was the Weights and Measures Act 1963.

Coal and Coke: There were difficulties in 1901 in applying the 1889 Act to the sale of coal. One concern was that a railway truck was not included in the definition of a "vehicle" and a coal merchant was left at the mercy of the colliery owner. In 1903, the Reference Committee of the Society considered the vexed question of the sale of coke, but they had to conclude that the 1889 Act dealt only with coal, not coke. In 1906, Cambridgeshire County Council and the Society proposed that there should be a Sale of Coke Bill similar to the Middlesborough Corporation Act 1910 which controlled sales of coke in that area. In 1913, the Liverpool Corporation Bill aimed to require a weight ticket for all deliveries over 2 cwt (hundredweight). It also required that keepers of weighing machines were licensed.

The Factory and Workshop Act 1901 extended weights and measures control to equipment used to ascertain wages in all industries. In 1911, an American magazine published news about the idea of selling eggs by weight. In 1907, there was a report that magistrates and licensed victuallers were reaching a consensus view that the "Long Pull" should be prohibited.

Bread: In 1903, there was a proposal for bread to be sold in standard weights to include a 2 lb loaf. However there was no consensus within local authorities because only 14 were in favour, with 11 against.

In 1909, there was a case against a Liverpool Inspector for libel because his report indicated that a baker's bread was often short weight, but he escaped conviction by using clever marketing ploys. The verdict was in favour of the plaintiff, but with only one farthing ordered to be paid in damages by the Inspector.

Fish and Cran Measures: In spring 1904, there was approval for a totally new unit of measurement in England. East Suffolk County Council proposed the use of the 'cran' for the sale of herrings. This evoked a response from the Board of Trade that the cran was a legal measure in Scotland but not in England. There were a number of objectors to its use. However, the Government did introduce the Cran Measures Act 1908, legalising the use of cran and quarter cran measures for the sale of fresh herrings in England and Wales. A cran is 37.5 gallons and a quarter cran is 9.375 gallons. Later regulations specified precise dimensions for wooden and woven measures.

Board of Trade: In 1901, a letter in the *Monthly Review* grumbled that if an Inspector sought advice from the Board of Trade the answer on 90% of occasions was that "it is a matter for the local authorities". There has always been a tussle between the comfort of ready answers from the Board of Trade and unwarranted interference from the Board with local autonomy. The Board of Trade Report for 1901 stated that 182 local authorities had stamped 2,569,368 weights, 6,148,634 measures and 216,557 weighing instruments and there had been 1,826 convictions.

Fees: There was growing dissent between Inspectors about verification fees. On one hand, the fees were regarded as useful income for local authorities, creating a temptation for Inspectors to reject equipment without good reason. On the other hand, there was concern about the practice of allowing a rebate to manufacturers on fees for any assistance provided or the size of a consignment. The upshot of many deputations and letters to the Board of Trade was a judgement in the case of Rex v Roberts in 1901. The decision was that

Inspectors and local authorities must charge the prescribed fees in all cases.

Food: Weights and measures work was the major occupation of Inspectors, but in 1900 some 53,046 samples were taken under the Food and Drugs Acts, of which 4,970 were found to be adulterated. There were 3,110 prosecutions.

In the previous century there had been concern about the adulteration of butter and the sale of butter substitutes. In 1907, the Butter and Margarine Act specified the maximum permitted amount of water in butter and butter mixtures. The Incorporated Society pressed the Ministry to give Inspectors the power to enforce the Act and this was granted everywhere except in London. Here the Board of Agriculture and Fisheries was given the task of approving trade names for mixtures of butter, and in December 1908 a list of 33 approved names included Alimo, Bradlac, Casmon, Esselbee and Pearksown.

At this time (1910), deputations and campaigns by the Incorporated Society on food matters had little effect. Progress was generally made when Inspectors prompted action via the local authority associations. In 1910, the County Councils' Association sent a deputation to the Minister proposing amendments to food and drugs legislation. The proposals included extended sampling powers, improved standards for dairy products, restrictions on preservatives, and a ban on vendors contracting out of the requirements of the Act.

There were many novel forms of food adulteration to increase profit margins. In 1906, there was a growing trend for traders to post inconspicuous notices stating that a food was "not guaranteed pure". In 1914, stale eggs from Russia were described as "new laid". In 1913, there were cases of the adulteration of jam, which included the addition of apple pulp and the addition of sesame seed to imitate strawberry pips. The products were euphemistically labelled as "improved".

In 1915, there was reference to the practice of "toning" milk by mixing separated or skimmed milk with fresh or whole milk. One reluctantly admires this euphemistic use of the word "toning". In a more shocking case of special pleading, the Federation of Grocers' Associations in 1916 made strong representations to Government about the undesirability of "highly technical" questions about adulteration being raised by Inspectors during wartime.

Petroleum: The first Petroleum Order dealing with light locomotives was published in 1900. In 1903, there were further regulations about the use of petroleum in vehicles. The *Monthly Review* published a lengthy report in 1902 about Inspectors' duties under the Petroleum Acts. This highlighted its importance and the importance of other so-called ancillary duties. In April 1908, it was noted that the flash-point of petroleum oil had risen with the growth of "automobilism" (sic).

There was comment on a proposal for an "immense" petroleum store in Fulham, and in 1911, it was announced that a licence had been granted for this store to contain 200,000 gallons.

In the Report of H M Inspectors published in 1913, there was reference to seven accidents involving petroleum in one year. One of them was a lady whose hair was being washed in petroleum near a gas stove at a hairdresser's in Hackney. In 1916, a 700-gallon underground tank in Dublin survived a fire above it caused by violent political disturbances.

Explosives: In 1902, there was a fatal explosion at Marple Cheshire in retail premises. One person was killed because illegal quantities of gunpowder were stored and some of the containers had leaked.

Ancillary Legislation: In 1904, Inspectors took samples of 671 fertilisers and 337 feeding stuffs. Many Inspectors also enforced the Shops Acts 1904. This Act required local authorities to establish an early closing day, but only if this was agreed by two-thirds of the traders affected. A few years, later the Shops Act 1912 introduced compulsory half-day closing.

In 1907, a correspondent in the *Monthly Review* drew attention to the Workmen's Compensation Act 1906 and suggested that it made the employer liable for injuries suffered by Inspectors at work. This was an early example of concern about health and safety.

Offences: At the end of 1915, there was a prosecution of a colliery for using a 'Billy Fairplay' spring balance which was a quarter hundredweight out of balance. In 1902, a weight marked 56lb was found to weigh 63.5lb and was being used to determine the wages of employees. In 1914, there was a case of an oilcan labelled as 5 gallons when it actually held 4 gallons because it had a false bottom. The oil company was not fined, but the lorry driver was fined £2 and costs. In 1900, the Editor of the Monthly Review wrote about a correspondent who, very diplomatically, drew attention to "Irregularities, due to the mischievous influence which is exerted on members of local authorities by parties in their constituencies who get into trouble with the Inspector". This led to an article about whether the decision to prosecute should be taken by an Inspector, the Council's Clerk or a Committee (often referred to as the "Star Chamber"). In 1918, an article in the *Justice of the Peace Review* questioned the tendency for legislation to be made by orders or regulations using delegated powers in acts of parliament. This is something which became more and more common and remains familiar in 2013.

Exams and Qualifications: In 1901, the Incorporated Society wanted to introduce a more severe examination than that set by the

Board of Trade. The law relating to the statutory qualification changed in 1904. In 1889, the examination had been *"...to ascertain whether persons acting or appointed as inspectors passed the examination..."* However from 1904 the purpose of the examination was *"...to ascertain whether applicants for the post of Inspector under a local authority recommended by that authority passed the examination..."*

In August 1905, the subjects of the Board of Trade examination were listed as Dictation, Arithmetic, Mensuration, Elementary Mechanics, Elementary Physics, Inspection and the Verification of Equipment. In 1906,the fee for the Board of Trade examination was £1.10s (£1.50). It was alleged that Smethwick had an excessive number of "applicants" "approved" by the Board of Trade. Council members took a critical view and, in 1908, the then Chief Inspector of Smethwick, Howard Cunliffe, resigned as Secretary of the Incorporated Society, a post he had held with distinction for seven years. *"Cunliffe of Smethwick"* also advertised private coaching in the *Monthly Review*. In 1911, there was criticism of misleading statements in advertisements because some candidates found out very late in the day that they had to be employed in a weights and measures department before they could sit the Board of Trade exam. There was also continued criticism about the practice of police officers being used to act as inspectors. Many believed this to be illegal.

Criticisms: In 1912, there were a number of articles in the *Pen Circle* under the title *The Incorporated Society Inspected*. This led to criticism under the rubric 'What has the Society done for me?' Complaints expressed included the following:

- The Executive Council not doing enough to get Inspectors to join
- Unqualified people acting as Chief Inspectors
- Some local authorities launching Inspectors who didn't have a berth or a job to go to
- Nothing happening about a Short Weight Bill
- Typical salary only £150 pa – the same as a mechanic
- Executive Council unrepresentative as 18 of 26 were Chiefs.
- Council having done nothing to prohibit police constables
- Society just a philanthropic body, not for the good of the profession?

Many of these issues still exercise members of the Institute in the 21st century.

Assizers: In 1911 the Society agreed that at the first opportunity the title "Inspector of Weights and Measures" should be changed to "Assizer". However no progress had been made by 1916 and the proposal was allowed to lapse. Nevertheless, from time to time, members suggested this would be a better alternative title, claiming that practice of assizing and marking of weights dated from the time of King Alfred in 871. It was noted that Board of Trade staff who tested local standard weights were called Assizers.

Membership: Most of the administration procedures of the Society for the next 50 years were determined during this period. One encouraging factor was that the membership of the Incorporated Society increased steadily. In 1901, 237 out of about 600 inspectors belonged to the Incorporated Society, and in 1910 there were about 540 Inspectors, of whom 365 were members.

In 1903, an impressively printed membership certificate was produced and later sold to members for half-a-crown (12.5p). The certificates were dated from the date of joining but were not numbered, as this was considered invidious. In 1903, there was a proposal that a Fellowship Certificate should be issued after 12 years' membership, but this was not adopted. However, the rules were changed in 1907 to add a category of Life Membership and the first Life Member was Thomas Jones of Liverpool. Also in 1907, a category of Associate Member was created. An Associate had to be 18 years old, working as a bona fide assistant in a weights and measures department for at least 12 months and must pass an examination set by the Incorporated Society. An Inspector appointed outside the UK could also be an Associate Member.

Society Officers: At the spring meeting in April 1901, it was agreed to dispense with the post of Manager of the *Monthly Review*, but that separate Editors and Secretaries would continue.

Subscriptions: The Society's budget was often in deficit from 1894 to 1900 due to the late payment of subscriptions. However, the overall financial position improved with the growth in membership. In 1905, the subscription for membership was 16/6d (82½p) and the subscription for the *Monthly Review* was 7/6d (37½p). In 1905, there was a major discussion to identify the "benefits of membership", a debate which continues to the present time. In 1912, the subscription for Associate Members was 10/- (50p), with a reduced subscription for members earning less than £104 per annum.

Corresponding Members: In 1900, there was a Chief Corresponding Member and 16 District Corresponding Members, 11 for England and Wales, 4 for Scotland and one for Ireland. In 1904, the Corresponding Department was reorganised with 16 members for England and Wales, seven for Scotland and one for Ireland. One observer sadly claimed that only 140 out of 540 Inspectors attended the AGM. Members suggested that the Executive Council should be chosen by districts. By 1917 there were 19 districts in England, 7 in Scotland and one in Ireland based in Dublin. It was also agreed that the *Monthly Review* should be free to members.

The next advance was to hold meetings in the districts. The first such meeting was held in East Anglia in early 1901. Four other districts – Midland, Lancashire, Cheshire and Derbyshire, and South and West Scotland – held meetings in the years from 1901 to 1904.

Pen Circle: In November 1900, an article on *The Dilemmas of Weights and Measures Inspectors* was published in the *Review* in a column entitled *The Pen Circle Bureau*. Many responses were published. A controversial issue was whether the stamp should be allowed to remain on a scale which was inaccurate because there was no specific power to deface it. In 1902, an Inspector in Bournemouth was fined for defacing the stamp on a scale because he did not have the specific power. He was fined 10/- (50p). *The Pen Circle* seemed an excellent way to air these issues and to provide ideas, criticisms and solutions.

Publications: Considering the limited number of Inspectors, a surprising number of publications became available. One of the first was the *List of Prosecutions,* published by the Society in 1901. This was known as the 'Blue Book'. A *Book of Tolerances* was published privately by an inspector in Dudley in 1904, and this became the precursor of the Incorporated Society's *Handbook*. In 1907, there was a call for a *Treatise on Weighing Machines*, eventually published in 1922 with a completely new edition in 1970. In 1909, the third edition of Roberts' *Handbook on Weights and Measures* was published.

In 1911, a new edition of the *Inspector's Handbook* became available. This edition included the fees charged by the Board of Trade, penalties for weights and measures offences and summaries of appeal cases. A review of the *Handbook* suggested that the gradual expansion in the contents may mean that it would become "too large to fit in a pocket!" In 1912, the *New Edition* cost 2s 3d (11¼p) and was planned to last for two years. A book published commercially by Howard Cunliffe and George A Owen in 1913 contained all the Board of Trade notices up to number 50. The book began with a history from 1866 and was 220 pages long. Price 5/- (25p).

Superannuation: The topic of superannuation for Inspectors was a preoccupation of the Incorporated Society for many years. In 1911, the Society donated £10 to the Municipal Officers Association to support a bid for legislation. In 1914, a Superannuation Bill was unsuccessful in Parliament, but the Society persisted with the campaign. In 1919, there was a White Paper about a superannuation scheme for local government staff, which the Government refused. However, an Act was eventually passed in 1922 which allowed local authorities to opt into an appropriate scheme.

Benevolent Fund: In 1909, the Thrift Scheme and the Mutual Benefit Branch of the Incorporated Society were inaugurated. The purpose was to provide for the dependants of any member who died in service. All members of the Society were invited to join. An example of the benefits was that on the death of any member the sum of 2s 6d (12½p) would be paid by each of the other members for donation to the widow. At the AGM in 1913, the Incorporated Society agreed to establish a Benevolent Fund to replace the Thrift Scheme and Mutual Benefit Branch. It was agreed one shilling per member (5p) should be transferred from the General Fund of the Incorporated Society to the Benevolent Fund.

Violent Deaths: In August 1917, there was a chilling alarm call for all inspectors when it was reported that an Inspector ST White was shot dead in Warwick by TE Vernon, a milkman, who also killed himself. The Inspector was on the premises to take samples of the milk.
Mr WE Hipkins, a director of W&T Avery, scale-makers, lost his life in the sinking of the Titanic in 1912.

The Lighter Side

In January 1900, a "Grave Slander of Inspectors" was causing consternation. Reports which originally appeared in the *Morning Post* contained the allegation that milk in London was often watered and that 75% of Inspectors accepted blackmail payments. Only one in fifty Inspectors was said to be honest.

In 1902, it was reported an American had thrown a 56lb weight a distance of 28 feet 5 in (8.66 metres). The '56 lb weight throw' was an event in the 1920 Olympics, when a record throw of 11.265 metres (36 feet 11½ inches) was made by Pat McDonald USA.

In 1915, a light-hearted correspondent in the *Monthly Review* asked whether automatic vending machines should have a half-day holiday under the Shops Acts.

The motorcar was very new in 1900 but was to have a profound effect on everyone's daily life, including Inspectors. In 1902, there was a fascinating article about the use of a motorcar by an inspector to replace the horse and trap. The speed limit at the time was 12 mph. There was a long list of problems such as loose wires, failure of the accumulator, trouble with the sparking plug and having to push the car home for two miles. The Inspector said he had begun with a motor tricycle and a 'Whippet' trailer. This debate went on for ten or more years. In 1914, a county Inspector sought advice on methods of transport for carrying out inspection. He said a bicycle was not suitable because it was not possible to carry sufficient weights. A horse and cart could only drive 30 miles a day. Was the motorcar an appropriate alternative? There was then a detailed comparison of the costs of using light cars, bicycles and horses and carts. The first Inspector's car was probably a De Dion single cylinder owned by William Crabtree in Nottinghamshire and this was certainly in use in 1902. Correspondents were then asking when the first Inspector would use an aircraft. In 1934, this speculation continued, especially in relation to inspections in the Western Isles.

On a related track, Henry Ford made the intriguing remark that consumers were not infallible. He said that if he had asked his customers what they wanted before the first Model T Ford rolled off the assembly line in 1908 they would have asked for faster horses that ate less.

'MacDuff' was the pen name of a frequent critic of Inspectors. In 1911, MacDuff called Inspectors an "unscrupulous pack of martinets". MacDuff wrote at length about the difficult plight of bakers at the hands of Inspectors. In September 1915, there was another lengthy article about 'MacDuff'. Some of his recent remarks appeared in the National Association Review. He said that the cases besmirched all bakers. Remarks by MacDuff were published until September 1922. To add a positive spin, it could be said that the articles tended to highlight the difficulties that Inspectors face in trying to be fair in carrying out their duties.

Wofflers. The earlier chapter refers to 'wofflers' or imitators of Inspectors. In 1911, there was a fresh call to outlaw bogus inspectors. Yet another Woffler appeared in court in Southwest London in March 1916. He was a scale-maker who attempted to obtain 30/- (£1.50) from a confectioner by representing himself as an Inspector. He had ten previous convictions dating back to 1896. He was sentenced to 18 months in prison, but without hard labour because he had only been charged 'with attempting to obtain money'.

CHAPTER FOUR – 1919 to 1939

Between the Wars - Quiet Progress

Introduction: This chapter covers the years between the two great World Wars. This period was a generally quiet time for weights and measures, but there were some significant changes. There were proposals to continue some wartime regulations in the plan for reconstruction after the First World War. The Incorporated Society continued to examine its proposals that district representatives should occupy at least some positions on its Executive Council. Weights and measures legislation made important advances, and there were also changes to 'ancillary' legislation.

Technological developments and an increase in the variety of goods accelerated in the 20th century. One aspect of growth concerned the safety of the community and general public protection. The Incorporated Society was at the forefront in demanding the law should keep pace with changes in trading practices. Recommendations were put forward, and evidence given to government departments proposing many forms of consumer protection. These included safeguards against adulteration of milk, foods and drugs, the safe storage of dangerous commodities such as petrol, explosives and poisons, and shop hours. After much discussion, petrol delivery systems, which were spreading rapidly, were brought within weights and measures control.

Although this was a quiet time for the Incorporated Society, it was a very busy period for the community in general. Oxford University awarded its first degrees to women in 1920, and universal female suffrage began in 1928. The partition of Ireland was agreed in 1921, and the first Labour Government was elected in 1924. Unemployment reached 17% in 1921, and the Jarrow march for jobs took place in 1936. The Gresford mine disaster killed 266 in North Wales in 1934.

Technological progress was marching onwards, with the first demonstration of the Baird mechanical television in 1926. Electronic TV was demonstrated in 1936, penicillin was discovered in 1928, the first talking film appeared in 1928, the first frozen food in 1937 and the Whittle Jet Engine in 1937. And of course Edward VIII abdicated in 1936.

The chapter will end with the beginning of the Second World War.

Local Government Reorganisation: In 1921, three boroughs agreed to have their weights and measures service provided by the local county council.

A Royal Commission on Local Government was set up in 1923 and took evidence on weights and measures enforcement. The report of the Commission was published in 1930. It concluded that some smaller weights and measures departments could not be effective and that normally county councils and county boroughs should have the duties of administration. However, the duty could remain with non-county boroughs that had their own police force and a population of more than 20,000. As far as food and drugs were concerned, the Commission recommended that the duty should lie with the county and county borough councils although district councils could retain the rights of enforcement and prosecution. County councils would be able to contribute to the costs of the districts if they wished. County councils and county borough councils should also have the power to set up gas meter testing stations.

Commerce: In 1930, the first true supermarket was opened in Queens, New York. It was run by Michael J Cullen and occupied 6,000 square feet. The first in the UK would come some 20 years later. The first home shopping (mail order) business was established in Britain by Littlewoods in 1932.

Citizens Advice Bureaux: The Society (and the Institute) has always had a particularly good relationship with the Citizens Advice Bureaux (CABx). In 1935, the Government considered the need for an information service linked to the fledgling social welfare service. In 1938, with the prospect of a world war looming, the National Council of Social Services (the forerunner of today's National Council of Voluntary Organisations) established a group to decide how to meet the needs of the civilian population in wartime. It was agreed a Citizens Advice Bureaux should be established throughout the country, particularly in the large cities and industrial areas where social disorganisation because of the war might be acute. On 3rd September 1939, war was declared, and on the following day the first 200 CABx were opened.

Weights and Measures: After World War I in 1919, a number of presentations were made about the reconstruction of the country. The Society's suggestions for improvement included scrapping exemptions from Government weights and measures such as post offices, and including weighing equipment in railways, docks and harbours and coalmines. There was also determination to continue the wartime requirements for sale by net weight. Inspectors anticipated regulations on measuring instruments for liquid fuels and oils, and clarification of the role of National Physical Laboratory. The Society urged a decision on the adoption of the metric system. Other issues included control of personal weighing machines and regulation of the sale of coke.

In 1919, the Consumers Council established during the war demanded that it should continue in existence until food control was abolished. A Sub-Committee of Council noted that no action had been taken on the recommendations about net weight. The Council also issued a list of foods that should be regulated, including tea, bread and jam. In 1921, the wartime food orders were rescinded. The first success of the Society's joint campaign came with the Sale of Tea Act 1922, which permanently confirmed the sale of tea by net weight. Four years later, it was followed by the important Sale of Food (Weights and Measures) Act 1926 which controlled a wide range of foodstuffs.

Importantly, the functions of the wartime Food Controller were transferred to local authorities with full enforcement powers given to Inspectors. The sale of bread was a cause of division within the Incorporated Society. One faction wanted to see the continuation of laws requiring the sale of loaves in fixed weights of 1 lb or multiples of a pound, which would lead to simplicity. Other Inspectors were sympathetic to the difficulties of baking loaves of fixed weight, because of uneven baking in the ovens and the subsequent loss of weight from evaporation.

In 1925, Inspector Allan Granger, Birmingham, echoed the thoughts of many when he wrote a wide-ranging plea for the revision of legislation. He mentioned the problems of short weight, net weight, evaporation and prepacked goods. He pointed out that still no action had been taken on the 1870 commission report which recommended the control of quantity marking on all prepacked goods.

Sale of Food 1926: A National Food Council was established to advise the Government. It met for the first time in July 1925 to examine supplies and processing of foodstuffs. The Council had two lady members and, to inform its work, established a Statistical Committee. The Council examined 60 complaints from the public and received evidence on behalf of the Incorporated Society from George Cole, Chief Inspector of Weights and Measures in Manchester. The main points of evidence (and recommendation) were that

- giving short weight and measure should be an offence,
- all articles should be sold by weight or measure, unless exempt,
- all sales by weight should be by net weight unless exempt,
- all items ready for sale should be marked or labelled with weight,
- the Orders for bread and tea should be re-enacted,
- milk should be sold by standard measure,
- meat, when delivered to the purchaser, should have a weight ticket,
- the scale should be visible to the purchaser, if weighed at time of sale,
- and that enforcement should be with the local authorities administering the Weights and Measures Acts.

The Grocer magazine protested that the evidence from the Incorporated Society was exaggerated and had painted all traders as habitually giving short weight.

The final 22 recommendations of the National Food Council were generally in line with the wishes of the Society, but with some exceptions. In essence, the Report identified that certain foods should be sold by net weight and others in prescribed quantities, that a weight ticket should be delivered with meat and that the law on warranties should be clarified. Inspectors would have powers to check the weights of foods at wholesalers. There should be a defence to allow for evaporation and/or mistake, but claims of average weight and false oral statements would be an offence. These recommendations were largely followed in the Sale of Food (Weights and Measures) Act 1926.

This controlled the sale of certain foodstuffs but did not make short weight a general offence for non-food. However, the Act did bring about a sea-change in the scope and character of the weights and measures service. The powers of Inspectors were no longer largely confined to testing, stamping and inspecting weighing and measuring equipment used in trade. Many commodities were now subject to inspection in depots and shops and on wholesale and packing premises and also in the course of delivery. This enabled control to be exercised throughout all the main channels of distribution. Despite the long wait most Inspectors were satisfied.

In 1927, regulations dealt with the manner of marking prepacked food and the manner of resealing after a check by an Inspector. A campaign to extend similar provisions to goods soon began. The approach of Inspectors to enforcement can be best summed up by quoting a paper given to the Incorporated Society's Annual Conference in 1927. The speaker said:

> "I feel that very few prosecutions will be necessary, let us always pause and consider what the law was intended for, namely, the suppression of the man who wilfully cheats or wilfully deceives as to the weight or measure of the goods he sells."

Despite this assertion, it must be noted that offences were absolute offences, subject to specified safeguards. The Act could be used to penalize serious carelessness or negligence as well as wilful fraud. From that time, there was continuous dialogue between the Incorporated Society and the Board of Trade.

In 1929, there were concerns about the scarcity of Inspectors following the impact of the 1926 Act. There were then 575 Inspectors in England, Wales and Scotland.

Milk Bottles: In 1932, a special general meeting of the Society was arranged to discuss the sale of milk in bottles. The meeting was held in response to a proposal from manufacturers that they should be able to apply a mark equivalent to an Inspector's stamp. The meeting opposed the idea and urged

- the licensing of manufacturers by the Board of Trade,
- the marking of a line on each bottle,
- the use of letters to identify the manufacturer on each bottle,

- an amendment of existing law to permit use of these bottles,
- a right of access to factories by Inspectors, with
- local authorities deciding on inspection criteria.

In January 1936, the provisions relating to milk bottles were deleted from the Weights and Measures Bill then before Parliament.

Sand and Ballast: In 1935, the Society commented on the draft Sand and Ballast Bill. They recommended that small quantities should be exempt, that sand and ballast should be clearly defined, and that laws should apply to carriage as well as sale. Inspectors should have power to demand to see delivery tickets which would be deemed to be statements by the seller.

The Bill led to the Weights and Measures (Sand and Ballast) Act 1936 which gave Inspectors considerable control over the sale of those commodities.

This was a unique piece of legislation because it was primarily promoted by a trade association – the Sand and Ballast Association. They reported that voluntary action had failed to prevent much of the short weight and that fraud was prevalent. The Act was difficult to enforce because of the freebooting nature of the trade. In spite of this, Inspectors turned the function into a valuable deterrent, particularly in dealing with 1939-1945 wartime construction sites and early peacetime reclamation after 1945. A number of large-scale frauds were detected and prosecuted.

Weighing and Measuring Equipment: Many changes were taking place in this period. Older types of weighing equipment were being replaced by machines that gave a visual indication of weight. More and more measuring instruments were installed for the sale of petrol. Electronic instruments were coming into use, especially for automatic weighing and packaging. In 1939, there was correspondence in the *Monthly Review* about the use of electric printers with weighbridges – another indication of technology striding forward. Inspectors had to learn how to understand and react to new developments of this type. This led to demands for more inspectors.

The measurement of leather and the use of counting machines became focuses of attention, and were prescribed in 1921 and 1926.

A *Monthly Review* letter suggested in 1919 that the acquisition of a vehicle with a gross weight of 25 tons was needed to test weighbridges, with a crane to lift 1-ton weights. This appears to have been the first vision for the creation of an Official Weighbridge Testing Unit.

The increasing complexity and ingenuity of weighing and measuring equipment is demonstrated by the fact that by November 1936 over 800 Section 6 Notices (*Board of Trade Notices*), had been issued.

Liquid Fuel and Lubricating Oil: Petrol pumps were quite common in 1921, but there were no regulations about testing and stamping. This was the subject of lengthy discussions prior to the introduction of the Weights and Measures (Amendment) Act 1926 which allowed the Board of Trade to make regulations. These were issued in 1929 for liquid fuel and lubricating oil instruments. The Society welcomed the regulations but regretted the long delay and the fact that instruments which did not comply with the regulations would be allowed to continue in use for some unspecified time: for example, there were in Glasgow in 1931 160 twin containers, 401 piston types, 29 subdivided containers and 5 flow-meters for the sale of petrol.

Despite the new regulations in September 1932, there was a letter from Sir Malcolm Campbell in the *Daily Mail* questioning the accuracy of petrol pumps (Sir Malcolm being the holder of the world land speed record at various times between 1927 and 1935 and the first person in the world to drive a car at over 300 mph).

Gas Meters: The fact that the testing of gas meters was carried out by another band of inspectors had been a frustration for Inspectors of Weights and Measures for many years. New gas measurement regulations were introduced in 1920. Under this Act examinations were to be held. At the first examination in 1921, five of the nine candidates passed, and in that year the Association of Statutory Inspectors of Gas Meters was inaugurated.

Inspectors: There was much speculation at the end of 1927 that more Inspectors would be needed to enforce the 1926 Act and worries that unqualified staff might be required to enforce the impending short weight provisions. The *Monthly Review* published a diatribe about the high cost of living and blamed bakers, drapers and dairymen, amongst others. It is interesting that the famous illustration of the trader and customer trying to manipulate the scales in their favour was based on a story imported from France, although it appears to be in an American style.

In 1935, RJ Trump of the Standards Department of the Board of Trade wrote about the interpretation of the well-known phrase 'facilitation of the perpetration of fraud'. He hit out, saying he was aware every one of the 600 Inspectors in the country was waiting to criticise each and every decision of the Board of Trade. He was also surprised that manufacturers continued to submit patterns of equipment that clearly failed to comply with the regulations.

Later in the year, the same RJ Trump claimed many Inspectors were too ready to prosecute, the outcome often being a puny fine and resentment from the trading community, which undermined respect for the law and the Inspectorate.

Standard Units: In April 1924, the *Monthly Review* featured another of the regular reports about the definition of units of length by reference to the wavelength of light, on this occasion the light from the element cadmium. In 2012, the definition of the metre by reference to distance travelled by light was a tiny fraction of a second. Shock, horror! In January 1931, the UK standard yard was found to be 0.0002 inches shorter in length than it was 80 years before. At that time, five duplicates of the standard still existed at the Royal Mint, the Royal Society, the Royal Observatory, the House of Commons and the Board of Trade.

The lead article in the *Monthly Review* in January 1935 called for another major review of weights and measures legislation. The Editor pointed to the continued use of customary units and the multiplicity of enforcing authorities, particularly in Scotland.

Metrication: In 1922, the Joint Board of UK Scientific Societies decided not to support the metric system because they saw clear advantages in an octaval system (base 8) compared with a decimal system (base 10).

Food Quality: Concerns about adulteration of food continued to be vexatious. The People's League of Health (founded in 1917) submitted evidence to the Minister which stated that "on every hand can be found examples of deception of the public in the matter of the sale of foodstuffs". The Sub-Committee of the Food Consumers Council recommended that wartime standards should continue. Regulations on preservatives and colouring matter were made in 1925 and consolidated in 1928, to provide that penalties in some cases should be paid to the local authority.

In 1934, another departmental committee on food reviewed the appointment of food and drugs authorities. It found that there were 61 county councils, 83 county boroughs and 51 non-borough councils enforcing the law. It recommended that future enforcement authorities should be county councils, county boroughs and urban areas with a population over 40,000.

Petroleum: In 1922, the Society sought improvements to the petroleum laws, including the imposition of an enforcement duty on local authorities and a requirement that Inspectors should pass a 'petroleum' examination. In March 1924, there were five appeals in Gloucester against the refusal of licences for installations with swing arms across the pavement. The appeals were dismissed. Swing arms were regarded as hazardous with smokers passing beneath them, but they continued in use in many other places for many years.

In 1924, there was an accident near Nuneaton. A passenger struck a match while the driver of an omnibus was replenishing the tank from a petrol can carried on the vehicle. Tragically eight people were killed.

The Petroleum Act 1926 made various amendments but did not entirely replace legislation dating back to 1871. In November 1936, an explosion in an above ground petrol tank in Hull with a capacity of one million gallons killed three people. A Petroleum (Consolidation) Act received royal assent in 1928.

Explosives: It is shocking to realise that 26 people were killed in one year in 1931 while keeping, making or using explosives.

Fertilisers and Feeding Stuffs: In 1920, the Society led a deputation to Government to press for improvements to the Fertilisers and Feeding Stuffs Act 1906. The demands included extension of time limits, power to fix responsibility for offences on the right person, extension of rules relating to limited companies, an obstruction offence and prohibition of contracting out. The Fertilisers and Feeding Stuffs Act 1926 was introduced and sufficed for the next 40 years.

Ancillary Legislation: At the AGM of the Incorporated Society in 1928 a paper was presented about "quasi-criminal" offences where there was no element of *mens rea*.

It was unusual for the enforcement of legislation about poisons to cause concern, but in 1933 various Grocers' Associations objected to Inspectors being given powers of entry under the Pharmacy and Poisons Act 1933. Their reasons were unclear.

In June, there was a conference paper about the practical aspects of enforcing the overloading provisions of the Road Traffic Act 1930, including the possible use of a 'Stop' sign. In 1936, a Magistrates' Court in Buckinghamshire decided that the Stop sign devised by the Society and used by Inspectors was legal.

Lay Advocates: In 1920, a judge commented on the undesirability of allowing police officers to act as advocates. His main criticism was that advocates were expected to assist the court and not go 'all out' for a conviction. The *Monthly Review* commented that similar considerations could be applied to other 'lay' advocates, including the many Inspectors who regularly presented their cases in court.

Whistle Blower: In January 1926, a trade unionist alleged that his firm was training staff to give short weight. Instructions to staff were:
- How to judge which customers can be given short weight with least risk.
- How best to divert the attention of customers from the actual weighing of the goods which were being purchased.
- How to place articles on the scale so that the balance should be turned by the force of the impact, and
- Various other artfully conceived ideas by which the customer could be defrauded.

Training: In 1919, Inspector WE Allen of Kent advanced the idea of providing apprenticeships and improving the training and qualification of Inspectors. He said this would raise status and levels of remuneration. In 1928, 86 people took the Board of Trade examination but only 14 were successful. Following this debacle, there were in June 1929 various suggestions about how to help train Trainee Inspectors. In April 1933, a correspondent suggested that Inspectors should re-examine themselves from time to time to ensure that they remained competent and up to date. This was the first mention of the idea of CPPD (Continuing Professional and Personal Development) with which we are now so familiar.

Scale-makers: The periodical concern about the relationship between the Incorporated Society and scale-makers reared its head again. Sixteen scale companies sent representatives to the AGM of the Society in 1926. However, a follow-up letter in the *Monthly Review* criticised the over-enthusiastic spirit of cooperation by Inspectors towards scale-makers. There were various opinions on the appropriate level of professional etiquette, fraternising and even "flirting" between Inspectors and scale-makers. In part of the debate it was noted that the Executive Council had agreed to ask manufacturers of weighing and measuring equipment to read papers at Conference from time to time.

The Incorporated Society

The Council: In 1928, the eight committees of the Incorporated Society were Parliamentary, Weights and Measures, Reference, General Purposes, Short Weight and Measure, Handbook, Membership and Finance. By 1935 the Weights and Measures and Reference Committees had merged, the Handbook Committee had been discontinued and two new committees for Service Conditions and Organisation had been created. This demonstrated the demands and priorities of Council members at this time. In 1933, the Editor welcomed the enthusiasm of district organisations and the likely move to district representation on the Executive Council. In 1934, the members of the Executive Council were 20 men who had all been elected by national ballot.

Status of Inspectors: The status of Inspectors was a 'burning' policy preoccupation. Some members were concerned that the qualification and the enormous growth in knowledge was not being recognised. In 1930, a spirited article spelled out the value of the weights and measures service to the nation. In 1937, there were yet more papers calling for recognition and extolling the benefits of the highly qualified service. The Incorporated Society vigorously pursued better conditions of service and remuneration.

Departmental Names: The Council dealt with views about the names of departments and the Incorporated Society. One group proposed the Society should be re-named the Chartered Institute of Assizers. Others pursed an application for the granting of a Royal Charter to the Incorporated Society. In 1932, that application was refused. In 1937, it was suggested that the titles of all Weights and Measures departments should be changed to Public Control Departments.

Districts and Branches: The Scottish District was established in 1928. In 1935, there were a total of 12 districts and these were East Anglia, East Midland, Lancashire Cheshire and North Wales, Midland, Northumberland and Durham, Scotland, South East Midland, South Eastern, South Wales, South Western, West and Yorkshire. It is therefore perhaps remarkable that the AGM of the Incorporated Society was never held outside London before 1933. In 1938, the Editor wrote about another odd predicament: a body of members was campaigning for the *Monthly Review* to exclude references to all ancillary functions because they felt the *Review* should deal only with weights and measures matters.

Handbook: Useful reference material was provided by the Incorporated Society. This included new editions of the *Inspector's Handbook*, published in 1922 and 1928. There was also the *Treatise on Weighing Machines* by George A Owen, published by Charles Griffin, and a book of the first 250 *Board of Trade Notices* (section 6 Notices), published in 1928.

Superannuation: The demand for a superannuation scheme continued into its fifth decade. In 1924, 66 local authorities had adopted the provisions of the Superannuation Act 1922. This allowed local authorities to establish their own scheme. In 1934, hope was expressed by the Incorporated Society that a Superannuation Bill to compel authorities to adopt a scheme would succeed.

Salaries: At the AGM in 1921 there was a debate on salary levels and optimism about a favourable Whitley Council Report and on-going work by NALGO on the subject. In 1937 and 1939, there were further reports on the campaign for national salary scales. These were not achieved until the 1950s.

On the Lighter Side...

A 1924 *Monthly Review* set out an Inspector's dream of the future. The dream included a weighbridge with a dial and a loudspeaker that announced the weight and worked using "steel bands, discs and rods and the like". Inspectors were no longer required for many functions because managers of businesses would stamp their own machines.

Finally, the Inspector stood on a scale which hit him hard and rejected him for being too sensitive and no longer able to withstand ordinary wear and tear.

A nostalgic leading article in a 1922 *Monthly Review* bemoaned the trials and tribulations of the modern Inspector. These included frustration over superannuation, problems of testing "monster" weighbridges and calculating scales, the monkey tricks of repairers and the "metric thing".

In September 1922, there were lengthy quotations from the anonymous 'MacDuff' about *Unspeakable Inspectors*. These included the allegation that Inspectors want the law on bread weights to be easy to enforce rather than fair to the baker.

In 1931, *Tit-Bits* magazine reported that a scientist had used a cosmic balance to calculate the mass of the Earth as 6 thousand trillion tons or 81 times the mass of the moon. That is 6 followed by 21 zeros. This was pretty accurate because the calculation at the time of writing (2013) is that the mass in tons is 5.886 followed by 21 zeros.

Great Guy (1936) was a very popular Hollywood film starring James Cagney as an honest weights and measures inspector taking on corrupt traders and politicians. It was originally premiered in England under the title *Pluck of the Irish* because the producers thought everyone might believe it was a film about Guy Fawkes.

In 1937, a poem appeared in the *Monthly Review* under the title *Ancient History*. It was the tale of a member of staff who allowed his attention to wander whilst adjusting a large quantity of weights. The final two verses reveal the outcome of his efforts while drilling a new adjusting hole:

"With thankful sigh he ceased his toilsome grind,
The drill was buried deeply in the weight,
He lifted it and then rejoiced to find
The hole was bored quite uniform and straight.

Then suddenly he stiffened and a glare
Of horror in his tortured eyes expanded,
He reeled and shrieked out in despair . . .
"Great Jupiter, I've drilled the Local Standard."

CHAPTER FIVE – The 1940s

War Peace and Reconstruction

Introduction: This chapter deals with just one decade, because so many things were happening in British society and within the 'Institute'. The first half of the period was dominated by the Second World War. This was a tragic time for everyone and a number of Institute members died on active service or as civilians. Shortages of food and other goods led to many control orders enforced by Inspectors. It also became a time to rebuild, and a small part of the reconstruction movement was a review of weights and measures and ancillary legislation. However, the priorities after the war were the politics of railway and industrial nationalisation and the creation of the National Health Service.

War: The Second World War was declared on 3rd September 1939. The Government and local authorities had been planning for the prospect of war for some time. Decisions had been made about the men to be called up and those who would serve in volunteer or territorial units.

There were to be nearly six years of relentless stress. The first member of the Incorporated Society to die in action was Sergeant-Pilot HE Black of Leicestershire, a member of the RAF, who died of wounds suffered in air combat on 9th November 1940. It is noteworthy that the first Incorporated Society member to die in the First World War was also named Black; he was James William Black of Edinburgh. Our Honorary Secretary, Alan Charles Ashburner, was killed by enemy action on 10th May 1941. He was at his office at the London County Council when it was destroyed, along with all of the records of the Incorporated Society. He had been Editor of the *Monthly Review* from 1938 and Secretary since December 1940. It proved impossible to replace many of the Institute's records. In 1941, the Offices of Coventry Weights and Measures were damaged and all local records destroyed. The AGM held in June 1943 reported that 120 members of the Society were serving in the Armed Forces.

The number of meetings were much reduced. In 1942, the *Monthly Review* was produced in smaller format, 10 inches by 7 inches (25cm x 18cm) instead of 12 inches by nine, and with fewer pages. Some monthly editions were combined.

In 1940, the Editor wrote that enforcement must continue, as experience showed that unscrupulous people often try to feather their nests in wartime. Public protection was important. However, unlike the First World War the job of an Inspector was not defined as a 'reserved occupation'.

Control Orders: There were many control orders setting maximum prices and much liaison between the Society, Food Control Committees and the Ministry of Food. The *Monthly Review* pointed out that grocers would be bringing back obsolete scales, beam balances and the weights needed to weigh out the small quantities of the foods which were now rationed, such as butter and sugar. The first Orders made in 1939 were for sugar, potatoes, eggs and herrings. They were not easy to digest. In February 1940, R Race of Tunbridge Wells wrote:

"Those inspectors who have not yet been caught up in the Food Control System and whose patriotic fervour is straining at the leash may be interested to know that 125 statutory Orders have emanated from the Ministry of Food by January 1940. A perusal of them is guaranteed to dissipate the eagerness of all but the most zealous."

The Editor of the *Monthly Review* wrote an open letter to the Food Minister drawing attention to enforcement difficulties. These now embraced 75 commodities from apples, bacon and bananas to tomatoes, turkeys and wheat. There were some rumours that the Ministry of Food was frustrated by inadequate enforcement and might therefore take over direct control of weights and measures. This did not happen.

Parts of the Food and Drugs Act 1938 were suspended. New regulations required quantity marking, the common name of the food, the name of the packer and a new offence of 'exposing food for sale in contravention of the regulations' (as distinct from it actually having been sold), requirements which are familiar today.

In April 1946, an Order reduced the weight of loaves to 14 ounces or a multiple of 14 ounces. The standard loaf then became 28 ounces instead of 2 lbs (32 ounces), a requirement which had existed since 1917. It was widely believed the change would be short-lived, but it lasted until the metric equivalent of 400 grams was introduced in 1988.

Europe: In 1946, Winston Churchill spoke of his vision for a United States of Europe. This was in distinct contrast to the posture of isolationism which he had adopted before the War. In 1946, he said:

"We must build a kind of United States of Europe. In this way only will hundreds of millions of toilers be able to regain the simple joys and hopes which make life worth living."

The Future: It is interesting that in February 1942 the Editor still found the time to lament that there was no general short weight offence in legislation.

At this time many organisations began discussing how they wanted to see the country modernised when the War was over – a process known as 'Reconstruction'. The Society agreed to be involved with the Reconstruction Committee of NALGO, and in June the Incorporated

Society established a Reconstruction Sub-Committee that began a lengthy consultation with members. An Interim Report was issued by the Council in November 1942. This was known as the 'Reading Proposals' and included the following conclusions and recommendations:

- There was an uneven distribution of qualified staff.
- Since 1881 lack of uniformity remained.
- Some offices had inadequate equipment.
- Some local authority committees exerted improper influence.
- There were wide variations in salaries.
- Income from fees led some authorities to view Inspectors simply as a fund-raising resource.
- The Board of Trade should set examinations, appoint and dismiss inspectors, and then set salaries and grades.
- There should be a national weights and measures structure with a Chief Inspector for the United Kingdom, Regional Superintendents and Area Chief Inspectors.

These recommendations generated many letters and articles. In 1943, the Society's AGM rejected the 'Reading Proposals' by the substantial majority of 90 votes to six. The antagonism was focused on opposition to the proposals for centralisation. However, the Incorporated Society made little impression on government until the mood for reconstruction became more positive towards the end of the War. In November 1943, an agenda was agreed with the Board of Trade. The purpose was to urge the President of the Board to establish an inquiry to consider improvements, including:

- Reduction of the six different systems of weights in use
- Elimination of local customary units
- Redefinition of the word 'trade'
- Review of powers to control local services
- Re-verification to be compulsory at given intervals
- Inspection of gas, electricity and water meters
- Better regulation of the sale of coal, coke and other fuels
- Revision of Board of Trade powers for pattern approval
- Setting of admission requirements for the exam qualification
- Extension of Inspectors' powers
- Proper control of short weight and measure
- Evaluation of High Court decisions
- Standardisation of packages
- Establishment of controls on oil tanks, barges and bulk containers.

A **Joint Committee** of six people was created with four members from the Society plus FS Barber and TG Poppy from the Board of Trade. Their report, known as *The Green Book*, was considered at a special meeting in 1945. It did not meet with universal approval. The South-East Midland District expressed concern about the idea of Assistant Inspectors. At the AGM in 1945, it was agreed the report was not yet ready for publication. The Council nominated TH Jenks, R Robertson and Tom Metcalfe to speak to an inter-departmental committee considering the future of weights and measures.

In 1948, another departmental committee was appointed to review the Weights and Measures Acts. The Incorporated Society formed a special team to prepare and give evidence. The Society produced a vast amount of written and oral evidence during its incredible life of 48 meetings. The Departmental Committee's Final Report was the first comprehensive survey of weights and measures law for over 80 years, but once again the Government was not prepared to take immediate action.

Despite achieving little result, the Society's reputation (and the status of Inspectors) was significantly enhanced by its contributions and was warmly commended for "promoting ever higher standards in all spheres of the weights and measures service". This seems to be the time when the Incorporated Society became recognized as a professional body.

The Government then set up yet another committee of enquiry and this eventually this led to the publication of the groundbreaking *Blue Book* or *Hodgson Report* in May 1951. This is considered in the next chapter.

Specialisation: In July 1946, Edgar C Writer of Liverpool published a review paper about the need for specialisation. It was accompanied by a table showing which legislation was being enforced by which departments. 752 Inspectors enforced weights and measures, 214 food and drugs, 270 pharmacy and poisons, 192 petroleum, 212 explosives and 170 road traffic. He identified three classes of inspectors, namely, [a] those who perform only weights and measures; [b] those who also carry out functions allocated to counties and [c] those who also carry out duties allocated to boroughs. He was surprised inspectors were not required to take examinations in any of the 'ancillary' functions.

Lady Inspectors: In April 1943, the Editor wrote about the sensitive topic of Lady Inspectors. He was notably chauvinistic and saw obstacles if they had to handle heavy weights or deal with awkward traders. In the same edition, there is a letter about a female in the Women's Auxiliary Police Force in Gravesend being transferred to weights and measures staff in order to take the Board of Trade exam. No record has been found of the outcome.

Weights and Measures: In 1943, Inspector A Granger of Norfolk advocated many familiar ideas for improvements to weights and measures law. He asked that the metric system be adopted, that gas and electricity meters should be tested by Inspectors and, most controversially, that the weights and measures inspection service should be centralised.

In 1946, the Heyworth Committee recommended that the Ministry of Power should take over responsibility for the testing of gas meters from the Board of Trade.

Food Law: In 1947, the Ministry of Food reported on the Advertising, Labelling and Composition of Food. This said that a central administration operating alongside local enforcement worked very well.

Prosecutions: There were many prosecutions during this period. One of the most serious was reported in April 1941 and involved the delivery (or non-delivery) of sand and ballast. The defendants were sent to the Assizes for sentence, and the ringleader was jailed for a substantial period of 22 months.

Examinations: In 1942, the Board of Trade examination was held in Blackpool instead of London because of the War. Eight candidates passed. At the end of 1943, it was decided that candidates in the Services would be permitted to take the Board of Trade Exam in two parts and in the candidate's own military unit. After the War, exemptions from parts of the exam were announced for candidates who had served in the Forces. These concessions were finally withdrawn after the examination in April 1948. Only 21 candidates passed the Examination in 1949. The first Training Secretary for the Incorporated Society was JR (Reg) Roberts of Manchester City. In 1949, there was a call for a post-entry training scheme for experienced Inspectors who wished to advance in the profession.

Board of Trade: In 1945, there was frustration at the high-handed approach of the Board of Trade in connection with the release of new instructions to trade interests before informing the Inspectorate.

After the war, there was a continuing campaign to increase the number of members of the Incorporated Society. The Honorary Secretary wrote to all Trainee Inspectors inviting them to become Associate Members. This had moderate success because the 16 Associates in 1949 increased to 89 by 1951. In 1948, the Executive Council welcomed a report from the Chief Corresponding Member, Harry Robinson, who recommended there should be more technical content in the *Monthly Review*.

Financial Crisis: In 1947, the Incorporated Society faced a financial crisis. The annual subscription had not been increased for 30 years. The Executive Council confirmed that expenditure exceeded income in the first five months of 1947 by £74 on an income of £402. However, a vote at a special general meeting in May 1947 to increase the subscription to £2 10s (£2.50) was unsuccessful, as it failed to achieve the required 75% majority. In October 1947, the overdraft had grown to £350. Finally, at a special general meeting later in the year, it was agreed to increase the annual subscription to 2½ guineas (£2 12s 6d, equivalent to £2.62½). The subscription for Associate Members was set at one guinea (£1 1s 0d, equivalent to £1.05).

Society Rules: At the Executive Council in October 1944, a motion from AGM to review the Rules was considered. It was agreed the proposals drafted in 1935 were a good starting point. These included a Memorandum of Association: Articles and Byelaws. Each district would elect a member of the Executive Council, and a national ballot would elect the other members. A postal vote or referendum could be taken on any important matter. In 1949, a proposal that district representatives should replace the nationally elected members was defeated.

Name Change: At the end of the War, many members believed the old title of the Incorporated Society was out of date. They began to consider a name change, although it is not absolutely clear where the idea began.
However, a debate in the East Midlands branch in February 1948 considered whether the name should change to either the Institute of Assizers or the Institute of Weights and Measures Administration. A year later, the Executive Council agreed to alter the title to the Institute of Weights and Measures Administration, despite a powerful plea from Roger Breed of Dorset, on behalf of the South-West District, that it should become the Institute of Assizers. In August 1949, it was confirmed the title had changed to the Institute of Weights and Measures Administration (IWMA), with a certificate from the Registrar of Companies.

Public Relations: In this decade a lot of members believed the Incorporated Society was not properly recognised and was inefficient in 'selling' the work of its members to central and local government or to the public. In 1940, Mr H Brentnall, a member in Uganda, suggested the Society should commission a film about the work of Inspectors. He listed some of the possible scenes, including small and large shops, Avery's factory and testing a weighbridge and a petrol pump. In 1947, JH Sowden Hall of Reading wrote an article on *Public Relations*. His suggestions included moving the Conference around the country, inviting councillors to tour their department while verifications were taking place, participating in local government exhibitions, speaking to schoolchildren and talking to groups of adults and trade associations. In 1948, John Horsfall of Wolverhampton expressed his concern that for generations the Incorporated Society appeared to have "sought shadows and obscurity". He thought the Society should improve relations with the local authority associations, NALGO, the Ministries and others with whom Inspectors came into contact. He suggested that the Society should set up a Public Relations Committee and appoint a Public Relations Officer. Some Inspectors were already taking positive steps. For example, in March 1948, LG Greenhill of Surrey gave a talk on *Weights and Measures* in the Woman's Hour radio programme on the Home Service of the BBC (now Radio 4). Pathe News made a film about weights and measures inspection in Lewisham Market, London. In 1948, the Editor criticised the press, including *The Times*, for unfair negative comment on the work of Inspectors. He too supported better public relations.

A presentation by Kenneth Nattrass of Dorset was published in 1949. He began with the premise that very few members of the public knew what local government officials, and weights and measures Inspectors in particular, actually did. He said that this was bad news for democracy. He suggested that public relations should include personal relations with the public, talks to schoolchildren, improved relationships with national and local press, more public meetings to find out what the public wants, better cooperation with voluntary organisations, local and national, setting up local information bureaux and the use of films and exhibitions.

Information Service and Library: In October 1945, leading figure Roger Breed of Dorset suggested that the Incorporated Society should establish a Central Information Bureau. The purpose of the Bureau would be to record all formal opinions which had been made on problems, important legal decisions and "danger spots". He thought that it should be a task for the Society, but that it might attract funding from one or more ministries.

No action was taken at this time, but Roger Breed presented a similar report to the Council three years later. He included estimates of the cost of printing and distributing information. It was resolved to accept the Report, but again no action was taken. In parallel with these ideas, there was a proposal that the Society should start a library, and in December 1949, Maurice Stevenson of Eastbourne published an article about his views on how the Institute could establish such a library. Maurice subsequently became the Institute's first Librarian in 1955 (see next chapter).

Trade Unions: All the trade union activities that had been carried on by the Incorporated Society ceased, with immediate effect, when the Society became the Institute in 1949.

Paid Officers: A unanimous vote at the AGM in 1941 resolved to investigate the idea of the appointment of a professional secretary. In 1942, the Executive Council saw difficulties in using the title of Secretary and decided to offer the post of Accountant to Mr C Dale of

Marshall, Hurst and Co. The appointment was made on an experimental basis and after only four years it was terminated. The Council appointed a shorthand typist in his stead.

On the Lighter Side...

In 1941 a member, F S Milner of Wolverhampton, was the referee at an international football match between England and Scotland at Wembley Stadium.

Stanley Gascoigne of Sheffield won three prizes in the 1947 International TT Race on the Isle of Man, including one for being the fastest rider to compete for the first time. He later became Chief Inspector in Sheffield and a prominent figure in the Institute.

Various sources give different opinions about the first self-service shop in Britain. The earliest suggestion is a Cooperative shop in Romford in 1942. There is also a plaque on the wall in Albert Road, Portsmouth stating "these premises were converted by the Portsea Island Mutual Cooperative Society Limited in March 1948 to become the first self-service shop in Great Britain". Another reference states that there were ten self-service stores in the country in 1947.

The *Daily Mail* complained during the war that beer was "deficient in kick", but yet there were no prosecutions. One outlandish suggestion was that coalhouses should be of a standard size so that customers could check deliveries more easily.

Conclusion: The 1940s ended on a high note of hope and expectation The Institute was confident that weights and measures administration would soon be updated and modernised. However, real change took a little longer.

CHAPTER SIX – The 1950s

Lobbying and Hodgson

Introduction: This decade found the country still recovering from the War with rationing of several staple foods still in place. Petrol rationing ended in May 1950, but the rationing of meat did not stop until July 1954. A major report on a review of weights and measures administration was published after considerable input from the Institute, but the recommendations were not implemented for many years despite persistent campaigns.

Memorable events included the 1951 Festival of Britain, staged to celebrate reconstruction after the war, and the opening of the first length of motorway as the Preston bypass in 1958. This ultimately became part of the M6.

Reorganisation (The Green Book): The controversy about which local authorities should be entrusted with weights and measures continued. In May 1953, there was a report from county councils and other associations (but not boroughs and county boroughs) entitled *Local Government Reorganisation*. The counties proposed that county boroughs with populations of less than 75,000 should lose that status, and urban areas with populations of more than 100,000 should become county boroughs. There was a recommendation that weights and measures administration should be dealt with by the counties and county boroughs. The Government merely agreed to consider the report.

In 1956, a Government White Paper was published entitled *Areas and Status of Local Authorities in England and Wales*. The Report favoured the creation of larger authorities in urban areas and a reduction in the number of small boroughs. County boroughs would usually exceed a population of 100,000 and in the conurbations would exceed 125,000. Two commissions were established for England and Wales to work up detailed boundary proposals. There were no concrete proposals for the allocation of functions such as weights and measures and food and drugs.

Yet another White Paper on the functions of local government was published in May 1957. The principle this time was in reverse and sought to allocate more functions to smaller authorities such as district councils. The implication was that weights and measures would be allocated to authorities with populations greater than 60,000 but food and drugs could be delegated to authorities with populations of at least 20,000. The Government repeated its commitment to county boroughs of over 100,000 or 125,000 in conurbations.

A special Royal Commission would be appointed to look at the situation in London. This would have led to some weights and measures authorities not having the food and drugs function. Another

Royal Commission would be established to give substance to these principles.

In 1958, the Institute found it difficult to reach an agreed position on a review of local government in London. The matter was referred back to the Council of the Institute for further consideration, and it was eventually agreed not to submit any evidence to the Royal Commission as the matter was so contentious.

Europe: There was a momentous event in March 1958 when the original six members of the European Common Market signed the Treaty of Rome. It came into force on 1st January 1959. The six members were France, West Germany, Italy, Belgium, Netherlands and Luxembourg. At this time the United Kingdom was no more than an interested bystander. Little did the Institute and its members anticipate the impact that Europe would have on trading standards less than fifteen years into the future.

Commerce: Self-service stores and supermarkets became firmly established. Despite earlier claims about the first self-service shop, it was recognised that the first self-service store in the United Kingdom was a branch of Sainsbury's in Croydon in 1950. The first supermarket was opened by Premier in Streatham in London in 1952. The UK was years behind the USA where only six per cent of grocery shops remained entirely counter-service.

Departmental Names: Following the renaming of the Institute, in 1951 the Executive Council was asked to recommend a suitable name for Departments more descriptive than the familiar Weights and Measures. Suggestions included Trade and Commerce, Standards and Public Control. The Council agreed not to make a recommendation pending the anticipated recommendations of the Committee of Inquiry into Weights and Measures (The Hodgson Report).

Organisations: There were more and more organisations being formed which impinged on the work of the Institute. In 1950, the Institute of Shops Acts Administration proposed to hold an examination. In 1951, the Coal Meters Protection Branch in London had increased the number of meters (inspectors) from five to six. This organisation was run by the coal industry without statutory powers.

In 1950, the Institute considered the impact of BSI (British Standards Institution) specifications on weights and measures. There were then just five relevant standards which were about graduated measuring cylinders, imperial dispensing measures, metric dispensing measures, weighing and height measurement for health purposes and cylindrical milk bottles. By 1954 the Institute was represented on three committees of BSI.

Michael Young (later Lord Young) became very influential as Research Director for the Labour Party. He proposed a Consumer Advisory Service in 1950, but this was rejected by Harold Wilson, then President of the Board of Trade (later Prime Minister). However, Young went on to set up the Consumers' Association in 1957. The first *Which?* Magazine was published by the Consumers' Association in 1957. He also founded the Open University.

In the same year the book *Shoppers Guide* was published by Elizabeth Gundrey. A review commented that this was a "donnish" book, but the aggressive undercurrent in it was that *"it was high time that the nation got off its knees praying for help to keep everyone honest and took up the nearest thick stick".*

Consumer Advisory Council: In 1958, the Consumer Advisory Council of BSI suggested that the Institute should produce information leaflets for consumers. The Institute (IWMA) agreed to investigate further. Also that year, the Consumer Advisory Committee of BSI was given a grant of £10,000 by the Government to develop standards of relevance to consumers. BSI Consumer Advisory Council was assisted by the Women's Advisory Committee. In February 1959, a report of a speech by a representative of the Women's Advisory Council claimed that housewives do not think about weights and measures because they believe the Inspectors have the situation under complete control.

The Hodgson Report: The Report of the Committee of Enquiry into Weights and Measures was published on 11th May 1951. The document was known initially as the *Blue Paper* but is now more usually called the *Hodgson Report*. This was a massively important report that reflected almost all of the recommendations put forward by the Institute in previous years. It came to be recognised as a model for the constructive revision of legislation. Despite the importance of the report the Government was not prepared to take immediate action, in part because of the pending recommendations of the Molony Inquiry into Consumer Protection.

Hodgson Recommendations: A few of these are illustrated below:
- Full metrication in about 20 years
- Imperial units defined by reference to metric standards
- A new definition of 'trade'
- Controls extended to bulk flow-meters, counting machines, volumetric appliances and personal weighers
- Prepacked liquids to be controlled
- Short weight a universal offence
- Fancy bread over 12 ounces to be included as bread
- Milk in one-third pint quantities permitted
- Fish, chocolate, fruit and vegetables sold by weight
- Draught ale to be sold only by lawful measure

- Spirits and wines sold in specified fractions of a gill
- Paint, knitting wool, tobacco, liquid fuel by quantity only
- Solid fuel only by net weight
- Enforcement only by larger local authorities
- Inspectors must be over 21
- Examinations to be kept up to date
- Penalties to be increased.

The Incorporated Society (as it was at the start of 1950) drew particularly high commendation from Hodgson for the scope and quality of its contribution, as well as its activities "in promoting ever higher standards in all spheres of the weights and measures service". The proposals were the catalyst encouraging members to strengthen the constitution and alter its title to reflect the new concepts.

Government Reaction: The Minister said there were a number of recommendations the Government could not accept at that time. These included:

- The adoption of the metric system in 20 years was rejected, as too many trading partners continued to use the Imperial system, especially the USA and Commonwealth.
- The recommendation that weights and measures services be located in larger local authorities was not acceptable.
- The Government would also not adopt the recommended extension of controls to fresh fruit and vegetables or to deliveries by rail and canal or wholesale transactions, nor more control of local authorities by the Board of Trade.

Institute Reaction: The Institute welcomed the Hodgson Report which had encapsulated many of its submissions. They also acknowledged Inspectors would now need to undertake refresher courses. The most contentious reaction related to the most appropriate tier of local government to be responsible for enforcement. This was a debate that would run and run for many years and, indeed, was still running at the time of writing in 2013. Comprehensive comments by the Institute on the recommendations were published in November 1951.

From 1953 onwards there was a steady flow of correspondence between the Board of Trade and the Institute. There was firm agreement that a Chief Inspector should have the power to prosecute without agreement of his Committee or Council. There was also an assumption that bread would return to multiples of a pound, although this never took place.

The Government's failure to implement the Hodgson Report within a reasonable time was the greatest disappointment to everyone connected with the weights and measures service. There was a leading article in July 1953 regretting the delay in implementing the Hodgson report. Little did the author know that the wait would extend for another ten long years.

The Institute could, and did, campaign and agitate for legislation. Chief Inspectors' annual reports in the 1950s repeatedly drew attention to trading practices that were prejudicial to consumers and about which they could do nothing. Local authorities and their associations joined with the Institute to press the Government for action. Members of Parliament, in the Commons and the Lords, were well briefed with compelling arguments. Private members' bills, in both Houses, were abortively introduced, but the Weights and Measures Act did not appear until 1963.

Industry Reactions: The evidence of the National Union of Scale-makers to the Hodgson Committee was that there should be statutory licensing of scale-makers. There was no such recommendation in the Report.

The Grocers' Federation said there should be an allowance for evaporation after packing and that stamping fees should be of only nominal value. The delay in legislation encouraged the trade in packaged goods free from legal constraint. Manufacturers put their goods, particularly foodstuffs, into packets without any indication of the weight of the contents. More and more commodities were being prepacked, and deceptive packaging, big packets with small contents, and other misleading trade practices became widespread. Inspectors were powerless. Complaints about deceptive packaging mushroomed, but little could be done by Inspectors, as they remained controlled by simple Victorian rules.

In 1958, the Council of the Institute reported on trends in business since the Hodgson Report was published in 1951. This showed a great increase in the sale of petroleum and lubricating oil and an increased use of bulk flow-meters. Another major change was the move to retail self-service stores and the growth of supermarkets. The Report needed to be revisited in the light of these trends. In 1960, the Institute sent yet another memorandum to the Board of Trade about the Hodgson Report. A sad postscript to discussion of his Report was that Sir Edward Hodgson died in February 1955, quite soon after publication.

Police: The Committee on Police Extraneous Duties recommended in 1953 that the police should no longer undertake "extraneous" duties including weights and measures and food and drugs. The three authorities involved were Lancashire County Council and the County Boroughs of Oldham and Oxford.

Weighing and Measuring Equipment: In 1950, the *Monthly Review* focused on the arrival of the electronic age and the numerous technical innovations. There were lengthy articles about technical aspects of electronic weighing. Later there were articles on automatic weighing machines and the electronic control of filling and weighing packages, and also articles about counting machines that had been a subject of debate for many years.

Some predictions of experts were wide of the mark. In 1958, Tom Metcalfe of Smethwick presented a paper in which he said he could not see much of a future for electronic (load cell) weighing machines except as approximate weighers, such as crane machines. In this case the respected Metcalfe crystal ball was cloudy; he did not foresee the credit due to engineers who were able to develop the load cell as a practical proposition for trade use.

Weighbridge Testing: The testing of heavy weighing machines and weighbridges had relied on the use of a small number of standard weights with a great deal of loose material provided by the scale-maker or the owner of the machine. The first vehicle recognised as a Weighbridge Test Unit in 1950 was privately owned by a Mr Lock. In the following couple of years, test units were purchased by London County Council, Worcestershire, Bedfordshire and Nottinghamshire. In December 1957, the leader in the *Monthly Review* expressed concern about the risk of injury to staff using these mechanisms.

Goods: There were many issues around the quantity of goods that it was hoped would be resolved by a new Act. In 1954, there was enthusiasm about the controversial subject of drained weights. In May 1955, the *Monthly Review* addressed the issue of dual marking, as when products, such as cream crackers, were marked with two weights, an average weight and a minimum weight. The leading article in January 1956 was about the problems of prepacking bacon in prescribed quantities. The Townswomen's Guild raised seven issues in September 1959:

- Too many claims of 'giant size'and 'reduced price'
- Failure to mark the quantity on detergent powder packets
- No weight marking on prepacked fruit and vegetables
- Difficulty of comparing value of canned foods
- Expensive price for the convenience of prepacked
- Price increases for seasonal foods
- Ignorance of housewives about the work of Inspectors.

Metrication: In May 1959, the Editor of the *Review* chose to write boldly that it was "now or never" for making metric units compulsory.

Food Quality: An Order was made in 1950 that continued the rationing of some food. Rationing was not to end until it was removed from meat in July 1954. Throughout this decade there was a steady flow of reviews of the composition, adulteration and misdescription of food and the increasing use of additives. There were reports by the

Food Standards Committee (FSC) on fish paste, ice cream, cream, metallic contamination, fluorine and jam. The FSC report on Vitamins in Margarine in 1954 demonstrated an early concern with nutritional content and recommended minimum levels of Vitamins A and D.

The publication of a Food and Drugs Bill was welcomed in 1953. The long-standing representations of the Institute on food and drugs matters found a place in the Bill's 32 clauses, though not all the Institute's wishes were fulfilled. The Bill gave more scope for making regulations and provided more detail on sampling procedures in line with the Institute's recommendations. However, the Institute was disappointed there was to be no standard for milk. The Bill became the Food and Drugs Act 1955.

Ancillary Legislation: The Merchandise Marks Act 1953 amended the Acts of 1887 and 1926 by extending the meaning of false descriptions to add to those that were misleading. It also increased penalties for offences. It was noted that it was a "common informers" Act and still did not give a power or a duty of enforcement to local authorities or the police.

The Council in 1958 tried to oppose the introduction of measures of 1/3 and 1/6 gill for use for the sale of spirits. These were probably the oddest fractions of units ever considered for approval.

In 1955, a pilot scheme allowing Inspectors to test weighing equipment in post offices was tried out in London and Northallerton. Four years later, it was reported that the trial had been successful, and the Post Office informed the Board of Trade that it would welcome national supervision in the future.

In January 1951, the Editor wrote about the task of checking the weight of prepacked goods. He returned to an old suggestion that public scales should be available so that customers could check weights for themselves. He also suggested that more Inspectors would be required when the Hodgson Report was eventually implemented.

Miscellaneous Legal: New Fertilisers and Feeding Stuffs Regulations were published in 1955 and the Petroleum Spirit (Conveyance by Road) Regulations in 1957. In 1957, the Institute sent a memorandum to the Committee on Horticultural Marketing, recommending that all sales should be by net weight and that short weight should be an offence.

In 1956, there were rumours in favour of the creation of a Council for Consumer Protection or an Institute of Good Selling Practice. A *Review* article suggested that the first step should be to close the loopholes in the law and improve enforcement; the creation of a new body must not be a façade to hide current imperfections. The article was signed "LCP" who is believed to have been Council Member LC Porter of Bootle.

In June 1959, the Government announced that it was intending to carry out a survey of consumer protection. It appointed a committee under the chairmanship of JT Molony QC to look at consumer protection more generally

Examinations: In 1953, it was announced that the Board of Trade examination would be held only once per year (instead of twice) because of the pressure of work at the Standards Department in preparing for the implementation of the Hodgson Report.

Institute Testamur: In 1950 the Institute devised its own examination called the Testamur. It was in two parts:
Part I
- English Essay and Précis
- General Knowledge and Current Affairs
- Arithmetic
Part II
- Legal General
- Summary jurisdiction, courts of appeal, weights and measures laws
- Technical – Theory and principles of weighing and measuring
- Mechanics and physics
- Care of standards and equipment
- Practical – Methods of tests of weighing and measuring appliances
- The adjustment of weights and measures
- Petroleum (optional)

There were 27 candidates for the first Testamur Examination in November 1951. There were 8 full passes and 4 passes in Part One only. In December 1953, the Board of Trade agreed to exemptions for holders of the Testamur. This had been a recommendation in the Hodgson Report. By 1962 there had been 624 registrations for the Testamur. Preparation for the examinations was seen as very important. Some branches, particularly the North West Branch, were very active in supporting students with evening classes. In 1959, the Council assisted the School of Careers in London to provide a course for the Testamur but would not give explicit approval. The trade union National and Local Government Officers Association [NALGO] was the leading provider of correspondence courses from an early date and the contribution of this trade union to the training of inspectors could fill several pages.

In 1959, a 4-page letter by Stephen Hargreaves of Warwickshire was published about the education and qualification policies of the Institute. He was concerned that the education and skills of Inspectors were not recognised. He proposed *Operation How-To* which would be a policy for the Institute to establish quickly a new two-part examination. At the AGM in June 1959, it was reported that the Board of Trade was going to review its own examination and its relationship to the Testamur.

Weekend Schools: Moves were made to improve the continuing education of Inspectors after qualification. The South-East Midlands Branch agreed to the organisation of weekend schools by the Branch Educational Secretary, JR Thornley of Essex. The first he organised was at Cambridge University. Other Branches followed with courses at Oxford University, Leicester University, Lancaster University and Nottingham University. In 1958, Stanley Gascoigne of Sheffield arranged a very successful weekend school for the Yorkshire Branch at York University.

Institute of Weights and Measures Administration: Following the change of name the previous year, the Institute agreed at an extraordinary general meeting in June 1950 to replace the Aims of the Institute with the following:
"*To advance the legal, technical, scientific, practical and general knowledge of persons engaged in the administration of the Weights and Measures Acts and other legislation or duties which can or may be administered or undertaken by its members*".
This can be compared with the original aims of the British Society in 1881 which were simply
"*the education of Inspectors and uniformity of administration*".
It is, perhaps, surprising that the aim of "uniformity" was not specifically mentioned in the new version. The AGM in 1957 agreed that full membership should be extended to all those with the full qualification and a suitable appointment and that retired Associate Members should be allowed to become Retired Members.

Towards a Profession: In the past the Institute had shied away from referring to the role of an Inspector of Weights and Measures as a 'profession'. This may have been because there was uncertainty about the relevant ingredients. In 1955, David Johnson of Weymouth approached the question head on. He said that ten years before he had been dismayed by the inward-looking attitude of the Incorporated Society and was excited when the "new" Institute was formed. He hoped that there would be a more progressive and professional attitude. He set out three essentials:
* The operation of a service using skills developed from lengthy and specialised training
* A sense of corporate responsibility which tested the competence and standards of conduct of the members
* Payment at a fixed salary or fee independent of the value of the service given.

Public Relations: In 1954, it was the turn of Ron Billings of Darlington to insist the Institute should adopt a public relations policy. He said the public should be aware of the weights and measures service and what it did. He suggested that there should be a Public Relations Committee, a Public Relations Officer, a panel of speakers and a group formed to write articles for use in a range of publications.

Branches: Districts of the Institute were renamed 'branches' from the beginning of 1952. In 1958, a Northern Ireland Branch was established by Inspectors who were employed as civil servants. At this time a discussion about membership of the Institute's Council, that had been going on for many years, was nearing resolution. A motion to change the membership of the Executive Council to consist of Branch representatives together with ten directly elected members was finally agreed in 1954.

Publications: In July 1950, another new edition of the *Inspector's Handbook* was published, and five years later it was agreed to print a *Third Supplement*. In 1956, it was noted that work on the *Measuring Instruments Treatise* and the *Weighing Machines Treatise* was progressing.
In 1955, the Council agreed to consider alternative titles for the *Monthly Review* but nothing was decided. In October 1958, the Council agreed to the distribution of a confidential *Information Bulletin* to be circulated, but only to members. John Graham of Cheshire was appointed as the Institute Information Officer.

Museum, History, Library: In October 1954, the Council finalised plans for an Institute Library and appointed Maurice Stephenson of Eastbourne as Librarian. In May 1955, he recommended how the Library could be established and managed. Initially the sum of £20 was allocated from Institute funds. In 1959, the Council agreed to consider setting up a museum of measuring instruments, but no action was taken.

Service Conditions: In May 1950, it was stressed again that the activities of the Institute relating to service conditions were not permitted by the Aims and Objectives of the Institute and must cease. This followed many years of activity by the Incorporated Society to improve the service conditions of members. IWMA deleted all reference to terms, conditions and salaries from the rules. A totally separate Association of Inspectors of Weights and Measures was created to deal with these matters. This new association had a separate subscription, rules and officers. In 1956, the basic salary grade for Inspectors was £630 –£735 pa.

College of Fellows: In 1950, the Institute agreed to revise the administration of its benevolent activities and, in 1951, the Council recommended a set of rules for a new College of Fellows. In April 1951, the first twelve Fellows were proposed and, in December 1951, a further four Fellows recommended. The first Fellows were formally elected at the AGM in Cheltenham in 1952. The College of Fellows was bound by a Declaration of Trust dated 6th March 1957, by a letter dated 27th March 1973 and registration as a charity in October 1962. In 2013, the official title remains the "College of Fellows of the Institute of Trading Standards Administration".

The College's early activities included recommending the appointment of Fellows and a charity fund to help members in difficulty. The College soon became involved with the development of education services and the Library of the Institute. Part of the impetus for the formation of the College of Fellows was to lend aid to the application of the Institute for a Royal Charter. A list of all the Fellows elected since the beginning in 1952 is included in Appendix 1. The College has since granted scholarships to members for research, overseas studies, young consumer competitions, and has sponsored the production of this book and other publications.

On the Lighter Side...

In April and May 1950, there were articles about the connections between weights and measures and William Shakespeare, the playwright, who lived from 1564 to 1616. There are apparently over 230 references to 49 metrological subjects – in every play except one.

In June 1957, a coal merchant company made a vain attempt to avoid liability in court for the delivery of short weight by claiming that "it had to be accepted that coalmen were usually dishonest".

Money was tight in the Institute's coffers at this time, but it was able to purchase a portable typewriter for £13.10s (£13.50) in 1955.

The popular English crime writer John Creasy described one of his leading characters as "very respectable, like a weights and measures inspector".

CHAPTER SEVEN – The 1960s

Into the Limelight

Introduction: The 1960s was a decade of excitement, anxiety and anticipation for the Institute, with two massive pieces of consumer protection legislation: the Weights and Measures Act 1963 and the Trade Descriptions Act 1968 (TDA). The Institute aimed to ensure the key enforcement role continued and with the uniformity for which they had striven for nigh on 80 years. However, nothing was secure, and not even the most supreme optimist could have anticipated the revolution to the profession brought about by new trade descriptions laws. It was the decade that propelled Inspectors into the limelight.

The Government established a National Economic Development Council in 1962 to arrest the severe economic decline, and Institute member Stephen Hargreaves of Warwickshire accepted an invitation to become a Consultant. The future Prime Minister Edward Heath, then Minister for Trade, largely abolished retail price maintenance by promoting the Resale Prices Act 1964.

Social change continued. The Beatles reigned supreme from 1960 to 1970. From 1961, it was no longer a criminal offence to attempt suicide, and the death penalty was for the most part abolished in 1965. The first credit card was issued in 1966. In 1969, Concorde made its maiden flight, and the first person landed on the Moon.

Technological Advances: There were many significant advances in technology and striking developments in the use of electronics. A series of articles entitled *Electronics in Practice* was published in the *Monthly Review* from 1962 to 1964. In 1963, Avery's announced that it was making a strain gauge load cell, and the first load cell weighbridge was made by this company and stamped at West Bromwich in that year.

Several new scales were launched on the market, including the Avery Aristocrat counter scale – for use in front of the customer – that incorporated a photographically produced disc to produce the illuminated display. One digit '3' was reversed and inadvertently reproduced on thousands of pieces of equipment, but to no detrimental effect. In 1964, Avery also announced their 'Autocrat', a ticket printing scale for rapid weighing of prepacked foods, which was followed in 1965 by their fan scale that uniquely remained accurate even when out of level. It was required to stay within tolerances when tilted 3 degrees. Inspectors puzzled how to measure 3 degrees when testing 'on the road'.

There are conflicting opinions about the location of the first self-service petrol station. Some sources say that it was at Southwark Bridge in London in November 1961, while others say it was Turnbull's Garage in Plymouth in April 1963. Whatever the truth, there was considerable concern about whether such systems were safe and complied with petroleum legislation.

Milk had been sold from farms in churns for many decades, but a trial collection of milk from refrigerated bulk tanks at farms began in 1957 with the measurement of the milk by dipstick. Concerning the measurement of beer, Jack Birch of Birmingham published a paper in 1962 about the use of beer meters, and John Corfield wrote a comprehensive article updating knowledge in 1966. Meanwhile, Chris Howell of Somerset explained the messy business of checking deliveries of ready-mix concrete.

Following years of speculation, the definition of the metre by reference to wavelengths of light was included in the Act of 1963.

The Marketplace: The number of supermarkets continued to increase and the ownership of businesses was concentrated into fewer hands.

Prepacking of goods became much more widespread, and the need for a statistical approach towards checking the quantities in packages began to be recognised. Quality Control and Quantity Control were everyday terms for most Inspectors, who had had to acquire a mathematical and statistical approach to the sampling of goods. In 1967, Thomas Kane of Lancashire suggested that Inspectors should use sampling procedures when testing equipment as well as goods, and that prepacked items should be checked at source.

A comprehensive series of articles under the title *Packers Have Problems* appeared in the *Monthly Review*. Contributors included Cadburys, British Oil and Cake Mills, Fish Processors, Smiths Crisps, Birds Eye, Petfoods, Soap Makers, Tin Box manufacturers and Three in One.

Local Government: This was the beginning of fundamental change in local government. As a precursor, in December 1964, the Board of Trade followed the requirements of the 1963 Act and announced that twelve local authorities were to become weights and measures authorities in 1965 when they reached a population of 60,000. At the same time, 13 existing authorities with populations smaller than 60,000 ceased to be such authorities.

A Royal Commission was established in June 1966 to review the structure of local government in England under the chairmanship of Sir John Redcliffe-Maud (later Lord Redcliffe-Maud). The Board of Trade told Redcliffe-Maud that they would prefer weights and measures enforcing authorities to have populations of at least 60,000 and would prefer them to be even larger so that they would be more effective at lower cost. The Institute was separately debating the idea of weights and measures becoming a regional or national service. There was no clear evidence to favour any particular solution and no convincing consensus among members.

The Institute policy decided to advocate a solution that produced enforcement units under the rubric "large enough to be viable".

The Maud report was published in 1969. The fundamental recommendation was that there should be unitary government throughout England, except in the conurbations of Birmingham, Manchester and Liverpool, where two tiers were favoured with weights and measures in the top tier. There was a Note of Dissent from Derek Senior, a journalist member of the Commission, who favoured two-tier administrations throughout England. This was fortunate for the Conservative Party, which came to power in 1970, and which also favoured this two-tier approach. This system was implemented in 1974.

The **Mallaby Committee Report** on manpower and training in local government was published in 1966. Mallaby was quite critical of the trading standards service, seeing it as a highly technical, inward-looking service which lacked a career structure.

Consumer Advice: One aspect of the work of Inspectors that was often discussed was the role of the profession in providing education and advice to consumers and businesses. A paper on *Advising the Citizen* was read at Conference in 1964 by Joan Pridham of the National Citizens' Advice Bureaux. However, the Editor of the Monthly Review, JT Graham, thought this would not be a quick solution and that enforcement would "have to continue as the bulwark" (October 1964). Nonetheless, Sheffield were providing consumer advice services in the weights and measures department in 1968, while Croydon opened an experimental advice centre in partnership with *WHICH?* These appeared to be revolutionary developments.

Consumer Organisations: A Consumer Council was established in 1963, following the recommendation of the Molony Report. This was an important initiative for consumers, although the decision led to some uncertainty within the Institute. Positioning the Institute in relation to a growing number of other bodies having a consumer agenda remains a balancing issue to the present day. The terms of reference of the Consumer Council included informing itself about consumers' problems, considering action to deal with these problems and providing advice and guidance to consumers, primarily through the Citizens' Advice Bureaux. The Consumer Council produced the first edition of a publication called *Focus* in 1966. The following year it introduced the 'Teltag' scheme for labelling essential information on products. The Director was the formidable Senior Civil Servant Elizabeth Ackroyd (later Dame), with TSO 'Jack' Brudenell, a Head of Division.

By 1968 the Government had established 36 Consumer Consultative Councils that monitored public services and utilities including coal, gas, electricity, transport and the Post Office.

In 1965, there was a proposal from the Government for a Parliamentary Commissioner of Administration, otherwise known as The Ombudsman. His role did not extend to the weights and measures services. However, this was a precursor for the nine Ombudsman organisations established in the United Kingdom by 2013.

Following the establishment of the Consumer Council, the BSI Consumer Advisory Council was dissolved, although the Women's Advisory Council of BSI continued.

The Standards Department in the Board of Trade changed its name to the National Weights and Measures Laboratory (NWML) in 1965. A year later, the British Calibration Service (BCS) was established to oversee calibration services in the United Kingdom. BCS accredited testing stations, which were established by some local authorities. It was later renamed NATLAS and then NAMAS, and is now part of the United Kingdom Accreditation Service (UKAS).

Advertising Standards Authority: In 1959, the voluntary Advertising Inquiry Council was set up by the advertising industry. AE Waller of Northamptonshire and FW Crabtree of Isle of Ely accepted invitations to become members of the Council in 1962. This Council later became the Advertising Standards Authority. The Code of Advertising Practice (CAP) was first published in 1962. The control of advertising became an issue of concern when the report of the Reith Commission was published in 1966. It advocated a voluntary system of control of advertisers and agencies policed by a body financed from a levy on advertising. Institute members were interested to see how voluntary controls could work alongside the statutory criminal provisions such as the Trade Descriptions Act.

A trade body, the Retail Trading Standards Association (RTSA), led by Director Roger Diplock, announced in 1963 that it would take a more proactive role in prosecuting traders for false advertising under the Merchandise Marks Acts. He subsequently waged a vigorous legal campaign against traders who falsely described the quality and feather content of pillows and duvets, a lucrative scam at the time.

The Weights and Measures Act 1963: Euphoria! By 1961 the members of the Institute had been campaigning for short weight offences for all goods for 80 years. The Institute had been acutely frustrated by delays in implementing the Hodgson Committee Report, which had been published ten years earlier. Several Bills introduced into Parliament had failed because of the pressure of other legislation. Following more lengthy delays, the Molony Report 1962 (see below) demanded that the Government bring in a Weights and Measures Bill without further ado. This recommendation was accepted, and the Bill cleared all hurdles to emerge, almost unscathed, as the Weights and Measures Act 1963.

Debates and Reception: Throughout the committee debates on the Weights and Measures Bill, in both Houses of Parliament, the Institute made a vast amount of written evidence available. Officers of the Institute were appointed to attend the debates and assist with expert advice. Fulsome tributes were paid to the Institute by leading members of both Houses of Parliament. Many amendments were promoted by the Institute, and accepted. Subsequently, the '63 Act was brought into operation, smoothly, efficiently and with no drama. This was seen to be a tribute to the commonsense approach of Inspectors and the Institute. Perhaps one of the Institute's finest hours.

The '63 Act - Brief Description: The first part was simply an update of existing legislation. The second part came into effect in 1965 and provided a general prohibition against selling short in any goods sold by weight, measure or number. This was a pleasing outcome for the Institute's campaign. Far more goods had to be sold by quantity, allowances for containers and wrappers for goods sold by gross weight were more clearly defined, and there were more stringent requirements about making known the quantity to the buyer. The commodities brought under control for the first time ranged from fish to stationery, sausages to paint, and toilet requisites to petrol and oil.

A number of Hodgson's recommendations were not followed. The absolute insistence on sale of all goods by net weight was not included, nor was a recommended requirement for each authority to have at least three inspectors. Much of the detail of the Act was set out in Schedules, and even more detail was to be included in a raft of Orders and Regulations. The schedule on foods divided them into twelve categories, and generally dealt with both prepacked and loose sales. Separate schedules dealt with solid fuels, sand and ballast and thirteen other categories of non-food goods. Inspectors had to reference a vast amount of information, and the Institute prepared an excellent series of *Aide-Memoires for Inspectors* for use in the field.

The third part, operative in 1966, required intoxicating liquors to be sold in specified quantities. Regrettably, the '63 Act specified not one but three separate sets of measures which could be used for spirits, based on one-quarter, one-fifth and one-sixth gill. As was to be expected, the smallest measure was the one widely adopted by the trade, except in some parts of Scotland.

Enforcement: The powers of Weights and Measures Inspectors were greatly increased. John O'Keefe of Middlesex was quoted in 1963 as predicting that 500 new inspectors would be needed; others thought more than 600 would be required. A clear policy of advising traders about the terms of the Act emerged, and this avoided many unwitting infringements – a policy exemplified later in the decade.

Many articles appeared in the *Monthly Review* picking over and interpreting the meaning of the Act in great detail. A small group of people emerged as experts. Some of the difficulties were resolved by *Guidance Notes from the Board of Trade* and advice from the Reference Committee of the Institute. Quite quickly, three Institute members, Roger Breed, John O'Keefe and Ken Shaw, published books on the Act, but the one that has stood the test of time was by John O'Keefe's. Inevitably, some of the uncertainties and problems had to be left to the courts.

The concern, indeed resentment, amongst some Inspectors was that no additional resources were to be made available for the enforcement of an Act that had so many new and important provisions.

Commencement: The new Act came into operation in stages to allow businesses time to adjust their trading practices. The Institute and its members were busy giving advice to traders so that the new rules produced surprisingly few prosecutions. Between 1966 and 1967, nearly nine million scales and other weighing and measuring instruments were tested and over 300,000 were found to be incorrect. The quantity of more than 400,000 packaged foodstuffs were incorrectly marked or not marked at all. But most of these were regarded as being of minor consequence and largely technical offences arising from inexperience rather than deceptive intent. The biggest proportion of offences occurred in the sales of solid fuels.

Metrication: The Institute submitted evidence to the British Association on the proposed adoption of the Metric System. The Institute had always been interested in the practical problems that would arise if this system were adopted, and papers on the subject were regularly given at annual conferences and branch meetings. In 1962, BSI published their ideas on a way forward. Metrication again came to the fore at the end of the decade with the establishment of the Metrication Board in 1969, following the advice of the Joint Standing Committee on Metrication. In May of the same year, the United Kingdom formally joined the International Organisation of Legal Metrology, which was pushing for metrication as the worldwide standard for measurement.

Decimal Currency: The Government stated in 1961 that there could be advantages in converting to a decimal currency, and the Halsbury Report on decimal currency was published in 1963. It was eventually announced that decimalisation would be implemented on 15th February 1971. There was urgent consideration of the conversion of price-calculating weighing and measuring equipment, and TSOs dealt with many complaints about mispricing.

Food Quality: The Local Authorities Joint Advisory Committee on Food Standards (LAJACS) was established in 1962. The Committee had equal representation from public analysts, weights and measures and environmental health, and was serviced by the local authority associations. It published Codes of Practice, in the absence of regulations, on such matters as the use of 'chocolate' coatings on bakery products, the use of the word 'brandy' and the crabmeat content of canned crabmeat products. These Codes were negotiated with trade representatives, often based on samples obtained by Institute members. The Codes were used in the enforcement of the Food and Drugs Act.

America: Many members enjoyed the Hornby Reports about the USA that resulted from the award of a Churchill Scholarship to Inspector Haydn Hornby in 1966. He presented a paper to Conference in 1968 about his experiences and what he had learnt, as well as publishing punchy reports in many issues of the *Monthly Review*.

The Molony Report: Many recommendations of the Hodgson Report could not properly be included in a Weights and Measures Act, and this led the Government to appoint a Departmental Committee on Consumer Protection in 1959, known as the Molony Committee, the Chairman being Joseph Thomas Molony QC. The collective knowledge of the Institute was presented in evidence, particularly their experiences of dealing with misleading descriptions of goods. For many years, Inspectors had been using the Merchandise Marks Acts to prosecute cases of misrepresentation. This wealth of experience proved very valuable. An Institute Consumer Protection Panel was formulated to give evidence, its four members being W Gray, TLE Gregory, LM Griffiths and JR Roberts. The evidence was published in the *Monthly Review* in March 1960 and ran to eight pages. It can be summarised as follows:

- There were two aspects to consumer protection: one to enforce controls and the other to devise standards for the use of businesses.
- Criticism of the delay in updating the weights and measures acts.
- The need for a National Advisory Service to advise businesses.
- The Merchandise Marks Acts should be extended to verbal representations, general trade descriptions, misleading price and quality claims, false advertisements and markings of origin.
- The enforcement duty should be with local authorities.

An appendix to the Institute's submission gave many examples of cases dealt with under the Merchandise Marks Acts. The Molony Committee received representations from nearly 400 organisations. The Final Report referred directly to the Institute and its outstanding contribution, both in the presentation of research material and in the commitment of its members to monitoring deficiencies,

The Molony Conclusions were finally published in July 1962. There were 214 conclusions and recommendations that affected virtually every aspect of consumers' economic interests, including quantity, performance, safety and finance. In some instances it was content to identify a problem and point the way towards further study, as, for example, in consumer credit, but in other areas it was forthright in recommending improvements.

It proposed the establishment of a Consumer Council and the concept of a suite of legislative controls administered by local weights and measures authorities, in what would become the Trade Descriptions Act 1968. The Committee saw that the main factors driving reform were technological advances, widening consumer choice, a wealthier community, more unfamiliar and complex products, the increase in advertising and the development of the art of salesmanship. Added to this was the perception that consumers were not well organised to fend for themselves.

In recommending procedures for enforcement, the Committee specified this should be in the top tier of local government. This latter recommendation focused the spotlight on members of the Institute. Despite the long list of recommendations, the Report was received by the Institute with faint praise. The general feeling was that the Committee had put too much faith in the ancient concept of *caveat emptor* and a virtually powerless Consumer Council.

In 1967, the Protection of Consumers (Trade Descriptions) Bill was presented to the House of Lords, and this Bill eventually became the Trade Descriptions Act in 1968.

The Trade Descriptions Act 1968: A second dawn. The Act placed Weights and Measures Inspectors at the forefront of a national discussion. Opposing the sweeping proposals, an MP gained headlines by asserting –

> *"these local inspectors would have more powers than those of the police in a murder investigation".*

In fact, the 1968 Act was short in length and had few detailed provisions. In addition to dealing with false descriptions of goods, the '68 Act had sections dealing with false and misleading price indications and knowingly false or misleading statements about services, facilities and accommodation.

Although the Act followed the principles of the Merchandise Marks Acts 1887, there had been very few appeal case decisions to help guide on interpretation. This soon changed, demonstrated by the size of the manuals now available from law publishers. In 2013, the latest edition of Butterworth's *Trading and Consumer Law* is in two large loose-leaf volumes and is priced at £594.

This was the major turning point for the members of the Institute, because it enlarged the consumer protection role in so many directions. There was a huge reaction from the media, trade and consumers. Great expectations were raised about the 'Shoppers Charter', and complaints to local authorities began to be numbered in thousands.

The first reported prosecution under the Act printed in the *Monthly Review* was in Mablethorpe, Lincolnshire, where a furnisher was convicted for claiming price reductions of 25% when they were actually only 16.8% and describing a bedroom rug as wool when it contained only 7% of this fibre. Fines of £30 were imposed. Only 29 prosecutions under the Act were reported in the *Monthly Review* in 1969.

TDA Committee: Uniformity was paramount if the Inspectorate was to retain its good reputation. Acting on the advice of George Darling MP (George Darling having been President of the Board of Trade though taken ill whilst steering the '68 Act through to conclusion), the Institute decided to create a Trade Descriptions Committee to give advice to Inspectors on the interpretation and administration of the law and to negotiate with trade associations on codes and good practice. Gordon Cottee, CTSO Somerset, was appointed Chairman and Jim Humble of Croydon the TDA Committee Secretary. This Committee issued hundreds of pieces of advice often on a daily basis, attended trade seminars and addressed meetings organised by many organisations including the CBI, the Retail Consortium, Motor Manufacturers and Traders and ABTA. George (later Lord) Darling was also responsible for 'opening doors' to ministers and top officials in local government, the civil service and industry. More than any other individual he probably single-handedly ensured the Institute 'came of age'. He was appointed President of the Institute from 1972 to 1974.

The '68 Act was generally perceived to have been the most sweeping and effective piece of consumer legislation any country had ever produced, and this helped to promote the Institute on a world stage. The advice of the TD Committee was rarely challenged, with one spectacular exception: a small number of Inspectors wondered whether the numbers on a motor car odometer could ever be a 'trade description'; the Committee considered, deliberated, took legal advice, and then gave the firm answer "No"; Charles Miller, CTSO North Yorkshire, thought otherwise and was the first to institute a 'clocking' prosecution. The rest is history. The flood gates opened and false and fraudulent cases involving the motor trade have topped the prosecution tables, every year, ever since.

As well as protecting consumers, the Act also provided protection for honest traders from fraudulent competitors. This was recognized with gratitude by many responsible trade associations.

Other Legislation: Soon after the Molony Committee started work, a number of tragic accidents alerted public attention to the need for control of potentially dangerous domestic appliances. The Committee published an Interim Report which quickly led to a private member's bill which became the Consumer Protection Act 1961. This provided protection, on safety grounds, in the design and sale of oil, gas and electric heaters. It was soon followed by legislation governing safety helmets and flame-proof materials for children's nightdresses. The Act enabled many regulations to be made controlling the safety of a long list of products in subsequent years. This was the beginning of a large body of legislation about safety to be enforced by members of the Institute.

Inspectors were being given other powers in their widening armoury, including controls on hire purchase, medicines, petroleum, explosives and road traffic. A paper about road traffic weighing at the Conference in 1968 drew attention to the colossal overloads and the subsequent damage to roads, building structures and the environment.

There was an alarming case in 1965 when petrol was delivered to a school instead of heating oil from a tanker carrying a mixed load. Fortunately catastrophic consequences were avoided.

The Criminal Justice Act 1967 was also significant because it streamlined a number of the investigation and procedural matters and sanctioned the reading of witness statements as evidence in court, instead of calling the witness to give evidence in person.

Education and Training: The Institute continued to focus on education. In 1964, Harry Robinson of Chester wrote an article on education policies. This included a detailed analysis of the Testamur and showed that the pass rate from 1951 to 1963 averaged only 16%. He advocated advanced professional courses to ensure that the members remained up to date in both skills and knowledge. In early 1967, the Institute held discussions with the Board of Trade about the examination for the statutory qualification becoming a two-part examination with the first part set by the Institute and the Testamur being phased out. A new syllabus was drafted in May 1967. In 1969, there were 186 candidates for the Weights and Measures Testamur examinations. Only 51 passed, 45 were referred and 90 failed. At this time the *NALGO Correspondence Course* and other *Special Notes* from NALGO were very important. The course was led by Regina (Reggie) Kibel, later an Institute Vice-President. During this decade, the first steps were taken to develop what was to become the immensely successful Diploma in Consumer Affairs.

The draft Syllabus appeared in the *Monthly Review* in May 1967. The plan was for the examination to be in three sections:

General law
- Trading standards and consumer protection law
- Civil law of sale of goods, hire purchase, monopolies etc
- Legislation in other countries

Trading Standards

- Technical background to goods and services
- Compulsory and voluntary labelling schemes
- Official and voluntary standards organisations
- Similar arrangements in other countries

Consumer advice, protection and education
- Domestic trade, problems of consumers and retailers
- Consumer advisory services
- Dealing with consumer complaints and enquiries

Many members were in debt to the first evening course for trainee inspectors in the 50s and 60s at the Ducie Avenue Technical College, Manchester, which eventually became part of the Manchester Metropolitan University. The profession owes a great debt to the many, many North West branch Inspectors, notably Tom Malone of Salford and John Grigg of Stockport, who gave their time to encourage trainees and to prepare and present lectures.

Institute Office: The difficulties of running an effective professional institute without any paid staff were discussed again and again. In 1964, a sub-committee reported that the cost of a permanent secretary with clerical support was beyond the means of an institute with only 900 members. Raising the annual subscription would lead to a reduction in the number of members and produce little change. The Institute continued with 15 voluntary positions coordinated by the Honorary Secretary.

In 1966, yet another sub-committee of the Institute considered the appointment of a full-time paid secretariat. It concluded that the appointment of paid staff would soon be essential, but there remained serious difficulties with funding. However, Articles of the Institute were amended to allow such appointments to be made when appropriate. This was approved at the AGM in June 1967. In addition, the number of elected Council members was increased from 10 to 12.

A Confidential Bulletin, initially for county council Trading Standards departments, was published weekly by the Somerset Weights and Measures Department from 1960.

The Future: The activities described above led to a resurgence of confidence and ambition within the Institute, following the grey days of wartime and the 1950s. Many positive articles on *The Future* were published in the *Monthly Review*. In 1962, Harry Rigby of Gloucestershire expressed his optimism that "the present time offers prospect of great change in our affairs".

Also in 1962, a paper by JR Thornley of Essex, advocated that weights and measures should be a national service with regional service boards. He believed this would improve the relationship of Inspectors with the Board of Trade, allow the Institute to establish an examination board and also enable improved technology to be developed for testing. He was very apprehensive about the transfer of many weights and measures services to local councils that had no experience of running them. Articulating a controversial view in March 1966, EH Griffiths of Hertfordshire wrote a paper in support of regional enforcement agencies.

Good Reputation: After the 1963 Act, the Institute appeared to have earned the confidence of Government by low-key but very sensible advice on consumer protection, given to ministers over many years. There were dissenting voices. A newspaper review of the book entitled *The Consumer Interest* by John Martin and George W Smith pooh-poohed the whole concept of consumer protection. In 1964, BA Smith of Leicestershire and Rutland published an article suggesting that Inspectors should concentrate more resources on helping traders to comply with legislation rather than penalising failures. This paper generated much adverse comment, primarily because it advocated a move away from traditional 'enforcement by inspection'. David Johnson of Weymouth was concerned about how the Weights and Measures Act 1963 might be enforced and wrote a lengthy letter in March 1960, of which the essence was:

> *"I venture into matters concerning individual status and opportunity within a changing Weights and Measures service ... there has been little or no heart-searching about personnel problems of an adequate Inspectorate in every sense. Prospects and status rest on two main points; the public view of the job and the recognition given to it within the system of administration."*

A different point of concern was raised by LC Porter in January 1961, namely that conferences were becoming too technical. The Editor of the *Monthly Review* confidently stated that that the legislation of 1968 "has provided a comprehensive pattern for the work which could remain fundamentally unaltered until the end of the 20th century." In the remaining chapters we will see whether he was correct.

Institute Name: Yet again there was a strong, but by no means unanimous, feeling that the title 'Institute of Weights and Measures Administration' did not adequately reflect the range of duties and functions. Early in the decade, the word 'Standards' was mooted as a more suitable word to be used to describe the range of the role. Stephen Hargreaves of Warwickshire wrote *"...the role of the present service is much wider than 'Consumer Protection' and words such as 'Public', 'Control', and even 'Trade', have unhappy associations. I should like to see departments renamed as 'Bureau of Standards' or simply 'Standards Department', as the word covers quantity, quality, conduct and accuracy."*

Other options mentioned included Public Control, Public Protection, Consumer Protection and, the eventual victor, Trading Standards.

Some of the members of the Institute strongly felt that the phrase 'consumer protection' excluded the role of the service in protecting businesses from malpractice.

In 1968, the Constitution and Membership Committee of the Institute considered the results of a ballot on a change of departmental title. 474 forms were returned, 329 were in favour of change, 145 were against.

'Trading Standards' topped the poll with 158 votes. The Committee decided the vote was inconclusive because only 33% of votes were in favour of the leading option. It was resolved to take no further action for the time being.

The Institute celebrated its 75th anniversary in 1969, marking the 75 years that had passed since the amalgamation of the Society and the Association in 1894, although many would have preferred the anniversary to be counted from the formation of the British Association in 1881.

The Institute recognised long-running similarities of role and rivalries with public health inspectors and a joint meeting was held in 1969, which was however inconclusive about working together in the future. The nature of the relationship between the two professions appeared to vacillate between suspicion, friction, rivalry and cooperation.

Publications: Publishing of reference works remained an important Institute role and the first part of the *Measuring Instruments Treatise* became available in March 1966. This was a well-illustrated guide and companion to the one on weighing instruments. The final edition of the *Inspectors Handbook* was again updated by the Institute at the end of 1969.

Library: The decision to establish an official Institute Library was originally approved in 1955. On the advice of Maurice Stevenson, the Institute Librarian, the Institute agreed to place the Library at the premises of the University of Sussex in Brighton.

On the Lighter Side...

We have seen a number of mentions of female employees over the years. Janet Popplewell was appointed as the first female Inspector of Weights and Measures in West Yorkshire in 1968. Janet had previously been both a professional photographer and a police officer.

In a surprising and welcome moment of levity, the inspector's stamp number 1066 was allocated to Hastings by the Board of Trade.

It is interesting to take a brief look at Health and Safety in the 1960s. In the *Monthly Review* 1962 the following incidents were reported:

- Milk sampling under the eyes of a farmer with a 12-bore, a worker with a pitchfork and a wife brandishing a carving knife
- Burly coal carters hurling sacks to the pavement from the top of a lorry
- Milk poured over an Inspector who wanted to take a sample
- A trapdoor behind a shop counter left open to trap the unwary Inspector
- Unfriendly large dogs
- The use of oxy-acetylene for adjusting weights
- In traffic, dodging between the wheels of 8-wheeled lorries.

Conclusion: This decade ended with the Institute's cup overflowing. New legislation had made it clear that the role was well valued and the performance of Inspectors respected. The main blot on the horizon was the impending local government reorganisation that threatened the status of the profession, promised uncertainty and held out the prospect of reduced budgets. Some members of the Institute favoured administration based on a national or regional organisation and this caused controversy. However, many members thought that the profession was set fair with a following wind to the end of the century.

CHAPTER EIGHT – the 1970s

The Comprehensive Service

Introduction: In the decade that followed the passing of the Trade Descriptions Act, legislation emerged in a constant stream, strengthening the civil law, regulating transactions and extending the role of criminal sanctions into new areas. The most important legislation affecting the comprehensive nature of an Inspector's work was the Fair Trading Act, the Consumer Credit Act and the European Communities Act. Demands upon the expertise of the Institute and its members grew rapidly as Government departments', members of both Houses of Parliament and national organisations sought Institute advice.

The continued assignment of responsibility in most new legislation to local weights and measures authorities caused local reform to become a matter of prime consideration. There was another Institute change of name and a major change to the qualification process.

New technology was an important driver, with colour television introduced in 1970, the invention of microprocessors in 1971 and the first (large) mobile phone in 1979. In the political arena, Scotland and Wales rejected devolution, and Margaret Thatcher became the first woman prime minister in 1979.

Local Government Reorganisation: Reorganisation was seen by many as a threat to the status quo, but by others as an opportunity to advance the ambition for a comprehensive service. In the debates leading to the new structure, the Institute, led by Chairman Frank Bucknall of Grimsby, strongly favoured placing the trading standards service "in the largest tier of local government" as Frank put it. The first decision on reorganisation was for Wales. In June 1970, the Secretary of State for Wales said that Glamorgan and Monmouthshire would be reorganised on the basis of three unitary authorities and the remainder of Wales would have four counties and twenty districts.

The eventual local government structure for England from April 1974, and for Scotland from 1975, enabled the upper tier authorities in both systems to provide the comprehensive trading standards service as advocated by the Institute.

Reorganisation in the counties placed trading standards in the county councils and environmental health in the districts. However, five massive metropolitan regional counties were created in Merseyside, Greater Manchester, West Midland, South Yorkshire, and Tyne and Wear. They became the flagships of the service in 1974. The innovative Stephen Hargreaves became Consumer Protection Officer of West Midlands County Council – the local authority with the greatest population. Greater London retained the alternative structure as established in 1965. It was run at that time by fifteen boroughs and five consortia, but most had poor establishment structures, a reduced range of functions and a noisy and difficult working environment.

David Tench of the Consumers' Association claimed the major step forward for consumers came when the Local Government Act 1974 was amended to allow weights and measures authorities to provide consumer advice. These later became known as Shoppers Shops.

In 1977, Tony Painter of West Sussex wrote about the continuing threat of a national service which, he alleged, would destroy the comprehensive services then being established. However, at Conference in 1977 the Minister said there were no plans for nationalisation and that he was happy to see local authorities running the trading standards service. This was greeted with much applause.

In 1978, David Thompson of Lambeth London Borough (later Chief Executive of Lambeth) wrote about the "standards" of the Service, claiming there was a wide variation of practice. His perceptions were that metropolitan counties had abundant resources and staff, shire counties offered a narrow service in not being interested in consumers and London boroughs provided limited services because of low staff funding and numbers.

The Institute Name: The Incorporated Society of Inspectors of Weights and Measures became the Institute of Weights and Measures Administration in 1949. At the AGM in 1972, it was reported that the British Standards Institution had withdrawn its original objection to the words 'Trading Standards', and by a vote of 702 to 68 the name Institute of Trading Standards Administration (ITSA) was adopted. But controversy simmered, and the colourful correspondent 'Old Rowley' said the change was unwise, as it failed to capitalise on the words 'Consumer Protection', which had a far more popular ring. However, this was disliked by many because it suggested a bias in favour of consumers.

Consumer Council: The Consumer Council was disbanded in November 1970 when the incoming Conservative Government simply withdrew its grant of £250,000. The respected Dame Elizabeth Ackroyd was due to retire, and her chosen replacement was believed to be Des Wilson, the charismatic leader of the radical housing pressure group 'Shelter'. There was a strong adverse reaction to the abolition from Women's Organisations and the Consumers' Association. The Institute was particularly disappointed because it had had the support of the Council and had to shelve the twelve joint projects under review. The Government seemed somewhat embarrassed by public reaction, but the Minister of Trade Geoffrey Howe wasted little time in creating an alternative.

Office of Fair Trading: A key moment in the decade was the Fair Trading Act 1973.This brought together three institutions, namely the

Monopolies Commission, the Restrictive Practices Court and, most importantly, from the Institute's point of view, Consumer Protection. In January 1974, John Methven (later Sir John), a Director of ICI, was appointed Director-General of Fair Trading (DGFT), alongside Institute Council Member Jim Humble, who became Assistant Director of the Consumer Division. The Consumer Division had four specific tasks: to sanction persistent offenders, to propose new legislation via a special committee, to promote codes of practice and to provide consumer information.

The Director-General moved quickly to secure the support of the Institute, its members and their employing authorities. The view was reciprocated. The Act introduced a novel power for the DGFT to take action against recalcitrant traders, requiring them to give an undertaking that they would reform their ways. Trading Standards Officers provided almost all the evidence in these cases. John Methven made it repeatedly clear to ministers, Whitehall, local government and trade that Trading Standards Officers were vital to the success of the economy. They were his "eyes and ears" and were the true protectors of consumers. Collaborations between ITSA and OFT are too numerous to mention, but it is also noteworthy that, on a voluntary basis, every single Trading Standards authority in the United Kingdom submitted detailed statistical submissions of every consumer complaint and legal action. The figures ran into several hundred thousand. These were all carefully analysed and formed the basis of OFT policies and priorities, and those of other ministries.

In 1977, Sir John Methven became Director-General of the CBI and was honoured to accept Vice-Presidency of the Institute. (Sir) Gordon Borrie became the new Director-General of OFT.

National Consumer Council: In 1975, the National Consumer Council (NCC) was created, with Michael (later Lord) Young as the first Chairman. He had a wide interest in a range of social affairs. The statement by Michael Young at his appointment was a thoughtful review of the situation of the consumer during the previous hundred years, having regard to a wide social spectrum including the trade unions, inflation and deflation, and the plight of the inarticulate and disadvantaged. Separate Welsh and Scottish Consumer Councils were appointed that year.

Europe: The United Kingdom joined the European Economic Community in 1973. The Institute became an active supporter in allowing the European Commission to present a 'European Day' at its annual conference. In 1976, the Institute took the annual conference to Breda in the Netherlands – the first local government body to hold a conference on the European mainland. There were excellent papers on European consumerism and a dramatic presentation from the Director of the German Weights and Measures Service, who insisted that

Britain would be forced to accept the 'average' system of quantity marking. He was roundly booed. However, in 1979 ITSA awarded scholarships to study 'average quantity', joined the European Food Law Association and helped create a United Kingdom branch, also producing the first *Directory of Trading Standards Legislation* combining United Kingdom and European issues. The Institute continues to monitor the impact of European initiatives and their impact on United Kingdom legislation actively.

The Government gave two single-issue bodies, the Wine Standards Board and the Eggs Authority, a duty to enforce European regulations.

Management: In 1974, Roger Manley of Warwickshire was appointed Chairman of the Local Authorities Management Systems and Computing (LAMSAC) Committee, looking at computer systems for trading standards. Two years earlier, Clive Howard-Luck of Tunbridge Wells had proposed a uniform management structure for the new Trading Standards departments with five branches: Trade Inspection, Consumer Affairs, Testing, Trade Licensing and Administration. In 1974, the Editor (of the *Monthly Review*) commented on the increased need for consumer protection in a poor economic climate. 'Old Rowley' was concerned that the flood of new duties meant that Trading Standards Officers knew "less and less about more and more".

Sampling: In February 1975, Roger Manley of Warwickshire suggested that each department should have a "rational sampling programme" based on complaints, previous problems and general enforcement priorities. The Institute then called for a nationally coordinated sampling programme, primarily aimed at food sampling, although it could be extended to consumer safety and trade descriptions. This was an early example of the need for risk assessment and prioritisation being articulated.

Consumerism: ITSA conferences became the 'shop window' for consumerist speakers throughout the '70s. In 1972, Max Wood of the Cooperative Union explained that the consumer movement had arisen from the affluent society, which had only existed in the West for ten to twenty years. Professor Aubrey Diamond provoked an audience by delivering a lecture in entitled *Consumer Protection - Too Much of a Good Thing?* He said the costs of compliance, failure and enforcement were simply being passed on to the consumer. In 1977, Conference asked "What Does The Consumer Want?" There were excellent presentations by Gordon Borrie of the Office of Fair Trading, Michael Young, Chairman of the National Consumer Council, David Tench of the Consumers' Association and Rosemary McRobert of the Retail Trading Standards Authority. Borrie disputed suggestions that it would be more efficient if local authorities were authorised to seek undertakings against persistent offenders under Part III of the Fair

Trading Act. McRobert electrified the audience by insisting that the users of schools, hospitals, railways and the energy companies equally fell within the definition of 'consumer' and that therefore TSOs should be prepared to offer help, advice and protection. In 1979, John Nott, the Secretary of State for Trade for the incoming government, spoke about the balance between rampant consumerism and proper protection. He wanted to cut down on bureaucracy and regulatory bumf. This was the first hint of serious criticism of consumer power.

"Two Hats": In 1972, the big debate within the Institute was whether a consumer advice service should be provided by an agency involved with enforcement or whether the operation of one of these activities compromised the integrity of the other. In the past, the 'rugged individualist' had been admired within the Service, and many insisted it would be impossible to be a 'two-hatted' inspector. The consensus argued that difficulties could be resolved by good management. In 1973, the Policy Committee confirmed its support for consumer advice services forming part of a local trading standards service. The first 'One-Stop Shop' was established in Sheffield during this decade. After this, London Boroughs took up the concept with alacrity. The next debate was whether consumer advice services should negotiate for consumers and even represent them in civil courts. The Council resolved to leave this to local decision. In 1976, the Government announced which local authorities would receive a share of £1.4 million to develop consumer advice projects. The aim was to serve 9.9 million people and establish 120 centres by the end of 1976. An independent Institute of Consumer Advisers was founded in 1974, later changing its name to Institute of Consumer Affairs.

LACOTS (the Local Authority Coordinating Body on Food and Trading Standards)**:** Its predecessor, the Local Authorities Joint Advisory Committee on Food Standards (LAJACS), a committee of public analysts, environmental health and Trading Standards Officers, had done a valuable, if unspectacular, job on food standards since 1962. However, it caused a major political incident for the local government associations in 1978. In essence, the professionals agreed a standard for tins of 'fruit cocktail' without including a single tropical fruit – no pineapple, mango, banana or other such. Ambassadors, particularly from commonwealth countries, demanded explanations from the local authority associations, whose secretaries had jointly signed the approval document. The policy committees of the associations had never had to face quite this kind of international criticism before. Decisions were taken quickly. LAJACS was disbanded and LACOTS was created: an organisation which had been in the melting pot for some time, with a committee of leading local authority councillors, its own secretariat and a decision that any professional advisers must be Chief Officers representative of the authorities themselves. The Institute

111

was delighted, because it meant the coordinating body was no longer restricted to food but could range across the comprehensive range of trading standards functions. Ministers were confident that the new organisation would answer the continuing criticisms concerning uniformity. However, it was recognised that a dividing line between LACOTS and the Institute might need to be carefully drawn.

Metrication Board: This was a busy and initially optimistic time for metrication, which had been supported by the Institute since the 1890s. The first report of the Metrication Board, entitled *Going Metric*, was published in May 1970. At this time, the Institute foresaw a big task for Inspectors and doubted whether the costs had been fully assessed, while a reluctant nation was being urged to consider the costs of *not* going metric and operating two systems. The building industry agreed to drop the 'metric foot' of 30 centimetres. A tentative target date for conversion was 1975. In 1974, the Metrication Board reported on *Metrication in the Retail Trade* and safeguards for consumers. Jim Humble became Director of the Metrication Board, but in October 1979 the Government decided there would be no more orders to make metrication compulsory and therefore the Metrication Board could be abolished.

Measuring Equipment: Despite multiple distractions many inspectors were still concerned with all aspects of weighing and measuring. In 1973, 'Old Rowley' expressed his pleasure that verification centres and the adjustment of weights were things of the past. In 1978, there was a note about work by the Department of Prices and Consumer Protection (DPCP) to develop a voluntary scheme for the testing of tyre pressure gauges. This became the TYPEAC Scheme that thrived for about five years. No such scheme now exists.

Average Quantity: The Institute, Inspectors and the consumer world were totally opposed to the European concept of 'average' quantity, but their opposition was ignored. What it means is that instead of each jar or package containing the minimum quantity stated, the consignment as a whole should contain the stated total weight, so that each item is correct on average. In 1975, the Government created a working party on 'Metrological Control Systems' chaired by Dr Tony Eden. The Institute was represented by Ivan Davys CTSO Northamptonshire and Jim Humble with instructions to advise on the statistical control of prepacked products and other matters arising from a European directive. Their findings, issued in 1977, became known as the Eden Report.

A new Weights and Measures Bill was published, including draconian proposals for control of local authorities and the introduction of the need to prove *mens rea* for retail sales of inadequate goods. The Weights and Measures Act 1979 created the National Metrological Coordinating Unit (NMCU) to assist uniformity, consider appeals and issue advice. Only Inspectors recently qualified (who had received appropriate academic and statistical training) were allowed to operate the new average weight controls. The Institute arranged training for the remainder and in less than two years some 1,300 officers had successfully completed a post-entry training programme – a quite brilliant logistical arrangement.

Trade Descriptions: The Trade Descriptions Act 1968 opened a new and vastly extended range of activities for Inspectors and the Institute. It received massive publicity and was presented both as a protection for consumers and a means of preventing honest traders from fraudulent competition. Customers with complaints were advised to take them to the nearest Weights and Measures Office. Within weeks, complaints were numbered in thousands, and the fact that most were quickly remedied to customers' satisfaction is a tribute to the integrity of most shopkeepers and traders. Nevertheless, it was reported that 6,556 prosecutions had been instituted up to November 1973, which offers another picture of certain parts of the trading community.

Complaints were generally what the Institute had expected: false car mileages, old car parts fitted as new, wrong petrol octane ratings, false claims of price reductions, faulty electrical and engineering equipment, false description of clothes, bedlinen and other textiles, and many goods wrongly advertised. However, few had anticipated having to deal with pedigrees of dogs, "qualified" driving instructors, badly fitted fireplaces, "table chickens" two years old, and a mink coat not from the country stated.

In 1972, the Institute said that the Trade Descriptions Act 1968 had done little to help consumers who were dissatisfied with overseas package holidays. The problem was showing that the offending statement was false to a 'material degree' at the time it was made and that the tour operator knew it was untrue or acted recklessly. Even if these hurdles were surmounted, a tour operator could escape by citing the fault of an overseas supplier.

The Methven Committee (Cmnd 6628) reported to Parliament on the effectiveness of the Act in October 1976. The Director-General relied heavily on the experiences and submissions of Trading Standards Officers and the Institute. Many of the recommendations were implemented during the course of the next 20 years.

False car mileages were (and remain) the most persistent and pernicious problem of fraud, resulting in a massive number of prosecutions. In 1973, Leicestershire County Council piloted a national programme for the monitoring of odometer readings. The Institute promoted the idea of a national register of vehicle histories, and in 1977, it was suggested this could be achieved by creating better links with the Driving and Vehicle Licensing Centre (DVLC; now DVLA). The DVLA later agreed to record vehicle histories on log books.

Consumer Credit: The control of the credit industry was the next major consumer protection initiative. The Institute presented written evidence to the Crowther Committee on Consumer Credit and in 1970 was invited to give oral evidence. The main thrust of this evidence was to convince the Committee of the competence of Inspectors to enforce complex financial arrangements alongside trade descriptions and consumer advice. Successful representations were made by the Chairman of ITSA, Frank Bucknall of Grimsby, and David Johnson of Manchester. The Institute welcomed the Crowther Report and drew further attention to their resolve to create the ideal of a comprehensive trading standards service. The Consumer Credit Act 1974 came into force the following year. Some provisions proved difficult, and in early 1978 the Fair Trading Committee of the Institute established a Consumer Credit Sub-Committee to advise on the Act. The OFT was the 'licensing authority' and welcomed this initiative.

Prices: Another furrow that became longer (or deeper) was the surveillance of pricing in an atmosphere of runaway inflation. In 1973, both the Editor of the *Review* and Old Rowley wrote critically about the counter-inflation orders which were intended to prevent price exploitation when VAT was introduced. Ministers were pleased the trading standards service were 'getting on with the job', but the Institute was concerned about being associated with an unpopular policy and fearful about the enormous volume of complaints. In the event, most problems were resolved relatively simply.

The Prices Acts 1974 and 1975 presented a new set of enforcement challenges with a range of price marking orders. In 1976, Ron Gainsford of West Sussex (later the Chief Executive of the Institute) wrote about petrol price displays and recommended that action should be taken against over-enthusiastic promotions by using Section 11 of the Trade Descriptions Act 1968. In 1977, the DGFT recommended there should be legislation about misleading bargain offer claims. This was the first recommendation under Section 2 of the Fair Trading Act. An Order was made in 1979.

Origin Marking: The Government decided in 1971 that all Origin Marking Orders would be scrapped. However, the Trade Descriptions Act 1972 was passed to deal with origin marking of imported goods, which had become a political issue *vis-à-vis* certain political regimes. In 1979, the Minister asked the National Consumer Council to carry out a review of origin markings.

Courts: This became known as the 'Decade of the Consumer' because of optimism about the effects of the Trade Descriptions Act, Consumer

Credit Act, Fair Trading Act, Consumer Safety Act, Unsolicited Goods Act, all with major institutional support. One less well-known change was the simplification of the procedures of the county court in 1975. This included new Small Claims Court procedures prompted by the Lord Chancellor's worries at the proliferation of 'rival' arbitration procedures in OFT Trade Codes of Practice.

Old Rowley wrote in 1974 about the thorny issue of prosecution policy. He had been very proud of a six-year record in which his department never lost a prosecution. However, he had lately formed the view that he had been over-cautious in only taking cases that he was confident he would win.

In 1978, members were discussing the status of the Judges Rules and the need and manner of cautioning suspects before questioning.

Other Laws: Other changes in the law included the Agriculture Act 1970, which replaced the Fertilisers and Feeding Stuffs Act, and the Poisons Act 1972, which replaced the Pharmacy and Poisons Act 1933 after 39 years. New regulations from the EEC included Cosmetic Product Safety Regulations.

The Health and Safety at Work Act 1974 replaced many existing laws, such as the Factories Acts, and embraced a wide range of safety matters that included the petroleum and explosives functions. The Institute was concerned that some enforcement functions of the trading standards service might be transferred to the Health and Safety Inspectors, but this did not occur.

The history of hallmarking dates back to 1300, when a statute of Edward I instituted the assaying and marking of precious metals. The new Hallmarking Act 1973 gave trading standards the duty to enforce hallmarking laws for the first time, and Bob Wright of Barnsley later became a leading member of the Hallmarking Council.

In 1978, Gordon Gresty of West Midlands described an exercise to test a contingency plan for a rabies outbreak, and TSOs used the Mock Auctions Act 1961 to deal with dishonest one-day sales.

In 1976, the Government was backing off from the idea of requiring the licensing of estate agents. After a long period where legislators were playing 'Will we? Won't we?' the Estate Agents Act 1979 reached the statute book. It was an early example of 'negative licensing' where an offending person could be banned from being an estate agent by the DGFT. The Criminal Law Act 1977 significantly increased penalties.

Civil Law: There were a number of changes to the civil law which helped consumers obtain compensation. In 1971, Jim Humble of Croydon drew attention to the award of compensation after a TDA prosecution, when Croydon Magistrates were persuaded to use their powers under the Forfeiture Act 1870 and the Magistrates Courts Act 1952. This led to new compensation powers in the Criminal Justice Act 1972. In 1978, Peter Green of Hampshire published an article about the Unfair Contract Terms Act 1977, which implemented an EEC proposal. In 1976, the Editor of the *Monthly Review* expressed reservations about the proposals in Europe for a directive on product liability. He thought there was a danger proposals would skew the law too much to the advantage of the consumer.

In 1979, it was announced that the Government intended to review the Sale of Goods Act 1893. This led very quickly to the Sale of Goods Act 1979.

Government Titles: There were frequent name changes of ministries in this period. The ministry responsible for weights and measures had originally been The Exchequer. These functions had been transferred to the Board of Trade in 1866. The Board merged with the Technology Department to become the Department of Trade and Industry (DTI) in 1970, which was the Department of Prices and Consumer Protection (DPCP) from 1974 to 1979. It is currently known as the Department for Business, Innovation and Skills.

Statutory Qualification: In 1970, the Board of Trade discussed the revision of the syllabus of the statutory examination. This led to a flurry of activity, which began in 1971 with exemption from English and Arithmetic papers granted to students with GCE O levels in English and Mathematics. In May 1973, a pre-examination minimum entry level was set at three O Levels in English Language, Maths and Physics. However, a difficulty arose with the preparation of a new Statistics examination paper as a result of serious objections from one of the training centres, Wandsworth Technical College. This was resolved by splitting the Statistics Paper between Parts I and II of the examination. Nonetheless, it was announced in 1976 that the Statutory Examination would end with the last Part I examination in 1978 and the final Part II examination in 1979.

This is an appropriate point to record the contribution of Institute members to the qualification of weights and measures inspectors in other countries. Between 1962 and 1970, Institute members trained and examined Inspectors from Nigeria, and in 1973 the Institute designed a syllabus and qualification for officials in Kenya.

Diploma in Trading Standards: The Institute had a long track record of setting examinations. For over twenty years it had mounted the Weights and Measures Testamur, which carried exemption from some papers of the Statutory Qualification. It had National Joint Council approval and was recognized for promotions. However, the aim of a comprehensive service demanded further development. In 1971, the Institute nominated Ian Welch, Education Officer, to collaborate with the Local Government Training Board to develop a new comprehensive qualification. In 1974, the Working Party issued Training Recommendation 18 and this led to the creation of the more demanding Diploma in Trading Standards (DTS). The DTS Controlling Committee had representatives from the Institute, the Local Government Training Board (LGTB), DPCP, OFT and academic institutions.

Three DTS courses started in September 1976 at Manchester Polytechnic Hollings College, South Thames College in Wandsworth and the South-West Provincial Council (SWPC), later to become South-West Provincial Employers (SWPE), at Weston-super-Mare. The full-time training officer on the Weston course was Tom Philpott, who had relinquished the post of Principal Officer, Consumer Advice, in West Yorkshire. Initially it was agreed that all Scottish authority trainees would go to the Manchester venue. In November 1975, it was estimated that it cost £36,500 to produce a qualified Inspector of Weights and Measures.

Testamur: The Institute's twenty-third and final Weights and Measures Testamur was held in 1973. There were 92 candidates of whom 21 passed and 29 were referred. The first examination had been held in November 1951.

Diploma in Consumer Affairs: A major advance for the Institute was the development of the Diploma in Consumer Affairs. The first DCA examination was held in 1970, and Bryan Dixon of Kent CC gave enthusiastic leadership. The DCA was initially designed as an additional qualification for Inspectors, but it was also taken up by those working in consumer affairs and consumer advice. Unfortunately, the introduction of the DCA deepened a controversy amongst Institute members about the enforcement role of officers who did not hold the Statutory Qualification. These arguments rumbled on for several years.

Training Courses: In 1970, the Policy Committee of the Institute decided that training courses, including courses for traders, should be run by the Institute to generate a valuable income stream. Many Inspectors had to master some totally different duties. In general terms, county staff needed training in petroleum, and borough staff needed food and drugs. As a result, the demand for courses greatly expanded.

The Institute established a Training Unit which offered post-entry training short courses and refreshers on specialist subjects. In 1975, the Institute's Education Secretary, Jack Brudenell, emphasised the importance of training for dealing with change, and by 1978 the role of Branch Education Secretaries had grown to become very important.

More About The Institute: The avalanche of changes in the 1960s and 1970s made exhausting demands on the Institute and its members. Their response was amazing. The contemporary image was of a small professional body in a highly complex field of public interest whose members were trained and sympathetic to the needs of the public. It was a service that was punching 'far above its weight'. This credibility had been won at some cost but could not be taken for granted in the turbulent economic conditions about to threaten.

Membership: There was discussion in 1970 about the need to increase the income of the Institute in order to fund the appointment of a paid secretariat. Options included extending membership to people in industry and seeking funding from local authorities and the Government, in recognition of the work done by the Institute for the educational activities provided for members, trade and business. By 1975 the Institute considered extending membership to people in advice services and also a category of life memberships. There were 21 Life Members in 1975.

Subscriptions: In 1972, a proposal to increase subscriptions to £12 for corporate membership was roundly defeated. A similar motion was defeated at an extraordinary general meeting held in November 1972. Following this meeting, the Secretary, Treasurer, Publications Secretary, Membership Secretary and Education Secretary all resigned. In 1976, subscriptions were raised to £16 but, in a period of high inflation, it was necessary to increase them to £18 the following year.

'Comprehensive' Service: In March 1970, George Darling, previously President of the Board of Trade, was one of the first to speak openly about the need for a comprehensive trading standards service. His reasoning was that fragmented enforcement would be ineffective. He hoped local government reorganisation would take a careful look at the most appropriate level. At the AGM in June 1971, the Institute adopted a policy supporting a 'comprehensive trading standards service', which would be based on existing weights and measures departments. The proposal included an Appendix listing the organisations with whom the Institute had an on-going dialogue, and this was published as evidence to the Redcliffe-Maud Commission.

Bain's *Report on Management Structures* of the new local authorities was published in August 1972. It recommended that a comprehensive Trading Standards department should be established in each county. David Tench of the Consumers Association told the Greater London branch that he supported comprehensive trading standards but feared local government reorganisation would not facilitate this arrangement in London.

In 1973, the Institute was heartened by talk of a comprehensive service during debates on the Fair Trading Bill. The Council of the Institute noted that most local authorities had decided to create a comprehensive consumer protection service including consumer advice. In terms of current expenditure, a comprehensive trading standards service had a miniscule effect on local government resources (less than ½%). However, public interest in consumer affairs led to greater concern about the ultimate vision. The Institute made it clear they wanted to see departments offering adequate staffing levels and the necessary spread of expertise, and provided with a full range of equipment and the necessary material resources. They considered the Service was making a contribution which greatly exceeded expectations of what could be achieved with a profession of just 1,600 members. In 1974, the Institute published an authoritative statement under the heading *The Effective Development of Consumer Protection and Advisory Services*.

Code of Conduct: In 1977, Peter Green wrote about professional responsibility. His concern about liabilities of officers when giving advice to consumers and businesses was timely. Roger Manley of Warwickshire went to the next stage and wrote about the need for a Code of Professional Conduct. A Code was finally introduced in 1981.

Institute Sections: Many members were discomforted by a long-running rivalry between inspectors in boroughs and those in counties. Despite this concern, the Institute Council approved the formation of a Borough Chief Officers Section in 1971. In 1973, the Council considered a proposal from the Borough Chiefs that they would disband if the County Chief Officers Section did the same. The County Chief Officers said it was a matter for the Institute Council, which then decided to take no action. In 1974, a section representing metropolitan councils was also established. This later also encompassed the London authorities, and in 1976 it became the Metropolitan Chief Officers Section, embracing 29 authorities and conurbations.

Coat of Arms: The crest or coat of arms had been used by the Institute since 1896 without having permission for the use of the crown. This was rectified on payment of £500 to the College of Arms in 1974.

Confidential Bulletin: The *Confidential 'Blue' Bulletin* was an insert in the *Monthly Review* from 1972 for members to use for controversial personal letters in addition to reports of Institute Council meetings and decisions of reference committees. This should not be confused with the *ITSA Confidential Bulletin* issued weekly by Somerset since 1960, which dealt with work in the field as distinct from Institute affairs.

Publications: After many years it was announced in September 1970 that *Weighing Machines – A Treatise in 3 Volumes* by TJ Metcalfe and EH Griffiths had been published. In 1972, the latest supplement to the

Inspectors' Handbook was ready. The first two volumes of the *Measuring Instruments Treatise* were published by the Institute in 1972. The final volume of this *Treatise* was published in January 1974. Each part was in two sections with text and diagrams.

Old Rowley: The first *Leaves from an Inspector's Notebook* column by Old Rowley was published in the *Monthly Review* in December 1972, the last column appearing in December 1977. "Old Rowley" was in fact the pen-name of Bob Kilsby of Surrey CC, who was appointed as Adviser on Trading Standards at the Department of Prices and Consumer Protection in 1977, along with Bob Insley of West Midlands.

Paid Secretariat: With so many changes to external relationships, it became impossible to continue with the existing structure. There were urgent needs for a secretariat to provide administration and an effective public image, together with an education and training function to complement the aspirations of the profession. In 1971, the Finance Committee reported the most effective option would be a full-time secretary with an assistant secretary and a clerk/typist, with office accommodation provided by the Institute. Further arrangements and costs were considered in 1972, and in 1974 job descriptions for staff were drawn up and an advertisement placed for a part-time general secretary.

In August 1974, Joe Fisher, formerly of the defunct Consumer Council, was appointed as the first paid Administrative Officer – some eighty years after such proposals had first been made. Joe served for 13 years and was well respected and went well beyond what might have been expected. In 1970, George Darling PC, MP, was appointed as Public Relations Consultant. Henry Martin of Cambridgeshire was Honorary Secretary during this very formative period.

Young Consumers Competition: The Young Consumers of the Year competition began in 1970. It was started by Birmingham City Council and taken over later by ITSA. The broadcasters John Stapleton and Lynn Faulds-Wood were closely involved. In recognition of their contributions, they were awarded honorary membership.

On the Lighter Side...

In August 1973, Old Rowley recalled attending a verification centre at which a trader submitted a 2 oz weight for testing which turned out to be his authority's working standard which had been given to him inadvertently the previous year.

The word 'metrology' began coming into more common use as a convenient shorthand for weights and measures. Dr Eden said that metrology was "weights and measures done up in a dinner jacket."

Members have always been able to laugh at themselves. In June 1979, an anonymous correspondent drew a distinction between three types of Trading Standards Officer. The first was the Traditionalist, who passed the "old exam" and knew only weights and measures and sadly rated only 1 out of 10. The second was the Meter Reader, who was like the first but a little more diligent; he once visited a consumer advice centre in the belief that it was a retail shop; he rated 5 out of 10. The third was the Professional, who was fully qualified and competent; he was a bit of a bore because he discussed work instead of football on a Monday morning; however, he scored 10 out of 10.

In Swansea, an ironmonger was fined for having unstamped and unjust scales. Subsequently he advertised nails at "2/- per handful". Trading standards quickly pointed out to the press that the hands were unstamped measures.

In many quarters the Institute was perceived to be a Chief Officers Club. In 1977, Old Rowley went as far as to suggest that Chief Officers should never be allowed to speak at branch meetings.

CHAPTER NINE – The 1980s

National Information and Average Quantity

Introduction: This was yet another event-packed decade for the Institute. In fact, the pace of change would be relentless for the next thirty years. There was a great deal of new legislation and reviews of local government. The Director-General of Fair Trading declared the Trading Standards Service was "under stress and under-staffed".

One of the key changes was the move to 'Average Quantity'. This required members to learn about statistical quantity control and the relatively new techniques of quality assurance. Alongside these innovations, the Institute again considered its future and whether it believed that the contribution of the Service to society was fully and properly recognised. The development of the National Information Service (NIS) was a major landmark for the Service.

The decade is noteworthy for the impact of the first woman prime minister, the Falklands War in 1982, the Miners Strike in 1984 and the invention of the World Wide Web in 1989 by Tim Berners-Lee. It was also the decade of Rubik's cube.

Local Government: Following successive reorganisations, there was a wide disparity in the size of trading standards authorities. In June 1983, they ranged in size from West Midlands, with a population of 2.5 million, to the Isle of Wight, with only 116,000 citizens. Arranging an optimum size for Trading Standards departments was clearly not a high priority. At the end of 1983, the Government published a White Paper entitled *Streamlining the Cities,* with the primary aim of abolishing the metropolitan county councils, their functions to be carried out by metropolitan borough councils.

In 1983, the Institute's Policy and Resources Committee approved the campaign document produced by the Metropolitan Counties Action Group that vigorously opposed the changes. A special ITSA Conference was held in the Palace of Westminster in 1984 to debate the issues. The Institute policy had two main threads: that the comprehensive trading standards service based on the larger units of local government had been a great success, and that in any future reorganisation the Service should be enforced only by authorities large enough to provide the necessary resources.

Despite every effort and massive support, on 1st April 1986 the six metropolitan county councils – the 'supertankers' of trading standards – were abolished and replaced by 36 smaller authorities. Many of these new services were then merged with environmental health departments.

One of the metropolitan counties that were abolished was West Yorkshire. Uniquely and inspirationally, the five councils Bradford, Calderdale, Kirklees, Leeds and Wakefield agreed to form a consortium to provide a single trading standards service under the control of a joint committee. In June, the Institute reaffirmed its support for a comprehensive trading standards service 'in the largest units of local government'. The vote was a resounding 368 to 36 in favour.

In 1988, the number of established TSO posts had increased from 1,757 in 1987 to 1,816, whilst the officers in post only increased from 1,463 to 1,486, leaving 330 vacant posts (nearly 20%). Despite fears the number of officers in training increased from 240 to 297.

Europe: Ideas for the future of ITSA in Europe included a European Interpol for trading standards, reduction in the number of consumer laws, harmonised levels of enforcement and better communications. The draft constitution for a United Kingdom branch of the European Food Law Association (EFLA) was drawn up in 1980, and it was suggested that all 14 branch secretaries should join along with five members of the Quality Standards Committee of ITSA. The first AGM in September 1980 had 80 in attendance, and Paul Allen, Chairman of Policy and Resources, listed the Institute actions already taken:

- 1980 to 1987 – ITSA speakers at European Food Law Congresses
- Founder member of UK Section of EFLA
- 1983 Contract with European Commission to produce the *Directory of European Consumer Protection and Trading Standards Legislation*
- 1977 to 1988 – College of Fellows Travelling Scholarships to visit Common Market countries
- 1985 to 1988 – Participation in discussions on safety and food law enforcement in Brussels
- 1987 – the *Directory* computerised
- 1988 – Study tour of member states for food inspectors
- 1988 – House of Lords committee publishes a favourable report on UK food law enforcement as part of its review of EC Food Inspection.

In 1989, there was a great deal of activity about completing the Single European Market (SEM), with 1992 as the target. Chris Howell of Dudley reported on the first European Metrological Enforcement Symposium, held in London in October 1988 with nine of the twelve member states in attendance. A key policy change in the "New Approach" Directives was to dispense with trying to agree technical detail and instead rely on "mutual acceptance" of procedures accepted in other countries.

The Single European Market was addressed by the ITSA Chairman, Bob Wright, in a speech in 1989. He asserted that the SEM would only avoid reductions in safety, choice and quality if policies were harmonised at the highest levels.

Computing: The decade saw the triumphant rise of the computer in daily affairs. In 1981 and 1982, Charles Allan of West Midlands, Phil

May and John Hammond of Derbyshire and Dave Sibbert of Oxfordshire all wrote about the benefits of using computers in the trading standards service for recording complaints, monitoring car mileage records, keeping food sampling records, monitoring disguised business sales and word processing.

Quality Assurance: In 1982, Geoff Souch, Director of NWML, thought that quality assurance (QA) would provide a radical new way for metrology and trading standards. Manufacturers would be able to rely on quality control and quality assurance systems to provide evidence that production met their specification. He reported that the European Commission was moving away from traditional verification procedures, which implied the role of inspectors was going to change. He was correct. Roger Wankling of East Sussex was awarded a College of Fellows Scholarship to study quality assurance in 1983. The Institute formulated a Quality Assurance policy in 1984.

Service Pressures: The growth in legislation was a constant preoccupation and put great strain on the Service. But the legislation was merely a response to the ingenuity of elements of trade and business to part their customers from their money unfairly. This was not new. The Institute warned of the need for additional resources on many occasions, but these warnings were invariably ignored. Sir Gordon Borrie, DGFT, in stressing the Service was under acute pressure, mentioned credit, price displays, consumer safety and misleading advertising, but emphasised that the pre-existing laws must also be enforced. In his opinion, the expectations of consumers could not be met unless local resources were increased. In 1983, there were 1,642 TSO (qualified) posts and 650 other enforcement posts in the UK, a total of 2,292.

One response was to form Special Investigation Units (SIUs) within Trading Standards departments. Their origins were traced to Kent CC in 1969 when a major investigation of the sale of solid fuel to county council premises took place. Alan Wardle of Surrey explained these should be distinct from Specialist Divisions as the SIUs should:

- involve serious and/or widespread crime;
- extend across more than one divisional area;
- be particularly complex;
- require sustained investigation over a prolonged period.

The concept of SIUs varied from place to place but quickly became a key local authority trading standards weapon against serious frauds and organised crime.

Consumer Advice and Education: A survey by the National Consumer Council of 2,000 people indicated that 10% had been sold faulty goods, but that most people did not complain. In 1983, the NCC produced a report about consumer information and advice services pointing out the patchy nature of services and the absence of liaison. In 1988, Philip Hulme-Jones of Fife explained his authority's concentration on money advice. Katrina Miller (later Katrina Ritters) of Warwickshire observed a National Consumer Conference discussion on consumer education and the roles of the trading standards service, NCC, ITSA and OFT. This group called on ministers to ensure provision of consumer education throughout the school curriculum. The first National Consumer Week was organised by the Institute in 1989, an event which has been held every year since then.

NMCU: In July 1980, Jim Humble, Director of the National Metrological Coordinating Unit (NMCU), began a series of articles in the *Monthly Review* on how the Unit operated. He outlined the position of the Codes of Practice for average quantity, the bottles that could be regarded as stamped measures and the situation of small bakers. Subsequent articles dealt with issues raised by Inspectors on average quantity, factory control systems, bread weights and retail monitoring. The NMCU Board praised the speed with which Inspectors had got to grips with the new regime and paid tribute to their professional training.

LACOTS: In the three years since its creation in 1978, concerns had continued to be voiced about the respective roles of LACOTS and ITSA. Trading Standards Chief Officers could make representations to LACOTS through their employers, but this left the question whether ITSA members could, or should, make separate views known, whether they could be distinctive and whether they would carry weight. It was resolved that the Institute must continue to express opinions on all relevant issues supported by the evidence of the membership. In May 1983, Bryan Beckett of Avon, Institute representative and leading Chairman of LACOTS panels, and Jim Humble, then CEO of both LACOTS and the NMCU, launched a new idea, namely 'The Principle of the Home Authority'. This was to have a most far-reaching effect on responsibilities and the manner in which TSOs prioritised their duties. It promoted economical harmony and uniformity and was the final death knell of the once admired 'rugged individualists'. These were big personality chiefs who had previously seemed to ignore advice, push the boundaries of the law and insist 'my patch – my decision'.

NWML: Late in 1980, the National Weights and Measures Laboratory (NWML) announced a wide-ranging review of the prescription of weighing and measuring equipment. The NWML moved to new purpose-built premises at Teddington in 1987. In 1989, NWML became an executive agency of the Department for Trade and Industry.

Metrication Board: The Board was wound up by the Government when contracts expired on 30th April 1980. It was confirmed that there were no plans for more metrication orders after those for the quantities for tea and suet: future metrication would have to be totally voluntary. The Institute thought this a foolhardy decision. A further 25 years of confusion indicates the Institute was absolutely right.

The Advertising Standards Authority publicised its Code of Advertising Practice with the slogan *If an advertisement is wrong, we're here to put it right*. The Code contained 462 Rules for advertisers. The *Monthly Review* Editor was concerned that whilst trading standards referred many cases to the ASA, the ASA rarely referred cases in the other direction.

Consumer Safety Unit: David Jones, formerly Chief Inspector for Tyne and Wear, was appointed Head of the DTI Consumer Safety Unit in 1983 – a further example of more influential positions for members of the Institute.

Environmental Health: Trading Standards and Environmental Health in metropolitan areas were now located with the same authority. In June 1986, the Institute pressed to open dialogue with the Institute of Environmental Health Officers (IEHO) on matters of mutual interest. In September 1987, the Institute sent a draft *Memorandum of Understanding* to IEHO. However, the IEHO were unwilling to sign but agreed to reconcile future differences, if any, at face to face meetings.

FLEP: Following an EC Symposium on *Food Control*, held in Rome in 1989, the Institute, IEHO and LACOTS collaborated with the Food Control Service in the Netherlands to launch the European Forum of Food Enforcement Practitioners (FLEP). This gave a practical, distinctive 'enforcement' voice to food controls. Tony Williams of Gloucestershire represented the Institute in this highly active European arena.

Eden Report: A Committee on the Metrological Control of Equipment for Use for Trade (Cmnd.9850) considered prescription, self-verification and other metrology matters. It first sat in March 1984 under the chairmanship of Dr EM Eden with Ivan Davys of Northamptonshire CC representing the Institute. The Institute submitted a great deal of evidence and participated in a number of specialist sub-committees. The Eden Report was published in June 1985 and made 24 recommendations. The more radical included:
- Manufacturers to become responsible for pattern conformity
- Creation of a new self-verification system (SVS)
- SVS available to manufacturers but may be extended to some installers and repairers
- Organisations must be accredited under BS 5750 (later ISO 9001) and audited by TSOs

- Batch sampling could be used for verification, if appropriate
- A duty for local authorities to inspect equipment periodically.

The Institute had two main concerns: firstly, about the lack of a role for TSOs in the initial assessment of large firms, and secondly, about the decision to allow repairers to self-verify. A Government White Paper one month later accepted virtually all the recommendations of Dr Eden - a record response. It came into force as the Weights and Measures Act 1985 and, rather surprisingly, continued the statutory trading standards qualification.

The Average System: The Weights and Measures Act 1979 came into force at the beginning of the decade and introduced the 'average system' for packaged goods. Packers codes were negotiated with many trades. In 1980, Steve Bolchover of the National Metrological Coordinating Unit (NMCU) wrote about the problems with bread. The following year, Yvonne Mouncer (later Yvonne Hunter) of NMCU explained the responsibilities of importers, and in 1985 Terry Morris of Suffolk CC the use of computers for average quantity checks.

Another milestone was the move to the sale of liquid fuels by metric units that began in September 1981. In 1983, there was yet another controversy about short measure due to the head on beer. Stan Gascoigne of Sheffield advocated the metering of beer or the use of line measures. Peter Doxey of South Yorkshire revealed surveys that showed that 'pints' of beer were deficient by an average of 5%.

Legislation: The Government actively promoted consumer protection with a motor car code of practice and origin marking requirements. However, the useful Business Names Register was discontinued. There was new legislation on consumer credit, product safety, food and drugs, furniture flammability, bargain offers, the supply of goods and services, video recordings, product liability, copyright and sales of tobacco to children in 1988. This new legislation required continuous reaction from the Institute's experts and innovative programmes for training Inspectors. The final parts of the Consumer Credit Act came into force in 1985, but many doubted the complex APR (Annual Percentage Rate) would be understood by consumers.

A proposed Consumer Safety Bill to deal with unsafe goods was welcomed by the Institute in 1984 and again in 1987. However, the prospect of consumer safety enforcement threatened to be a hopeless task without sufficient resources for sampling and testing.

In 1988, Peter Mawdsley of Liverpool reported on surveys to establish the level of compliance with age restrictions on the sale of cigarettes. Keith Hurley of West Yorkshire recommended risk-based sampling and 'risk assessment', which soon became a focus for prioritising virtually all trading standards work.

Counterfeiting: A trade association, the Anti-Counterfeiting Group, welcomed the Copyright Designs and Patents Act 1988 and urged Institute members to become more active. Dennis Cronin of Birmingham hoped an EC directive would plug gaps in legislation about the package travel industry. Sir Gordon Borrie DGFT spoke about the dangers of the 'closed shop' in professions such as solicitors in conveyancing, opticians, accountancy and veterinary services. In 1986, Christine Wade produced a challenging paper on deceptive packaging, whilst in 1984 the Editor of the *Monthly Review* had been one of the first to advocate the creation of a statutory 'Duty to Trade Fairly'.

BSE: In 1986, a cow was found to be infected with bovine spongiform encephalopathy (BSE). This was the beginning of a widespread outbreak which led to the deaths of 106 people with variant Creutzfeldt-Jacob Disease (vCJD) by 2004. Over 180,000 cattle were infected in the United Kingdom. This involved a huge amount of extra work by trading standards staff. The Economist Intelligence Unit calculated the cost of enforcing all consumer protection laws was 0.14% of average household expenditure.

Scams: In the '80s there was a sharp escalation of 'scams'. These involved 'timeshare', 'counterfeiting', 'forgery', 'loft insulation', 'Gucci and Rolex watches', 'loan sharks' and pirated copies of popular films such as 'ET – the Extra Terrestial'. Dishonest traders were prosecuted, and the courts began to impose lengthy prison sentences for trading standards offences. In 1983, the DGFT announced that 809 credit firms had been warned about their trading practices, and in 1988, David Roberts of Shropshire CC warned about the 'Golden Tap', a mechanical trade device for debasing meat with added water.

General Training: Good training is the lifeblood of any profession. In 1982, Julian Golbey of Surrey wrote that practical experience should be at the heart of the examination. The Institute and the Local Government Training Board announced a new syllabus for the Diploma in Trading Standards (DTS). Courses would be held at three centres: Hollings College in Manchester Metropolitan University, South Thames College London and Dauncey's Hotel Weston-Super-Mare.

The Weston-Super-Mare venue caused raised eyebrows in more academic circles. However, they had not catered for the inspirational and enthusiastic Course Leader Tom Philpott. His students and courses out-performed their university equivalents, time and time again, year after year. Hundreds of trainees and the Institute owe him a great debt of gratitude.

In March 1988, the DTS Council granted exemptions from academic papers for applicants who had an appropriate first degree. During that year, eight of the papers of the DTS were reviewed to make them more relevant to operational duties. Quality Assurance was later added to the syllabus.

Pump Maintenance continued to provide training on petrol pumps. This began in 1962 and accepted up to 90 trainees per year in the '70s and '80s. Avery Scales provided practical training for trainees for many years, and it later became common for students to travel to other authorities to gain specific experiences to complete their workbook projects.

Quality Assurance Training: John Parton of West Yorkshire drew attention to training arranged by the Institute of Quality Assurance. There were three-day introductory courses and five-day events for prospective assessors. He referred to the White Paper issued in 1982 under the title *Standards, Quality and International Competitiveness*. The Institute advocated the use of QA when advising local authorities on compulsory competitive tendering, and also a scheme known as 'Total Quality Management', as practised by Japanese manufacturers and others.

Centenary of the Institute: In 1981, the Institute published *The Centennial Review* to celebrate 100 years of the union of Weights and Measures Inspectors. This publication was written by David Johnson and Maurice Stevenson and has been a great source of inspiration in writing parts of this book. A centenary symposium was held in Manchester on 27th and 28th October 1981 at the Midland Hotel, with an exhibition at the Arndale Centre. There was a 'silver service' celebration gala dinner in the Great Hall of Manchester Town Hall which was reported as a "right gradely do". A conversation piece was the artistic masterpieces of Ford Maddox-Brown, one of them *The Proclamation Regarding Weights and Measures 1556*.

The Future: Rising out of the centenary celebrations, Roger Manley of Cheshire challenged that in looking at the past hundred years, we must ask a number of questions about the future of metrology:

- Is retail checking going up, staying the same or going down?
- Why not check chickens on the average system?
- What are we doing about imported goods?
- Do we really know what we are doing when we stamp electronic scales?
- Why not use quality assurance for all initial verification?
- What more can be done about coordination and uniformity?

Hugh Scully, presenter of the BBC *Watchdog* TV programme, said his programme received 3,000 consumer complaints each week. *Monthly Review* Editor, Ken Shaw of Buckinghamshire, praised the ways in which the Institute responded to the appearance of LACOTS and the NMCU and supported the emergence of regional groupings and Technical Liaison Groups.

In 1985, Roland Rowell of West Midlands wrote a controversial letter about ITSA, which he saw to be in crisis. He urged the Institute to relocate to Central London, appoint a full-time director, widen the membership, reduce the number of committees and generate more income from selling information. The Institute was to follow much of this advice in future years.

In 1987, Paul Allen of East Sussex analysed a report by the Institute of Local Government Studies on the future of trading standards. The report had been commissioned by ITSA. The report noted the avalanche of new legislation, the competing objectives of serving consumers and businesses, and the unevenness of resources in different authorities.

In 1988, Peter Nelson, Honorary Secretary of the Association of Trading Standards Officers (the staff union), wrote to the Institute demanding that the title of Trading Standards Officer should be reserved for officers who held the statutory qualification. Many Inspectors may have sympathised with this view, but the Institute did not ultimately have the power to take action.

In 1989, Bob Gale, Chairman of ITSA, looked forward to a day when a Royal Charter would be granted. He said that he had spent much time as Honorary Secretary preparing evidence; the file had grown from a mere six pages to one that was eight inches thick. The case was presented to the Privy Council as a formal petition but subsequently refused.

Membership Rules: There was a schism in the Institute on the question of allowing holders of the DCA (usually Consumers Advisors) to become full members. A move in 1980 to exclude holders of the DCA from full membership was narrowly defeated by 186 votes to 179. A lengthy correspondence ensued, and another motion to the same effect was also lost. This controversy about membership rules raged for some time. Full membership was available only to a person who held an appointment in a Trading Standards and also held DTS, DTI, DPCP, BOT certificate or DCA qualification.

A statesmanlike speech by David Johnson of Greater Manchester said the important principle was that members of ITSA should honour the value of all of the qualifications granted by the Institute. A referendum was carried out in 1981 to determine the views of members. The result was that 371 favoured granting full membership to people who held any Institute Diploma, but 550 did not. The Institute finally agreed to revise the membership rules in 1985.

On a different topic, the 1982 AGM voted to increase the subscriptions to £30 for full members, £20 for associates and students, and £10 for retired members. A proposal to appoint a Public Relations Director was narrowly defeated.

Code of Conduct: A draft ITSA Code of Professional Conduct was issued in September 1981 for consultation with members. The Code was confirmed by Council in 1983.

Public Relations: In October 1988, the Institute issued the first publication entitled *PR News,* edited by Gay Jordan, the Director of Administration and Public Relations. The document included information about press releases, press enquiries, meetings with friends of the Institute and Conference. In 1989, schools from over 60 local authorities entered teams for the ITSA Young Consumers of the Year Competition.

The National Information Service (NIS): The *Confidential Bulletin* for Trading Standards departments had been published weekly by Somerset CC since 1960. It was originally the brainchild of Chief Inspector Gordon Cottee and was developed by his then deputy Edgar Mundy. It was known by various nicknames such as *The Bulletin*, *The Somerset Echo* and *Munday's Mouthpiece. The Bulletin* ceased publication in 1984, and the National Information Service (NIS) was developed for the Institute by Noel Hunter of Warwickshire CC to fill the huge gap. The Institute pump-primed the initiative with a grant of £11,000, and this was repaid in two years. The NIS was the beginning of the many excellent information systems the Institute provides today. It initially covered eight topic areas:

- Lists of legislation, issued immediately after enactment,
- Enforcement notes, with full guidance on interpretation and precedents,
- Administrative guidance notes and standard information,
- Updating on law, enforcement practice and legal precedents,
- A technical information service on all aspects of equipment,
- News-sheets on LACOTS/ITSA expert panels and other publications,
- A confidential bulletin to help build the service,
- Consumer safety test results to share and avoid duplication.

One consequence of NIS was that the Institute required larger office premises to house new staff. In October 1982, the Council agreed to move away from Hadleigh, Essex and rent offices in Southend-on-Sea. Dallas Willcox was appointed Director of Information. One of his first statements was to encourage members to "think NIS" and share information. Soon there were 100 local authority subscribers. The NIS was transferred to Warwickshire's mainframe computer in 1986, and local authorities were then able to gain remote access.

In 1987, there was a need for even more rapid communications, and the Institute developed TS-Link and later HAZPROD for dangerous and unsafe products, plus further developments to extend to the motor trade and animal health.

In 1987, the *Monthly Review* was renamed the *Fair Trader*, but in 1988 the title was altered again to the *Trading Standards Review*.

Staff and Accommodation: Joe Fisher retired in April 1987 after serving the Institute for nearly 13 years as the first full-time Administrative Officer. He orchestrated the office move to Southend-on-Sea in 1983. Adjacent accommodation was added in 1986. However, notice to leave these premises was received in 1989. The replacement office in Hadleigh was purchased for £193,000. The new Director of ITSA, from July 1987, was Gay Jordan. In 1988, Joyce Blow, former Director of OFT, was appointed as the Institute's Public Relations Adviser.

On the Lighter Side...

Throughout the life of the Institute there has always been a significant number of members who are interested in the history of metrology, and many are collectors of equipment. In 1987, some of these members mounted an exhibition at the Annual Conference. They belong to organisations such as the International Society of Antique Scale Collectors and the Weights and Measures History Group. There is also an excellent collection of weighing equipment at the Avery Historical Museum in Smethwick.

The obituary for the *Confidential Bulletin* or 'Taunton Express' in 1983 included the words: "Remembered by all trading standards officers and several others who should never have seen it".

A *Monthly Review* jotting reminisced about an occasion when a 56lb weight fell from the open back door of an inspection van, causing the following driver to react more quickly than he ever imagined possible.

A survey in 1980 revealed that 51% of men wanted a rapid change to metric units but only 37% of women agreed.

A City correspondent in 1985 wrote of examination success and applying for a job advertised in the *Monthly Review*. He was interviewed by a County but thought the office had a funny smell. It turned out to be fresh air.

An office received a postcard from a staff member on a package holiday. He wrote: "All of the resort staff are very helpful. The doctor says that I should be out of plaster in a few days."

CHAPTER TEN – The 1990s

Consumerism and Europe

Introduction: In this decade there were two general elections with two very different results. Following the general election in 1992, there was a deal of apprehension about a key plank of Tory policy, namely local government reorganisation. By 1997 'red tape' was an issue, and the manifestos of all three parties set out plans for reducing the meddling state and the excessive regulation it was claimed was "hindering" businesses. For the first time, Inspectors were subjected to ministerial and media criticism, and in the first half of the decade the Institute and its friends had to defend themselves from accusations that had become overzealous and nit-picking. These widely reported allegations were eventually shown to be untrue.

Before the 1997 election, the Conservatives 'promised' a paper on rabies and more action on animal welfare, a voluntary ID scheme for young people and a food safety council.

The Labour Party listed legislation on utilities, a ban on tobacco advertising, a food standards agency and stronger protection within the financial sector.

The Liberal Democrats wanted a cabinet minister for consumer affairs, better guarantees, more stringent laws on financial services, labelling of genetically modified foods, tougher laws on animal welfare, an independent food commission and a ban on tobacco advertising.

Tony Blair won the election in May 1997 with a landside victory and there was keen anticipation his government would support more effective consumer protection. However, at the end of the decade the Institute was still waiting for the Government plan to implement the White Paper entitled *Modern Markets, Confident Consumers*, a National Audit Office report on the OFT and the Audit Commission Report on Trading Standards.

For younger readers, and those with shorter memories, this decade saw Tim Berners-Lee actually use the internet for the first time, and in 1994, we saw the triumphant opening of the Channel Tunnel.

Funding and Staff: In 1991, the Editor of the *Review*, Alan Street, pointed out that there was a lack of resources in most trading standards services to cope with increasing duties arriving with the Food Safety Act, animal health regulations and the Construction Products Directive. The situation was not improved by the Government falsely claiming these laws had no resource implications.

David Roberts of Shropshire reviewed the use of CIPFA statistics to measure the performance of Trading Standards departments, and was particularly critical of misleading figures for expenditure per head of population. Analysis of the annual workforce survey showed an alarming shortfall in the number of officers, with 7% of posts unfilled.

Only 20% of officers were female. The numbers of trainees had halved in six years.

Local Government Reorganisation: In 1991, the Government set up a Local Government Commission that aimed to recommend changes in the structure of English counties from April 1994. ITSA submitted its response, confirming that uniformity was best administered by the largest units of local government. In 1992, the President of the Institute, Sir Gordon Borrie, wrote to the Prime Minister, John Major, to express concerns about reorganisation plans. The Prime Minister replied by saying *"there has to be a balance between providing a local focus for the service for consumers to use; and an efficient and effective service".*

The Local Government Commission Report was published in 1993. In Wales eight trading standards authorities were set to be replaced by 23 or more unitary authorities. Bob Wright of Barnsley gave a spirited defence of unitaries, writing that they could be responsible, accessible, resourced, high profile, committed and supportive.

In April 1995, the number of Trading Standards departments increased from 125 to 175 smaller authorities. Noel Hunter wrote a leading article entitled *Trading Standards Under Threat*, claiming the plans for reorganisation were like a *"cure for no known disease".* Gordon Borrie continued to warn that the delicate balance between trading standards and its clients could be put at risk. In 1995, most environmental and trading standards services in London were under combined control. The sadness was that this led to the early retirement of many experienced and valued officers.

Office of Fair Trading: In 1990, the OFT published the Trading Malpractices Report. A major feature was feedback on the idea of a general 'Duty to Trade Fairly', suggested by the Institute in 1986. In 1991, Sir Gordon agreed the law was inadequate because of the generally unfair balance in the bargaining position of the buyer and seller. He referred to a list of 23 unfair practices that had appeared in a 1990 Report. However, in June 1993, the new Director-General of Fair Trading, Sir Bryan Carsberg, expressed his view that encouragement of competition in the market place was more important than regulation, claiming it encouraged efficiency and innovation.

Trade Descriptions: There continued to be deep concern about the shortcomings of the Trade Descriptions Act. Lord Ezra, President of ITSA, introduced the Motor Trade (Consumer Protection) Bill to the House of Lords in 1990. He pointed out that second-hand motor vehicles always topped the list of complaints. The Bill was designed to deal with unroadworthy cars and clocking, but it was not supported by the Government.

DVLA: In 1992, the Government announced that the DVLA would begin collecting records of mileages of some vehicles. This was welcomed by Inspectors, and by 1997 the Minister announced that the mileage of a car was to be recorded by DVLA every time it changed hands.

Property: False and misleading descriptions of property were a great concern, and the Government enacted the Property Misdescriptions Act in 1991, which again gave trading standards the duty of enforcement.

Holidays: Some consolation was imminent for holiday complaints. In 1992, Bruce Treloar of West Sussex, financed by a College of Fellows scholarship, wrote about the Package Travel Directive. Statistics on complaints dealt with by ABTA showed an increase of 44%, and OFT logged nearly 34,000 complaints from the Trading Standards Service alone. The EC agreed to strengthen the Directive. In the years leading up to 1990, there was a growth in timeshare scams. Other expanding scams in 1991 were one-day sales, home work schemes and "slimming" tea. In 1996, the Institute warned about future deceptions in cyberspace – the use of the internet to deceive. This is a technique with which we are very familiar today.

Credit Scams: An article about experiences in bringing loan sharks to justice in Strathclyde was published in 1990. The main difficulties for investigators were the lack of written records of transactions and the reluctance of witnesses to give evidence. In one case, 62 benefit books were recovered from a suspect's home. 82 cases were investigated, and 20 individuals prosecuted. In 1993, there was massive reporting of the *Hoover Free Flights Fiasco*. Although many consumers were disappointed not to receive the free flights they were promised, the trading standards investigation concluded that Hoover had simply underestimated demand and legal action was not possible.
In the autumn of 1993, the OFT held public consultations about improving the Consumer Credit Act. Tower Hamlets London Borough promoted credit unions as a way of preventing borrowers falling into the clutches of loan sharks and, with Institute support, this initiative was taken up by other local authorities

Consumer Safety: The Kinder Eggs case caused much publicity in 1990 and 1991 and established an important precedent. A child swallowed part of a pink panther toy from within a Kinder egg and choked to death. Birmingham issued a suspension notice, and the company appealed by seeking judicial review rather then the normal appeal process. The Queens Bench at first overturned the suspension order, but this decision was overturned in the Supreme Court.
In 1992, Ron Gainsford, LACOTS, wrote about the impact of European legislation on the safety of fireworks. The decade ended in December

1999 with the Liverpool baby-walkers case, in which it was ruled that a press notice warning about unsafe baby-walkers was illegal.

Hallmarking: Bob Wright drew attention to the harmonisation of hallmarking requirements in the European Community, in 1993. It was expected that the proposals would not be as rigorous as the United Kingdom hallmarking regime. In June 1997, there were proposals to introduce new levels of fineness of gold, silver and platinum.

Age-Restricted Sales: In 1991, the Children and Young Persons (Protection from Tobacco) Bill was introduced, which included enforcement by Trading Standards. This was described as a "poisoned chalice" for the Service, because it might lead to a similar duty in relation to alcohol, solvent abuse, truancy from school and attendance by children at fairgrounds. The Institute subsequently collaborated in the development of a protocol for test purchasing using young people.

Animal Health: This remained a very important area of work for Institute members. In 1990, there were still reports of hundreds of cattle being infected with BSE. In 1996, Graham Godbold of Shropshire wrote about the legal changes that had been made to prevent the spread of BSE in farm animals.

Copyright: A bill was proposed in 1991 to protect trade marks, which eventually became the Trade Marks Act 1994. Local authorities were given a duty to enforce the Act, but in 1997 there were growing concerns about software piracy and theft.

Energy: In 1995, there was speculation about the possible consequences of the deregulation of the energy industry and telecommunications. This led to troublesome cold-calling by energy companies, which was not properly dealt with until 2012.

Weights and Measures: In April 1991, the Institute responded to the proposal for the implementation of the Non-Automatic Weighing Instruments Directive. ITSA had serious reservations about the ability of repairers to self-verify. Deregulation of verification eventually happened in March 1999, when a manufacturer, installer or repairer who was an "approved verifier" could self-verify.

In 1992, Chris Howell of Dudley reviewed the legal position of froth on a pint of beer. The saga had begun in November 1963 when an Inspector made a test purchase of Guinness in a pub in Bristol. Chris anticipated that all would be clear when Section 43 of the 1985 Act was implemented in April 1994. On the contrary, this Section was repealed.

A survey in the East Midlands in 1995 showed that 40% of re-verifications were requested by petrol station owners i to reduce the measures to exploit the legal tolerances. The following year saw the introduction of portable weigh pads that fitted in the boot of a car.

Food and Drugs: The Food Safety Act 1990 replaced parts of the 1984 Act and added controls on novel processes. Date-marking of food was updated. The new system continued to use "best before" dates but replaced "sell by" with "use buy" on short-life foods.

MAFF wrote about developments in the genetic modification of food, and there were calls for food containing genetically modified food ingredients to be labelled. A wide range of food was found to be "irradiated but unlabelled" – including paprika, lemon grass and whole prawns in shell. There seemed to be no end to the range of new and novel products released onto the market.

Water was also under the spotlight. The enthusiasm for water filters provoked an article in 1991 about seven different types of filter and their dubious effectiveness. By 1997, concern had shifted to the mineral content of bottled water, where the word "natural" seemed to be inappropriate.

Maggie Gibbons-Loveday of Walsall wrote about the green revolution and the growth of environmental claims. In 1995, Roger Manley of Cheshire was appointed Deputy Chair of the Food Advisory Committee of MAFF. The FAC were first to advocate the creation of a Food Standards Agency (FSA) with powers of surveillance form "plough to plate".

Europe: Rob Taylour compiled a *Directory of European Enforcement Agencies* in 1991. The President of the Board of Trade called for a report on implementing EC Law in the United Kingdom. The four questions to be answered were:
- When transposing legislation, should the UK add extra requirements?
- Do other member states under-implement by omitting provisions?
- Is the UK more zealous in enforcement?
- Can we ensure the UK adopts a proportionate approach?

The comprehensive range of TSO functions meant that the Institute and LACOTS could act as a unique catalyst, able to bring many different types of specialist European enforcement officers together.

PROSAFE: The Product Safety Forum of Europe, PROSAFE, was founded in 1990 at a meeting arranged by the European Consumer Safety Association, which was hosted by Mike Drewry and Trading Standards in Edinburgh. The hosts identified responsible people in each member state and created a framework for problem solving and sharing best practice. PROSAFE has grown in importance as the EU has increased in size.

WELMEC: Standing for European Cooperation in Legal Metrology, WELMEC was founded in London in June 1990. The word 'Western' was originally used, but it should be noted that it is no longer appropriate, as the European Union now embraces Eastern Europe. Main achievements were establishing EMPADS, later EMeTAS, (the database of type approvals), producing guidance on weights and measures directives, setting up a type approval agreement, examining verification procedure costs and putting inspection information on line.

FLEP: The last chapter mentioned the creation of the European Forum of Food Enforcement Practitioners FLEP. FLEP and EFLA were able to focus on different aspects of food inspection and control. This meant that the Institute and its members made a significant impact on the improvement of food standards and contributed to an excellent European network of communications to deal with food safety and hazard.

GINTRAP: On behalf of the Institute, *Guidance to Industrial Trading Practices in Europe* (GINTRAP) was researched by Paul Allen in 1979. A new edition was published in 1991 ready for the Single European Market. In general terms, referring problems to other member states had not been a straightforward process, as it was often difficult, or impossible, to track down the officials responsible. In 1994, a list of "New Approach" EU Directives was published, and trading standards was given the duty of enforcement.

Overzealous – Says Who? It is not surprising that the avalanche of laws and regulations over two decades stimulated a strong reaction from small and medium-sized businesses (SMTs). This was because many did not have the resources to digest the manner in which they may or may not be affected. Ministers and government proved 'old hands' at passing the buck. They briefed that problems arose because of the insensitive and bureaucratic nature of enforcement. Media columnists took up the theme, and in some sections of the press the allegations of zealous, nit-picking, mad officials became increasingly hysterical and exaggerated.

The Institute and LACOTS decided to react. A review team carefully researched the last 100 national media TSO complaint stories. The results were unsurprising. Some 96% of the stories were either apocryphal, not about TSOs at all, misleading reports on court decisions, or accusations which were demonstrably untrue.

One particularly distressing example related to a banner headline in a London newspaper. The story claimed that a popular London shop was closing down because of victimisation by Trading Standards Officers. The truth was the Authority had arranged for a single member of staff to give helpful advice on forthcoming price legislation. On entry the TSO was told to "Get out" as "No black (expletive) Inspector is ever going to set foot on these premises". The TSO was distressed but received good support from Human Resources, as well as from other satisfied traders. The story was never retracted. However, details of all the exaggerated claims were sent to ministers, senior civil servants, newspaper editors and columnists. The criticisms abated almost overnight, and by 1996 TSOs once again featured as the champions of consumers and the protectors of fair and honest business.

The Institute of Trading Standards Administration

Structure: Before handing over the role to Phil Bottomley, the Treasurer, Ron Carroll of Newham, saw the annual turnover of the Institute exceed £1million for the first time in 1990. In the same year ITSA embarked on a strategic review to prepare the Institute for the next century, and in 1992 a Strategy Group reported on the Institute's structure. The main recommendations (which continue into 2013) were:

* Establish a management board,
* Appoint a chief executive,
* Form a trading company,
* Appoint directors,
* Produce a business plan and
* Take all necessary legal and financial advice.

Most of these changes were agreed at an extraordinary general meeting in November 1992. This became a major turning point for the Institute. In December 1993, the Management Board was elected, with Noel Hunter of Warwickshire becoming an outstanding first Chairman. This led to the creation of a trading arm under the name ITSA Limited with Alan Street as Company Secretary.

Excellence: In 1995, the Institute published *Realising the Potential,* which described the role and achievements of the Service under the heading "Cohesiveness, Consistency and Clout". The Management Board provided a strategy to assist members affected by local government reorganisation, including an *Agenda for Action* and a five-year plan. These were designed to counteract the fragmentation of the Service.

In 1996, John Bridgeman, Director General of Fair Trading, announced the awards for 'Excellence in Trading Standards'. The winner in 1998 was Warwickshire CC, receiving their award from Princess Anne. The winner in 2000 was Warrington Council.

Income: In 1990, the turnover of ITSA was over £1 million a year, but only 10% of this was raised from members' subscriptions, the remainder coming from trading activities. One venture to increase income was the sale of Christmas gifts – clocks, pens, and so on – embossed with the ITSA logo.

In 1997, the ITSA subscription at £72 per annum was the lowest of the seven major local government professional societies. For example, members of the Environmental Health Officers Association paid a fee of £111. In August 1999, the AGM agreed to scrap the charge for members to attend the ITSA Conference.

Membership: There were contentious debates about membership that lasted throughout the decade. One faction wanted a category of membership for members who left local government to pursue a connected career in trade. In 1991, David Johnson reprised his view from many years before that the simple criterion for membership should be that it was available to anyone successful in one of the Institute's own examinations. These proposals were regularly defeated until 1999, when the Council devised an acceptable compromise. This was to the effect that DTS or DCA holders could become full members, whether or not they held a local authority appointment. However, they must be in a full-time Trading Standards post to stand for Council or the Management Board.

Lead Officers: In 1994, the Institute decided that the existing structure could not respond to the huge volume of consultations and requests for advice. Instead 42 Specialist Lead Officers were appointed. The subjects included all the major areas of legislation plus: communications, deregulation, health of the nation, privatisation, the motor trade and bilateral liaison with Northern Ireland, Scotland and Wales.

Sections: A major step was taken when a new single Society of Chief Trading Standards Officers was formed, replacing the separate county, borough and London Chief Officer sections. It held its first meeting in January 1997. In a hotly contested election Robert V Wright of Barnsley was the first elected Chairman.

Publications: In 1996, there was an assessment of the *Monthly Review*. The following year, the first edition of *Graffito* was issued exclusively to ITSA members to inform them about urgent matters in intervals between *Review* publications. A publication called *Communiqué* replaced *Graffito* in 1999 and became a supplement to the *Monthly Review*.

College of Fellows: In 1996, the College was concerned that members did not fully understand and appreciate its charitable purposes. The Registrar John Corfield explained how the College was funded, its educational role and the charity work it did for members and retired members who needed help and assistance. Branches subsequently made very generous donations.

DTS Qualification: In 1991, Diploma in Trading Standards centres were established at The Queen's College in Glasgow and at Teesside

Polytechnic in Middlesbrough. These were additional to Weston-super-Mare, Manchester (Hollings College) and London Roehampton. The qualification was also under review. Some suggested the alternative of a modular approach, others solely a postgraduate qualification or, again, that the existing DTS should continue. The *Review* led to massive debates and disagreement. Suffice it to say, it was eventually agreed that the DTS should follow the model of a postgraduate qualification with some departments appointed as regent bodies to oversee the practical training and the assessment of prior learning. The Council rejected an alternative proposal for qualification through an NVQ process.

In 1998, it was announced that the DTS in its present form would disappear and that therefore the last retakes would take place in 2002. There was much sadness that the successful DTS courses at Weston-Super-Mare, after 25 years, would not survive. Dave Marshall, the Lead Officer for Training, confirmed that the old DTS was dead but declared a new version would rise from the ashes.

In October 1999, there was a Council discussion about the proposal that the statutory qualification should be discontinued. However, it continues today, in 2013, by virtue of the Weights and Measures Act 1985.

Diploma in Consumer Affairs: In 1996, Gordon Gresty, Lead Officer for Education, reviewed the DCA with the help of Reggie Kibel who had retired from the Training Unit at NALGO. The review recommended 17 optional papers including four new papers that would be valuable in providing exemptions from parts of the DTS. In 1994, there were 593 candidates entered for the DCA. In February 1998, 150 students registered for DCA Part I and over 100 for Part II. In a six-month period in 1995, the Institute organised and provided 45 courses.

Information: A TS-Link newsletter in 1991 described the impressive range of services available from the Institute, which included the NIS database, a BBFC information, Telecom Gold and HAZPROD. Planned for the future were a link to GINTRAP (The Guide to Industrial Trading Regulations and Practice in Europe), a car mileage database, a quality assurance volume, a food alert system, with a Europe and the OFT conviction database. The European database of pattern approvals of weighing and measuring equipment (EMeTAS) was made available in electronic form with the help of Cornwall CC to complement the UK version (PADS). For the most part TS-Link was distributed on a CD-ROM.

However in March 1992, the Council approved a move towards a PC-based service, and in 1993 the Institute established its Information Centre in its Head Office. At this time only 50% of businesses and 20% of consumers had access to the worldwide web. In 1999, the

Institute was alerted to growing concerns about the impact of the Millennium Bug approaching in 2000 (or Y2K as it was known).

Quality Assurance: Roger Wankling, ITSA QA Committee, wrote about the struggle to obtain recognition of the QA skills. It was agreed the Committee would assess individual applications for registration as QA Assessors. However, in 1996 some members of the Institute were beginning to question whether ISO 9001 was over-rated. They felt there was a danger that it was becoming a cult objective without any real understanding of the costs and benefits involved.

Performance Measurement: The Audit Commission published a report about local government performance entitled *Citizens Charter Indicators – Charting a Course* in 1993. Noel Hunter and David Sibbert met the DTI on behalf of the Institute to discuss a draft agreement on 'Performance Indicators'. They left expressing optimism.

Recording Systems: A number of computer systems were developed in the 1990s to enable departments to record work to produce summaries of data and targets. These included Flare, MKA Software, Sanderson/ITECS, Norsk Data and David Edkins Associates. All had advantages and disadvantages but 'coding' was a constant problem.

Enforcement: Bob Wright of Barnsley wrote in 1990 about the need for a coordinated programme of food control, while Ron Gainsford of LACOTS wrote about toy safety in Europe. In 1993, the Editor wrote light-heartedly about the more relaxed approach to enforcement in other countries, termed the "Latin touch". A document entitled *Working with Business: A Code for Enforcement Agencies* was issued in 1993 by the Prime Minister, but in 1997 the Government started to encourage the 'naming and shaming' of offenders. There was a sharp rise in counterfeiting cases.

Consumer Advice: In 1991, Ian Nelson of Cheshire used a series of cartoons to convey consumer advice and a display car called ROT 10 to demonstrate the dangers of unroadworthy vehicles. Many such ROTs were used in the following years. In 1998, the first 'One-Stop Shop' was opened in Barnsley. This brought together the council reception area and advice services on housing, welfare rights and consumer protection. National Consumer Week in 1993 began in spectacular fashion with a consumer advice line staffed by 20 people at the BT Tower in London. Over 2,000 inquiries were received on the first day. In 1999, the Young Consumers Competition included an award for children to design safe toys. TSI worked with the British Toy and Hobby Association to develop the competition, which continues today as Playsafe.

142

Fair Trading Award: The Institute launched a Fair Trading Award (FTA) to provide a resource for businesses to train their staff and provide independent verification of that training. There were six compulsory modules, and the first award certificates were presented in 1996. In a separate initiative in 1998, the Institute won a contract to provide training for the insurance industry.

Chief Executive: The post of Chief Executive of TSI was advertised in 1992. Alan Street (previously Chief of Nottingham and Greater Manchester) held the position from May 1993 until May 1999, when Allan Charlesworth took up the post. The Institute then employed a total of 14 people.

Home Authority Principle: The Home Authority Principle was evolved by LACOTS in the '80s. In 1992, EFLA approved a European "Principle of the Home Authority", and it was also announced LACOTS was redrafting the principle to take account of its extended role with food safety and hygiene. In response to the consultation, the Institute said that it was enthusiastic, but concerned that it was being ignored by authorities with massive enterprises on their patch as they were hampered by lack of resources. There was also a suspicion that some manufacturers 'hid' behind their home authority, and in 1994 Nigel Smart of Oxfordshire wrote about the "home authority syndrome" where some authorities seemed to be becoming over-defensive, thinking their packers and manufacturers should be free from the threat of prosecution by others.

LACOTS: In May 1997, Lynne Skelton of LACOTS wrote about the future agenda for the organisation. A major aim would be to promote more dialogue between those who draft the law and those who enforce it. Key thoughts were that law is not always the best solution to problems and that codes and self-regulation had a role to play. In May 1998, Jim Humble OBE retired after eighteen years as Chief Executive of LACOTS, following a successful career which embraced OFT, Nigeria, the Metrication Board, NMCU, Croydon CTSO and the ITSA Council.

CATS: The All-Parliamentary Group on Consumer Affairs and Trading Standards (CATS) was launched in 1996 following conversations between the President, Vice-Presidents and parliamentarians on how best to act as parliamentary friends of the Institute. Paul Allen of East Sussex became its Executive Secretary and during the next 18 years arranged many excellent meetings of support within the Houses of Parliament. Ron Gainsford has recently succeeded him.

Partnerships: Partnership and working together became common themes. In 1992, Paul Allen wrote about efforts to improve cooperation and partnership with the police. Bob Wright spoke to the

143

Environmental Health Congress and asked why the two services, seen by the public to be closely related, remained largely remote. The Council urged local authorities to tighten relationships with CABx.

In 1997, the six county departments in the West Midlands and the South-West developed a joint food policy, serving a population of 3.5 million. The aims were to produce information for consumers and businesses, joint food sampling projects, inspection targets, investigation of criminal complaints, rapid exchange of information about suspect foods and joint staff training.

Deregulation: In 1996, the Editor of the *Monthly Review* drew attention to the report of the Government Deregulation Task Force. The section on consumer affairs stated "The Government operates an extensive framework of consumer protection. We will be examining both the way in which these regulations are enforced and the extent to which they are needed at all. We also propose to look critically at any 'gold-plating' or 'double-banking' of EC requirements."

Paul Galland said that 'Enforcement' seemed to have become the 'E' word not to be mentioned in polite society. He questioned the whole idea of "business-friendly enforcement". The first edition of *Graffito* in April 1997 announced that ITSA had joined with other enforcers to halt a proposal for a 'Crooks Charter' under which offenders would be given two weeks' notice of any investigation.

Consumer Charter: In 1997, ITSA called for a Charter for Consumer Rights and identified five rights, namely: the right to protection of economic interests, the right to information and education, the right to representation and consultation, the right to protection of health and safety and the right to redress.

After the 1997 election, the Institute struggled to respond to the landslide of consumer protection consultation documents from the new Government. They are dealt with in the next couple of paragraphs.

Best Value: In 1997, the Government announced that a regime of Best Value would replace the more prescriptive compulsory competitive tendering (CCT). CCT had not been applied to the Trading Standards Service but Best Value certainly was. In 1997, ITSA was represented on the ministerial working party and campaigned for a better partnership between central government, local government and business.

The Better Regulation Task Force reports were released in 1998, and Bob Wright drew attention to the British Quality Foundation Excellence Model as a possible self-assessment framework.

DTI Consultations: In 1999, a DTI consultation document entitled *Fair Measure* reviewed the Weights and Measures Act dealing with prepackaging. In August 1999, the White Paper *Modern Markets:*

Confident Consumers was published. The Institute had been represented on the Advisory Committee. The White Paper called for closure of loopholes, improvements to parts II and III of the Fair Trading Act, changes to section 14 of the Trade Descriptions Act and the provision of a 'proper' consumer advice service. It also promised a boost of £30 million for trading standards in order to make effective use of the new powers.

A Darker Side: On the darker side, there was a suspicious or malicious fire in 1996 which virtually destroyed the head office of the Trading Standards Department in Worcester. Fortunately nobody was injured and no evidence was destroyed.

On the Lighter Side...

In April 1991, Alan Blyth, Scottish branch representative, reported on the Council meeting where the strategic review was debated. He opened his report with the following poem in the style of, and with apologies to, William McGonagall:

Hail to the Council of the Institute of Trading Standards
Administration
The controlling body of a unique Organisation
Which has spent two agonising days
Critically discussing its operational ways
Which have been for as long as anyone remembers
A source of concern for all its Members.

Puns appeared to be the fashion. The media reported that Trading Standards "got into a flap" about short-weight birdseed in 1997, while Gloucestershire, Brent and Harrow reported a carpet scam that had cost customers a "pile". Estimates for carpeting a room varied by about 10% because a number of firms were still using Imperial units. Roll on Metrication.

CHAPTER ELEVEN – 2000 to 2009

A Firestorm of Change

Introduction: This was yet another frantically busy period for the Institute. The Council wanted the Institute's influence to be more effective, and this required additional finance. The aim was to enlarge membership and to raise more income from other sources. The Council revisited the rules relating to people with a Trading Standards qualification but who no longer worked in local government. Further income generation came from the delivery of training courses and the provision of information to local authorities and others, especially using information technology.

There was a Labour Government through much of the period, arguably a government having inherent sympathy with the plight of consumers. Local authorities were encouraged to spend more on the Trading Standards Service, especially consumer advice. This enthusiasm was accompanied by a wish to ensure the Service performed well and followed sensible, justifiable priorities. However, there was also an opposing wish to reduce 'red tape' and "burdens on business". The firestorm of government reports was a breathtaking and bewildering.

There were other distractions, ranging from a foot and mouth disease outbreak to the so-called 'Metric Martyrs', and a surge of new and amended legislation from the European Union.

On the political stage, ten new member states joined the European Union in 2004. In 2008, a period of economic decline began, and funding fell away, while, not surprisingly, the temptation for rogues to defraud consumers increased.

Another New Name: At the AGM in July 2000, it was agreed to change the name from the Institute of Trading Standards Administration to the Trading Standards Institute (TSI), this being short and to the point. There was no objection from BSI about possible confusion, and this name first appeared as the publisher on the cover of the *Review* in November 2000.

Reviews, Reports and More Reviews: This was a decade peppered with government-sponsored reports about consumer protection: *Best Value Services*, *Performance Measurement* and *Working Together*. The White Paper, *Modern Markets: Confident Consumers*, mentioned in the previous chapter, was published in 1999 and had an important influence. We will consider the reports, rather like Noah's animals, briefly one by one.

"Measure for Measure" – the Audit Commission: This was published in January 2000. It was a report on Trading Standards Services and how they should respond to the 'Best Value' framework.

It built on the White Paper already mentioned and included proposals to update weights and measures legislation. It emphasised the concepts of Best Value and Modernisation again and again and gave hints on how 'value' might be measured, such as by comparing the opening hours of advice services, prioritisation of traders, inspection frequency, preventative actions and measuring expenditure per head of population. The current range varied from £1 to £6 per citizen.

The Hampton Report: The Hampton Review, entitled *Reducing Administrative Burdens: Effective Inspection and Enforcement* was the single most influential document. It was written by (Sir) Philip Roy Hampton in early 2005 when he was Chairman of Sainsbury's. Hampton's aim was to reduce administrative burdens by promoting more efficient approaches to compliance. The Report acknowledged that society had increased expectations that regulations would protect consumers, businesses, workers and the environment. He asserted that the regulatory system had the pivotal role in resolving conflict between prosperity and protection. It was recommended that:

- comprehensive risk assessment should be the foundation of all enforcement programmes,
- there should be no inspections without a reason,
- data collection for less risky businesses should be lower than for riskier enterprises,
- resources released from unnecessary inspections should be redirected towards business advice,
- there should be fewer, simpler forms, and their re-design coordinated across regulators,
- thirty-one national regulators should be reduced to seven thematic bodies.

The first significant outcome of the Report was the creation of the Local Better Regulation Office (LBRO). It also suggested that a new Consumer and Trading Standards Agency should be formed. The only concern of the TSI was that the emphasis on self-regulation would become a reason for reducing the already inadequate resources allocated by local authorities. TSI adopted many of the Hampton recommendations when modernising the Institute.

The Macrory Report: The Macrory Report of 2006 dealt with the sanctions to be imposed when there was regulatory non-compliance. Richard Macrory was a barrister and professor of environmental law. He found that existing sanctions were ineffective because they relied largely on criminal prosecution and lacked flexibility. He recommended they should give criminal courts new powers to punish regulatory offences by fixed monetary penalties, compliance and restoration notices, voluntary undertakings, stop notices and pilot schemes to gain restorative justice. A Working Group of Regulators should be established to share best practice and publish enforcement information on a regular basis. The Government accepted the Report's nine main recommendations; most were taken forward by the Regulatory Enforcement and Sanctions Act 2008. This Act also established LBRO and the Primary Authority system, which is an enhancement of the Home Authority Principle mentioned in earlier chapters.

The Rogers Report – Health Priorities: This review was set up in 2007 in the wake of the Hampton Report. It was commissioned to list the areas of enforcement with the greatest impact on health. Peter Rogers, Chief Executive of Westminster Council, and said enforcement priorities should be based on the evidence of risk. This would help to tackle the biggest risks nationally, as well as helping those regulated to know what was expected. The Rogers Report set five priorities for local regulatory services, namely:
• Air quality,
• Alcohol consumption,
• Entertainment and late-night refreshment licensing,
• Food hygiene,
• Improving health in the workplace and fair trading.

Arculus Report – Better Regulation: Sir David Arculus presented a separate report on Better Regulation to the Conservative party while in opposition. It was mostly about relaxing the burdens of regulation on business. He said that good regulation provides a necessary framework for all economic activity, but bad regulation imposed unnecessary costs on everyone – costs that cannot be afforded in difficult economic times. It wanted fewer regulatory bodies and far more use of alternatives.

Consumer Protection or Red Tape? We have seen the impact of the Labour Government immediately after it came to power in 1997. Their apparent enthusiasm for consumer protection was tempered by a wish to reduce burdens on business. This was (and remains) a difficult balancing act, which caused problems for the Institute because Officers were certain that serious criminal activity was escaping the net to the detriment of consumers. This activity ranged from loan sharks to misleading practices by larger companies, some of which seemed to consider themselves invincible.

Better Regulation: One emphasis of the Labour Government was on Better Regulation. The Institute embraced this and offered many helpful suggestions. As the concept of Better Regulation evolved, there was an explosion of government agencies, including the Better Regulation Task Force, the Better Regulation Commission, the Better Regulation Executive, the National Regulatory Forum, the Local Authority Better Regulation Group and the Local Better Regulation Office. In 2005, the Institute developed a plan for Better Regulation

action within a document entitled *Towards a Vision for Trading Standards*. The ingredients included:
- a risk-based approach to regulation,
- 33% cut in inspections,
- 25% less form-filling and
- regulators to work jointly.

The Local Better Regulation Office (LBRO): There was much discussion of the Regulatory Enforcement and Sanctions Bill in 2007. It was to establish LBRO and introduce the Primary Authority System as an upgrade on the original Home Authority Principle. The Chief Executive of LBRO was Graham Russell, previously Director for Trading Standards in Staffordshire. In 2008, the strategy of LBRO was launched with the following main objectives:
- to deliver consistency through Primary Authorities,
- to improve local authority regulatory services and
- to remove cultural separation between trading standards, environmental health and fire safety.

In 2009, LBRO made £132,000 available for pilot areas to test new ways of integrating regional trading standards and environmental coordination. The Chief Executive of the Institute provocatively suggested a National Better Regulation Office to monitor the performance of the OFT, the Food Standards Agency, Financial Services Authority, Health and Safety Executive and the Environment Agency.

Local Government Reorganisation: At the start of the decade, the Government was discussing regional government for England, the outline proposals to begin in the North. The Institute agreed to take part in consultations. After much soul-searching and debate, the Institute submitted evidence on regionalism in 2004, but this again repeated calls for adequate resources, consistency of approach and a comprehensive level of service with a critical mass. Once again, there was no Institute consensus about which tier of government should become the home for the Trading Standards Service.

Devolution: The Government of Wales Act 1996 devolved legislating on food safety and consumer protection relating to food to the Welsh Assembly. In Scotland, customer protection was a reserved subject and, therefore, not devolved.

European Principles: In 2009, in yet another addition to the debate, the European Commission published a list of basic consumer protection principles, including
- Buy what you want, where you want
- If it doesn't work, send it back
- High safety standards for food and consumer goods

- Know what you are eating
- Make it easier to compare prices
- Consumers should not be misled
- Protection while on holiday
- Effective redress for cross-border disputes

European Regulation: There was a miscellany of consumer protection regulations and proposals from the European Commission. These included a Directive on Injunctions 2000 and an announcement that the *General Product Safety Directive* was being revised. In 2001, a European Commission *Green Paper on Consumer Protection* and a Directive on Consumer Guarantees were both featured. The name European Union (EU) replaced the title of European Community (EC) after the Lisbon Treaty in 2007.

The *European Consumer Protection Cooperation Regulation 2004* added new enforcement powers and provided a network of contacts for cooperation. The United Kingdom contact point was the OFT. In April 2009, there was a proposal for a new EU Consumer Rights Directive. The Directive would consolidate four existing directives on unfair contract terms, sale of goods and guarantees, doorstep selling and distance selling. A new central plank of consumer protection was established by the *Consumer Protection from Unfair Trading Regulations*, which took effect in 2008.

Computer Technology: It became clear that information technology had become indispensable to many aspects of Trading Standards work. It was a tool for communication, sharing information and training, recording systems and producing performance reports within the Service. It was also becoming an important tool for purchasing goods and services and for identifying rogue traders who were misleading customers on their own websites or on auction sites. Information technology was being widely used as just another tool for distributing counterfeit goods.

Information Technology: In 2001, the Institute embarked on a major project to integrate the information systems of Trading Standards departments under the code name 'The Castle Project'. This would involve partnership with a number of organisations. The complexity of the project was such that the Institute would need extensive financial and legal advice, and in 2002 it was agreed the project was not viable.

Instead, a new information and computing package was launched under the name TS Interlink. This replaced TS-Link-PC and included the Pattern Approvals Information Service, the News Service, BBFC Classified Films Register, LACOTS Circulars, Contents of TS-Mail Messages, Main Volumes, Animal Health prosecutions, RAPEX Notifications from DTI and the TS Directory.

In 2004, the Council launched a new website which provided access to TS Central, TS Courier and Trading Standards Specialist. A project named E-Trading Standards National (e-TSN) was granted funding of £1.3 million by the Department for the Environment. In 2007, e-TSN was partially integrated with TS Interlink, and in 2009, the Institute made TS broadcasts available to help TSOs present a useful and locally branded website to their citizens.

Quality Assurance: Despite earlier misgivings, almost all Trading Standards Services readily achieved quality assurance certification, as did the Institute itself.

Funding of Trading Standards: In 2000 the Minister announced that extra funding would be available for Trading Standards Services for four years. Most of this would be to fund new duties under the Fair Trading Act. In addition, £1.5 million would be available for training to reduce staff shortages, and £500,000 would be available to promote regional groups. In 2001, it was confirmed that the £30 million promised in the Consumer White Paper would be available in three annual tranches of £5 million, £10 million and £15 million via a 'Modernisation Fund'. At the end of 2003, the Institute of Public Finance reported that expenditure on Trading Standards was planned to rise by 7.9%. An independent assessment commissioned by OFT showed that its consumer protection activities saved £243 million each year for consumers.

Directly Funded Enforcement: In 2002, it was announced that new national standards for consumer protection would be informed by pilot projects launched in 2001 under the DTI Modernisation Fund. The results led to the National Performance Framework, launched the following year.
Loan shark teams had been established in Birmingham and Glasgow in 2004 and the *Monthly Review* headlined that they had received £1.2 million of DTI funding to cover the central regions of England and the whole of Scotland. A further £2 million was added in 2007 to extend the scheme to the rest of England and Wales.

Staffing Issues: In 2001, it was becoming more common for independent contractors and companies to advertise the availability of staff posts for trading standards, enforcement officers and advisers. In 2003, there was concern about the thorny problem of recruitment and retention of good quality staff within a local authority Trading Standards Service.
Also in 2001, an increasing number of Trading Standards departments were located within other large departments managed by Strategic Directors. Many of these had had no direct experience of Trading

Standards. The Institute advised members to take all possible steps to ensure that the scope and value of the Service was well understood.

Performance Measurement: At the Institute Conference in 2000, the Minister for Consumer Affairs dropped a bombshell by announcing OFT would set national standards for Trading Standards consumer work, whilst the Food Standards Agency would set standards for food enforcement. In October 2001, a letter from the DTI was sent to Chief Officers giving advance notice of the implications of the proposed Trading Standards National Plan which had been piloted with sixteen local authorities. This plan was launched in March 2002.

In 2002, the first Audit Commission report on *Best Value Inspections of Trading Standards* was published. The overall conclusion was that Trading Standards fared better against the 'best value' criteria than most other local government services. The Service achieved high levels of public satisfaction; it offered a quality-assured level of service, with the consumer advice services performing well. Criticisms were that services often did not involve closely with partners and that it was difficult to make contact out of office hours. Less common failures were poor choice of priorities and evidence of the profession's oldest bugbear: inconsistency.

A separate Accounts Commission report on Trading Standards in Scotland found that small authorities performed less well than larger ones. The Commission urged local authorities to join up their Trading Standards Services to provide better services and better value.

Regional Groups: In early 2001, the DTI invited bids for the funding of 'Regional Coordination' and 'Cross-Boundary' projects under the £30 million Modernisation Fund. Some £500,000 was available for the appointment of Regional Coordinators for Trading Standards. A report on the work of six regional groups was published in August 2004, which noted that they had all worked effectively, but had each developed their own agendas and styles of cooperation.

Primary Authority Schemes: The Home Authority Principle had been around since the 1980s under the hand of LACOTS. The latest evolution of the principle was promoted by the Local Authorities Coordinating Body on Regulatory Services (LACORS) in 2002. LBRO arranged a three-month consultation on how a Primary Authority (PA) scheme would work and officially launched its own Primary Authority Scheme in September 2008. It became a central plank of the Regulatory Enforcement and Sanctions Bill 2008. 17 local authorities trialled the scheme in 2008. Local authorities were able to charge businesses for the Primary Authority Service, and in 2011 one trading standards service alone had generated income payments of £100,000 in six months.

Enforcement, Inspection and Scambusters: In February 2000, Sally Harber of Worcestershire wrote about her research with a Churchill Scholarship in New Zealand investigating the use of risk assessment for the safety of consumer goods. It was a period of heart-searching about traditional enforcement and the alternatives to inspection. The Audit Commission published a document on the future of local government enforcement that aimed to build on the Comprehensive Performance Assessment and risk-based assessment approach. Two main concerns were that businesses regarded regulation as a burden and complained about lack of consistency.

The Institute supported the adoption of a National Intelligence Model in 2004, which was intended to share information about rogue businesses operating across regional boundaries. However, it was often difficult to take action on nationwide scams, and so the OFT established the 'Scambusters' team in 2005. This was given the task of tackling mass-marketing schemes which were creating problems for consumers. In June 2008, Government funding of £7.5 million was granted to continue the existing three Scambusters teams and to develop teams in the remaining six regions.

Enforcement Concordat: This was essentially a Code of Practice for the fair enforcement of the regulation of business, launched by the DTI in 1998. It was announced in 2000 that over 300 local authorities (not only Trading Standards) had signed up to it.

Peer Review: The DTI invited LACORS and TSI to devise a system for Peer Review. In 2004, a pilot of a computer-based peer review system was created, which was trialled with regional groups involving 11 local authorities. The Institute supported necessary training, and in 2008, a 'Peer Challenge' was developed by CIEH, LACORS, LBRO and TSI. Additional funding was provided by the Department of Communities and Local Government.

Consumer Advice: In 2000 the chances of a consumer finding advice was becoming a 'postcode lottery'. Many advice services were being closed. To counteract this trend, the Minister for Consumer Affairs launched the Consumer Support Network with funding of £1 million per year for the next three years. Initial grants were made to six Trading Standards Services but the Minister emphasised the service could be provided by any suitable provider.

Consumer Direct: In 2002, the Consumer Minister called on local authorities to help set up an organisation called 'Consumer Direct', based upon a successful pilot scheme in Yorkshire. In 2004, proposals for the provision of Consumer Direct from four of the six original pathfinders (all from Trading Standards consortia) were accepted by the DTI. Three more Consumer Direct Centres were opened in spring 2005, and the process was completed across the country in 2006.

UK ECC-Net: In 2006, the Institute made a successful bid to become the UK provider for the European Consumer Centre Net service (ECC-Net), to deal with consumer complaints and inquiries about transactions across European boundaries. The service had previously been provided by Citizens Advice. TSI took over the active running of UK ECC-Net in 2007.

Consumer Education: 'Ask CEDRIC' (Consumer Education Resource and Information Centre), an inspirational on-line consumer education and information resource, was developed by Cambridgeshire Trading Standards and launched at the TSI Annual Conference in 2002. In 2007, the schools section of 'Ask Cedric' moved away from Cambridgeshire to be hosted by TSI.

In 2008, the Consumer Challenge Quiz was part of the Annual Conference where teams from about 50 local authorities took part. It is a quiz originally developed by Birmingham Trading Standards for children with learning difficulties. In 2008, it won an award in the European Consumer Champion awards as Europe's most original consumer initiative.

Office of Fair Trading: In December 2003, the first page sponsored and written by the OFT appeared in the *Monthly Review*. John Fingleton became Chief Executive of OFT in October 2005 and pledged the OFT would become the Champion for Trading Standards at national level.

LACORS: In 1998, Institute member, Nick Cull, Hertfordshire Chief, had been appointed Executive Director of the Local Authorities Coordinating Body on Trading Standards (LACOTS). In 2002, LACOTS became LACORS, the Local Authorities Coordinators of Regulatory Services. The role was extended to include the registration service, public entertainment and liquor licensing.

Organisations: In 2006, a new organisation named Consumer Focus was to be formed to bring together the National Consumer Council, Energywatch and Postwatch. In the same year, the OFT took over the running of Consumer Direct from the DTI, and it was confirmed that Consumer Direct would also deal with inquiries about the utility sector. The Institute continued to foster and maintain good relationships with an increasing number of organisations which had an interest in its activities.

Following successful pilots with Birmingham and Somerset Trading Standards, a Quality Mark Scheme was launched with the aim of getting rid of 'cowboy builders'. Builders would be registered and have their work assessed and guaranteed for up to six years. Other organisations working with TSI included the Alliance Against Intellectual Property Theft and the Performing Rights Society. In 2007, the Financial Services Ombudsman took on responsibility for dealing with consumer credit complaints. The Assets Recovery Agency was subsumed into the Serious Organised Crime Agency (SOCA) in 2007.

Metrication and Metrology: The President of the Institute, Baroness Wilcox, wrote to the DTI about metrication, referring to rising opposition to metrication led by UKIP and the anti-metric British Weights and Measures Association. She said local Inspectors were being goaded and defied by local traders, with signs that some multinationals – under the guise of being 'metric martyrs' – were joining in. In 2008, the Innovation Minister said traders should not be prosecuted for breaching laws about imperial and metric measurements. The following year, Lord Howe (formerly Geoffrey Howe and one time Consumer Minister and Chancellor of the Exchequer) argued that the Trading Standards Institute should be vigorous in support of metrication, reminding them of their campaigning historical background and quoting Chris Howell as saying that "everyone needs a system of measurement, nobody needs two".

A metrology seminar was organised by TSI and NWML to consider the future. The DTI-funded Modernising Metrology project was a key report. Many TSOs were dismayed that metrological control was suffering from a low profile.

In 2004, the Institute pledged absolute support for the "full pint" campaign, the controversy about whether the head on a pint should count as part of the measure having raged for well over 40 years. The Audit Office revealed the shocking and sensational fact that the retail drinks industry sells about 200 million more pints each year than it purchases.

In 2008, LACORS and TSi arranged a national project for Trading Standards to test hospital scales, there having been reports that inaccurate scales had led to patients receiving incorrect treatments, including wrong doses of radiation for cancer. A year later, it was found the checks had led to great improvements in accuracy.

Yorkshire and Humberside explained the steps they had taken to cope with the Measuring Instruments Directive 2006. The *Monthly Review* published a series of four articles in 2008 about the importance of metrology in trading standards. It was asserted that weights and measures still remained the cornerstone of modern consumer protection.

Food Policy: In February 2004, a website entitled 'Food Vision' was launched jointly by LACORS, the Food Safety Agency and the Local Government Association. The aim was to help people achieve a healthy balanced diet. Warwickshire TSI members provided case studies for the website, and in 2004, TSI urged the Government to bring in laws to control fat and salt in food as a means of tackling obesity. At the end of 2009, the Food Safety Agency wrote about the UK Food Surveillance System database, intended to provide a complete picture of national sampling and help with future targeting and coordination. In 2005, local authorities were praised for reacting quickly by providing information to businesses and consumers about the safety of the food colorant Sudan 1.

Trade Descriptions: In 2001, the Institute again called for a Motor Trade Act to deal with multifarious misdeeds. The Executive Board received a report alleging the Good Garage Scheme was ineffective in promoting improvements in the motor trade. In 2004, the OFT approved new codes for the Society of Motor Manufacturers and Traders and the Vehicle Builders and Repairers Association. In 2009, a new company called Motor Codes Ltd was established to administer a number of codes of practice relating to the different sectors – the latest attempt to deal with persistent problems.

Consumer Credit: The Minister announced a major review of consumer credit laws in a report entitled *Tackling Loan Sharks – and More*. In 2007, Trading Standards control pilots on loan sharks in Birmingham and Glasgow were extended to West Yorkshire, Sheffield and Liverpool. The DTI made £1.2million available for new projects.
The new Consumer Credit Act 2006 came into force in 2007 with the promise that it gave consumers more opportunities to challenge unfair treatment by lenders. There was a broader fitness test for licence holders, and 'irresponsible lending' became an unfair business practice.

Explosives: At the end of 2006, there was a fire and explosion at the Festival fireworks factory near Lewes in East Sussex, in which two people were killed. This refocused attention on this aspect of the work of Trading Standards that had been pushed lower and lower down in national priorities.

Other Legislation: In this decade, the Trading Standards Service never stood still. Members were also ambitious to do more to protect consumers and improve trading standards – as were other stakeholders. This section describes a few of the influences. In 2004, the DTI launched a consultation paper entitled *Extending Competitive Markets: Empowered Consumers, Successful Businesses*. It concluded "We want to see services that are well-led, coordinated and targeted – and which provide value for money". In May 2008, the Business Secretary took a slightly different tack and announced a review of consumer law with the purpose of reducing burdens on business. He said the cost of compliance for businesses was £1.25 billion each year.

His department was totally focused on the economic aspects of regulation with no interest in health, safety, fair trading and sustainability. There was also no mention of foot and mouth disease and other animal health and welfare activities.

The White Paper *A Better Deal for Consumers* was debated in Parliament in 2009. The main proposals were for a dedicated team to tackle on-line sales, improved cross-border enforcement, cooperation between enforcers and proper qualifications for enforcement staff. The priorities were to be compliance, recompense and, only as a last resort, prosecution.

Age-Restricted Sales: By 2001, age-restricted sales were under the microscope. The Criminal Justice and Police Act 2000 gave Trading Standards a duty to enforce in relation to alcohol sales and sanctioned test purchasing by children. In 2006, the Home Office issued a Code of Practice controlling test purchasing. The Connexions Project issued 2.4 million membership cards to verify the age of the card holder. The Policing and Crime Act 2009 gave more powers to Trading Standards to deal with under-age drinking. TSI worked with business and the police to set up an accredited national proof-of-age scheme (PASS).

Foot and Mouth: Unfortunately, a major outbreak of foot and mouth disease began in February 2001. LACOTS and Trading Standards departments had to take on massive additional enforcement responsibilities and worked very long hours with minimal recognition. Later in 2001, the Government commissioned three inquiries into the foot and mouth outbreak, to which the Institute provided evidence. It expressed particular concern about the quality of the pre-existing contingency plans which the Institute believed to be the major reason for the rapid escalation of the disease. The effect on expenditure and the diversion of resources of Trading Standards was also highlighted. Of less importance in a time of national emergency was that TSI itself lost about £50,000 income from cancelled courses and examinations.

Copyright: The *Gowers Review of Intellectual Property* was published in 2006. One of the conclusions was that the Trading Standards Service should be given the power and the duty to enforce the law for copyright and related infringements.

Cold Calling: The Campaign against Cold Calling continued in 2004 under the name 'Doorstoppers'. A number of Trading Standards authorities signed up to provide training. Banks and building societies agreed to help by notifying TSOs of unusual financial activities, such as elderly or vulnerable customers withdrawing large sums of money.

'Stop Now': At the start of 2001, Trading Standards Officers were given 'Stop Now' powers under eleven sets of regulations implementing EC directives. These included misleading advertising, doorstep selling, consumer credit and package travel.

The Regulation of Investigatory Powers Act (RIPA) became law in 2000. The intention was to limit intrusive and covert surveillance and the use of informants and undercover agents. In 2009, the Home Secretary announced that RIPA was to be reviewed on the grounds of abuse by some officials.

Internet Crime: A growing challenge for TSOs was accessing and analysing data on computers which may have been used in the commission of offences. A North Yorkshire TSO unit known as DERIC (Digital Evidence Recovery and Internet Crime unit) began operation in 2002. In its first year, it reviewed the equivalent of 4,000 million A4 pages of text and helped many Trading Standards departments and other regulators with their investigations.

Proceeds of Crime: The Proceeds of Crime Act 2002 was used in a number of Trading Standards cases. In Leicester, a dealer in counterfeit clothing had over 8,000 items in his possession. He was ordered to pay nearly £73,000 restitution. In 2004, a car boot trader in Leeds was ordered to forfeit £39,000. A grandmother in Merthyr Tydfil was ordered to pay £86,000 after being found guilty of charges relating to counterfeit clothing and unsafe tobacco products. A dealer in counterfeit computer games was ordered to pay £69,000. In a large-scale car-clocking enterprise, a Surrey trader had to pay £354,049. A timeshare conman was ordered to pay £2.7m compensation to his victims, with another £33m confiscated.

Scams: It was ironic that at a time when enforcement policy was turning away from punitive prosecution the number of prosecutions reported in the *Monthly Review* continued to increase. The following list of examples has been heavily pruned but gives a taste of the variety. Sampling projects in 2000 showed that the proportion of fruit juice in fruit drinks fell from an average of 25% to 10% after deregulation. Hair sold as being 'from virgins' was found to be synthetic. A device for altering odometers was advertised to the trade. A businessman was fined £12,500 for advertising a bogus MBA. A car clamper claimed a false reference to a "Royal Warrant of Approval".

Home working scams became particularly prevalent. An estate agent who defrauded a 92-year-old man of £7,000 was banned from estate agency for life. In 2005, a duck farmer from Worcestershire was found guilty of buying in ordinary commercial ducks and selling them to restaurants as his own special breed. He was fined £12,000 and ordered to pay £6,000 costs.

In August 2006, it was found that the length of chocolate fingers made by Burtons was only two-thirds the width of the box. They were prosecuted for deceptive packaging and fined £3,000. Contaminated petrol was being sold in the South-East, including by a leading supermarket chain. A mock auctioneer was given a three-year ASBO in addition to a six-month jail sentence.

A market trader in Hampshire was tagged for eight weeks for selling counterfeit CDs and video games. A counterfeiter in Leicester was jailed for having 39,000 counterfeit items. In 2009, a family of three DVD counterfeiters were jailed for a total of 16 years.

A farmer in Scotland was fined £1,000 for falsifying the age of a cow to bypass the 30-month rule. In 2005, a prominent retailer was prosecuted under the Control of Misleading Advertisement Regulations for its permanent "70% off" price claims. TSOs had to investigate widespread concerns about the safety of mini motorbikes.

A thoughtful article written by Bryan Lewin, under his pen name 'Cytringan' (the ancient name for Kettering), appeared in *Communiqué* on the question of *Blaming, Naming and Shaming*. The key point was whether advance publicity could make a fair trial impossible.

A Liverpool appeal about an unsafe pushchair held that the issue of a press release, without statutory authority, deprived those affected of some of their rights under the law.

Diploma in Trading Standards: In 2000, the Institute took over responsibility for running the DTS. Some 40 candidates took the new style DTS examination; 51% passed and all others were referred. In 2005, it was confirmed that the Government had provided £245,000 to local authorities to assist with DTS training and to provide work experience. The last DTS examinations were to be in 2009.

Diploma in Consumer Affairs: In 2002, a total of 400 candidates took various examinations under the umbrella of the Diplomas and Certificates offered by the Institute. 170 candidates sat Part I of the DCA examination and 98 sat Part II; 56% passed Part 1 and 70% passed Part 2. However, two years later, 504 candidates attempted the DCA examination. The last DCA examination was held in 2006.

Qualifications Evolve: In April 2005, a review was completed that led to the development into the Trading Standards Qualifications Framework (TSQF). It was recognized that a balance must be struck between creating a qualifications framework that enhanced the professional standing of the Institute and the possibility of excluding some genuinely valuable officers. It was also essential for the framework to recognise people who held pre-existing qualifications such as the DTS, DCA and its antecedents. Some local authorities were looking towards a more generic qualification for a range of regulatory services, not trading standards alone. TSQF consists of five qualifications:

- Certificate of Competence
- Foundation Certificate in Consumer Affairs and Trading Standards

159

- Module Certificate in Consumer Affairs and Trading Standards
- Diploma in Consumer Affairs and Trading Standards
- Higher Diploma in Consumer Affairs and Trading Standards

Statutory Qualification: *TS Today* in September 2006 drew attention to the impracticalities of introducing the Trading Standards Qualifications Framework into a Trading Standards department. This required an understanding of the framework, assessment of training needs and the appointment and training of supervisors, mentors, assessors and verifiers. The detailed arrangements then had to be ratified by TSI and NWML/DTI. The syllabus for the Statutory Foundation module and 10 modules for the TSQF were finalised in March 2006. In July 2007, the South-Western Provincial Employers advertised dates for 18 courses for various modules of the TSQF.

Professional Development: The pilot stage of the paper-based scheme for Continuous Professional and Personal Development (CPPD) began in 2001. At the AGM in 2002, members agreed to introduce a new 'Accredited Category' of membership for those who had satisfied the requirements for CPPD. The full launch of CPPD was in 2004. The basic requirement was for 20 hours of qualifying activities each year. Entry to the scheme was free for members but was also available to non-members for £50.

Distance Learning: In 2001, the DTI agreed to provide £500,000 to TSI for distance learning materials, and by March 2002 an e-learning project was being developed. The *TS Desk Companion* was launched in May 2005. It was an online learning facility and knowledge bank available at all times. It included work-based learning for entrants to the profession, support for students undertaking structured learning and support for practitioners as a job aid. It was compatible with the requirements of CPPD and included most areas of Trading Standards work with automated tests and assessments. In 2007, the Institute advertised 44 individual courses for Trading Standards staff.

Trading Standards Institute

Chief Executive and Staff: The resignation of Allan Charlesworth, the second Chief Executive of the Institute, was announced in 2001, and TSI member Ron Gainsford, previously Assistant Chief Executive LACOTS, took up the position in January 2002. It was an inspired appointment.

Dallas Willcox retired in 2007 after nearly 25 years leading on the development of information and on-line services. Dallas reflected on his career and said that it began with the National Information Service in 1983. Many innovations were implemented as the range of Trading Standards services and the capabilities of information technology increased. It was interesting to note the intention to phase out paper copies of the NIS, but they were still being produced in small numbers 21 years later.

In 2003, TSI had outgrown and sold its office at Hadleigh in Essex and gone on to purchase new premises at Southfield Business Park, Basildon. These were modern offices that provided a refreshing and attractive ambience for staff, visitors and members.

Institute Manifesto: The Institute sought to influence its areas of concern – for fair, honest and safe trading – and establish a recognised status for itself and its members. In 2001, the Institute published an *Election Manifesto* setting out what should be done about these important issues, which was distributed to all the political parties. In 2005, the Institute was represented at a breakfast meeting with the Prime Minister, Tony Blair, to discuss age-restricted sales and, in particular, the sale of alcohol. Mr Blair said that Trading Standards powers needed to be clear with new powers to close offending premises.

In 2009 Baroness Christine Crawley became the new Institute President and Ron Gainsford, TSI Chief Executive, was moved to remind ministers that consumers are the drivers of the economy and business behaviour and that it is consumers who vote. The TSI Chairman, David Sanders, made it clear he believed that the work of Trading Standards with weights and measures continued to be very important.

In 2003, the Management Board of the Institute was reorganised and renamed the Executive Board.

Corporate Plans: The Institute took an increasingly formal approach to planning its activities. It produced important strategic documents: a framework for a National Trading Standards *Plan of Priorities*, a *List of Issues for Government to Address* and a *TSI Mission and Vision Statement*. There were also decisions about the accountability of the Executive Board, about Lead Officers, raising the profile of TSI with local authorities and liaison with the Chief Officer societies. It was agreed consultation with a wider group of stakeholders should be carried out through the Warwick University Institute of Governance and Public Management (IGPM).

Products and Finance: In 2009, TSI set out a portfolio of products and services. This included TS Interlink, e-Books, the pattern approvals database, free entry to Conference for members, TS Broadcast, the e-learning college for students and the Fair Trading Award. These activities generated a surplus of about £250,000 per annum, which TSI used to support its member services.

161

Modernisation: The word 'modernisation' became part of the Institute's lexicon, and it embarked on its own modernisation programme. This would be a wholesale review of what the Institute was for, what it did and the way in which it operated. Main topics would be development of the DTS, Lead Officer arrangements, the use of IT, preparing a business plan and establishing the Institute's identity. An Organisational Strategy Task Group (OSTG) presented 76 recommendations and a programme for consultation and review.

Following debates on the structure of the Institute, the New Articles, Memorandum and Bye-Laws for the Institute were agreed at the AGM in 2002 and at an extraordinary general meeting in February 2003. Some 22 motions were proposed and 18 agreed. Two were lost and two were referred back for further consideration. One result was that the Management Board was renamed the Executive Board. It was also agreed to establish a Section for Outside Local Authority Members (SOLAM). This was a key event in the evolution of the Institute and contrasted sharply with the suspicion of scale-makers in the 19th century. TSI was now a broad membership body embracing a wide spectrum of Trading Standards professionals.

From May 2006, Council consisted of chairman, vice-chairman, second vice-chairman, immediate past chairman, 15 branch and section representatives and only three elected on a national ballot.

New Rules: At the AGM in 2002, there were a number of proposals about rules. It was agreed to delete the requirement for a member to have an appointment in a Trading Standards department. It was also agreed that retired members could vote and be members of the Council. However, a proposal that branches should be able to nominate people as members who did not hold a qualification was not approved.

A new category of Accredited Member was approved for those who had completed Continuing Professional and Personnel Development (CPPD). It was agreed that members could use the following titles after their names: 'Student Member of the Trading Standards Institute', 'Corporate Affiliate Member of the Trading Standards Institute', 'Affiliate Member of the Trading Standards Institute', 'International Member of the Trading Standards Institute' or 'Honorary Member of the Trading Standards Institute'. A proposal to use the title 'Chair' in place of 'Chairman' was defeated.

Chairman and Membership: Maggie Gibbons-Loveday was elected as the first female chairman of the Institute at the AGM 2002, a year in which 239 members had not paid their subscriptions. In 2006, it was announced 230 employees of Consumer Direct in eight contact centres had joined the Institute, and a few months later TSI had a record of over 3,000 members in all categories.

Press Coverage: Despite small reservations, there was positive exposure for the Service in the media, initially in the printed press but increasingly on television. One example was the 'Sorted' column in the *Daily Mirror*. Reporters were keen to find and pillory conmen and sought the cooperation of TSOs, firmly pledging not to prejudice ongoing investigations. They stuck to their word.

In 2000, the *Monthly Review* wrote of the success of the *House of Horrors*, set up by Granada TV with help from Warrington Trading Standards. The Institute debated the ethics of being involved in such stings and of 'naming and shaming'. In 2004, five Trading Standards departments in Scotland took part in a BBC programme called *The Enforcers*, and in 2005, TSOs were heroes in the peak viewing BBC TV show *Watchdog*. Producers and programme-makers constantly appealed for stories about fraud and scams. In August 2006, Steve Playle of Surrey wrote of his experience as Guest Editor of *The Guardian*'s 'Capital Letters' complaints column.

Fair Trading Award: The Council agreed to proceed with the marketing of the Fair Trading Award and the Fair Trading Certificate in 2004. In 2008, the Fair Trading Award was recognised by the Local Authority Assured Trader Scheme Network (LAATSN).

Branches and Sections: At the AGM in 2001, it was agreed to redefine the Welsh Branch to cover the whole of Wales, a change which would affect the boundaries of other branches in the North-West. This followed the devolution of some Trading Standards matters to the new Welsh Assembly.

In 2004, SOLAM (the Section for Outside Local Authority Members) held its first AGM with 25 members. Two years later, the Section had increased to 68. This showed the impact of Trading Standards Officers within trade and businesses.

The Society of Chief Trading Standards Officers (SCTSO) became the Association of Chief Trading Standards Officers (ACTSO) in April 2009. Jacqui Kennedy of Birmingham explained the change by saying that SOCTSO wanted a wider sphere of influence, and members agreed that rebranding might help achieve this objective.

Library: The Library of the Institute had been at the University of Sussex at Lewes since 1956. Unfortunately, it was flooded in October 2000, and the total contents were destroyed. A surge of water from the River Ouse inundated the rooms to a depth of 3 metres and turned much of the contents to papier-mâché. The oldest item destroyed was a copy of *Arbuthnot's Tables* from 1727. The Librarian, Clive Howard-Luck said it was a bitter blow for the Institute. Maurice Stevenson, the founder of the Institute's Library, would have been greatly saddened. The Library was re-established at the NWML offices at Teddington in

2004, thanks to very generous donations of publications from many sources around the country.

The College of Fellows: Towards the end of 2005, a review of the College of Fellows was completed under the Chairmanship of David Sibbert of Oxfordshire. The main recommendations were that the nomination process for Fellows should be revised, the educational opportunities should be promoted more vigorously and more effort should be used to identify members in need of help and assistance. It was decided to recruit a representative in every branch to improve communications and to provide a regular report to the TSI Council.

On the Lighter Side...

Nigel Smart of Oxfordshire told the story of the father of a friend who went to a pub just after the war in his demob suit. He enjoyed a very acceptable three-course meal and was told it was on the house. He assumed that it was because he was a demobbed serviceman but discovered that he had been mistaken for a weights and measures inspector.

Robin Middleton CBE presented a novel College of Fellows Lecture at an Annual Conference on the subject of *Short Measures to Shipwrecks*. Robin was a Council member of the Royal National Lifeboat Institute who formerly worked as CTSO at Waltham Forest but became the highly acclaimed and respected Secretary of State's Representative for Marine Salvage and Intervention (SOSREP).

The Alternative Metric Martyr arrived in Worcester in 2002. An Austrian was in trouble when he opened a restaurant and sold beer in one-litre mugs.

CHAPTER TWELVE – 2010 to 2013

Bulldozers on the Landscape

Introduction: The big issues for the Trading Standards Service in this period were the economic downturn which began in 2008 and the frantic determination of the Coalition Government to carry out yet more reviews on nearly everything. These led to massive unbearable cuts in budgets for local authorities. Trading Standards were not excluded.

The economic crisis of 2008 showed few signs of real recovery by 2013. Many experienced and well-respected members of the Institute lost their jobs. There was a consequent loss for customers of the services provided by the Institute's members. TSI income was significantly reduced, and Head Office staff reductions were necessary. Salaries of local government staffs were frozen, as were subscriptions to the Institute. The Government cuts announced in 2010 reduced the budget of the Department for Business, Innovation and Skills (BIS) by 25% and DEFRA by 29%. A report in 2011 indicated an average reduction of 8.8% on regulatory services compared to the previous year. The average 'hit' for Trading Standards was greater, at 11%, although this masked changes for individual authorities ranging from devastating cuts of 40% to an increase of 10%. In Wales, the cuts ranged from zero to 10% with an average 7.4% reduction.

Reviews of Trading Standards: Following the General Election in May 2010, the new Coalition Government was keen to search for the means of emerging from recession. This included looking at ways of freeing businesses from unnecessary restraints, including regulation. It began a number of reviews which were to have a serious impact on the Service. There was trenchant criticism of a Government Adviser by the Institute for ill-informed remarks. He asked why 60% of Government contracts could not go to small companies – the reply was that small businesses do not build aircraft carriers. He also suggested that when one new regulation was made, two old ones should be scrapped.

In 2010, LBRO and TSI called together a group of regulators led first by Clive Grace for LBRO and then Lord Currie, Chair of the Better Regulation Executive. It met to discuss strategic issues affecting the members. The group included the Chairmen and Chief Éxecutives of OFT, HSE, FSA, NMO, CIEH and the two founding organisations. Review followed review. In April 2011, the Government launched the 'Red Tape Challenge' with the aim of reducing an alleged 21,000 rules that were said to affect business. In August, it was announced that regulation of Christmas crackers, imitation dummies, pencils, liqueur chocolates, bunk beds, prams and hood cords would be scrapped. A report by the National Audit Office in 2011 found that the system of consumer protection failed to evaluate the scale of harm to consumers, particularly relating to doorstep sales. The Report was the subject of a Parliamentary Public Accounts Committee inquiry, where the Institute's Chief Executive gave evidence alongside the Chair of OFT and the BIS Permanent Secretary.

Trading Crime: The National Audit Office estimated the cost of harm was £4.8 billion each year. The Minister for Business, Innovation and Skills, informed by TSI, announced that £213 million spent on consumer protection in 2011 would fall to £140 million in 2014. He also claimed the system of governance was too fragmented between BIS, OFT, local authorities and regional arrangements.

In 2011, the Consumer Affairs Minister launched a more sympathetic 'Consumer Landscape' consultation at the TSI Conference. This proposed that Citizens Advice would become a 'One-Stop Shop' for consumers in order to help bolster the Trading Standards Service. TSI's response was positive but called for all the new structures to be stronger, more coherent and fit for purpose. TSI confirmed it was keen to work alongside Citizens Advice and OFT, and in 2011, the OFT recommended the establishment of a Joint Enforcement Board to determine priorities. In 2011, TSI launched a TSI National Trading Standards Conversation with the intention of capturing the best ideas. BIS said they favoured an incremental review and not major overhaul. Others wanted something more fundamental.

National Conversation: In 2011, the TSI Chairman, Nigel Strick, and the Chief Executive, Ron Gainsford, staged a written public debate in the *Monthly Review* asking whether 'Inspection' was a dirty word following the Hampton Review. They supported the ten Hampton principles but also advocated that risk-based inspection had a place in the modern Better Regulation environment in support of good business and consumer protection.

In November 2011, the Public Accounts Committee found that consumer detriment was £6.6 billion each year (the National Audit Office had put the figure at £4.8 billion) and called for more consumer protection enforcement – not less. It noted central Government provided £34 million to support regional and national enforcement and some £8.5 million for OFT. The Institute expressed concern that excessive belt-tightening was a frightening prospect that would work against economic recovery, as criminals would eat away at honest businesses and devastate the lives of consumers.

The Institute welcomed the consultation document on *Transforming Regulatory Enforcement*, which BIS put forward in 2011. The proposal identified a number of ways in which enforcement could be improved, which included helping businesses comply and making fewer inspections of compliant organisations. The Institute recognised the importance of the focus on targeted, consistent and proportional enforcement and the need for professional standards for regulators.

A year later, in April 2012, BIS announced the results its Consumer Landscape Review, entitled *Empowering and Protecting Consumers*. This Review made the following changes relating to the Trading Standards Service:

- A National Trading Standards Board (NTSB) managed by TSI,
- An Enforcement Work Plan developed by NTSB agreed with BIS,
- Trading Standards to be responsible for business education and information
- TSI was invited to tender for a new Consumer Code Approvals Scheme (CCAS) and set up a database of approval schemes,
- TSI to take over the roles of OFT for policy, international links and training, and
- An extra £10.5 million funding to be made available for Trading Standards.

In addition, Citizens Advice took on a number of new roles and responsibilities, including consumer advice and education and consumer advocacy. The Regulated Industries Unit (RIU) within BIS would move to Citizens Advice in 2014, and this might include postal services, energy and water. OFT would hand over all consumer work.

Ministers: The Institute was pleased to note that Baroness Judith Wilcox, who had been President of TSI from 1995 to 2006, became Parliamentary Secretary at BIS after the General Election in 2010, (a position she unfortunately lost in the 2012 reshuffle). The new Consumer Minister spoke in March 2011 about respect for Trading Standards, funding for the Money Lending and Scambusters teams, and the role of CABx in providing consumer advice. He also spoke optimistically about surviving budget cuts, liaison between authorities and the proposed organisational review of OFT.

Direct Funding: In January 2011, BIS announced that the Illegal Money Lending Team (IML) would receive funding of £5.2 million in 2011 and that the Scambusters team would receive a further £3.2 million. This was very positive. The regional IML teams would be merged into one team for England, alongside separate teams in Scotland and Wales. The English team would be coordinated from the successful team based in Birmingham Trading Standards.

Work Planning: The Retail Enforcement Pilot organised by the Local Better Regulation Office (LBRO) in 2009 involved 30 local authorities to follow up the recommendations of Hampton. The conclusions were that the 'single inspection' target was difficult to achieve and that management improvements were necessary using information technology. Many authorities did not have the resources to maintain a complete record of traders, and this made prioritising and planning difficult. LBRO launched 10 toolkits of ideas, which were:

- Primary authority partnerships schemes
- Primary authority database available at LBRO
- A scheme for assessing the value of regulatory services
- Placements of regulators with businesses
- Reducing under-age sales of alcohol
- An excellence framework to identify areas for improvement
- National enforcement priorities, initially in Wales
- Supporting businesses towards recovery,
- Best practice case studies
- A Year Ahead Conference

In 2011, 19 local authorities in the South-East established their liaison group as Trading Standards South-East Ltd. This enabled the group to negotiate and enter contracts with private and public suppliers to achieve savings.

ECC for Services: In 2010, the contract was awarded to the Institute to deliver the European Consumer Centre for Services for the UK (UK-ECC Services), as described in Article 21 of EU Services Directive from 2012.

Organisations: In 2010, both LBRO and the Food Standards Agency were under scrutiny in the 'Review of Quangos'. The review of LBRO decided that it should continue. The review of FSA saved it from abolition but reduced its duties so that Nutrition Policy moved to the Department of Health, while Origin Marking moved to DEFRA. An Excellence Framework for local authority regulatory services was developed by LBRO and endorsed by LACORS, TSI and others. The four themes of the Excellence Framework covered leadership and strategy, customer focus, resource management and achievement of sustainable outcomes.

In October 2011, a Joint Statement of Commitment between LBRO, CIEH and TSI was signed. The statement emphasised the importance of environmental health and trading standards and the Government drive for co-regulation. The parties agreed to work for greater clarity, efficiency and sustainability. Joint work would focus on the following four main areas:

- Support for officers: a framework to ensure professional competency
- Support for business: Home/Primary Authority Schemes
- Support for networks: establish professional policy/advisory groups
- Support for advisers: accessible advice via websites.

In 2012, the OFT wrote about its Internet Enforcement Laboratory.

The Office of the Surveillance Commissioner was established in 2010 to supervise the application of RIPA and the Scottish version of it. It was concerned with the use of covert surveillance, but not telephone intercepts.

LACORS was renamed Local Government Regulation (LGR) in July 2010 but was disbanded a year later by the Local Government Association, the TSI assuming responsibility for the Primary Authority Principle.

Legislation: In spite of concerns about 'red tape legislation' the flow continued in something approaching a torrent. Priorities were frequently reviewed. The range of legislation in the first two years of the decade included a Video Recordings Act, a Digital Economy Act, the Unfair Commercial Practices Directive, pricing practices guidance, RIPA and the General Product Safety Directive.

The 'Stop Loan Sharks' campaign gathered strength. In 2012, the Government moved to limit the marketing of Pay Day Loans. Some companies were boldly advertising loans on TV with a declared APR of 1,743%. Clearly many customers had no idea what APR represented.

The Minister announced a proposal for a Consumer Rights Bill in 2011 which followed the adoption of the European Consumer Rights Directive in the same year. This included:

* Elimination of hidden internet charges and costs
* Increased price transparency
* Banning pre-ticked boxes on websites
* Allowing a 14 days cooling off period
* Better refund rights
* Eliminating charges for the use of credit cards
* Clearer information on the costs of returning goods
* Common rules to make it easier to trade across the EU.

The Minister claimed that the Bill would consolidate, clarify and strengthen consumer laws and would bring together the provisions of 12 existing acts or regulations.

On a more controversial issue, the UK Metric Association criticised the Institute for not supporting metrication. TSI had taken the view that its role was to enforce the law and not take sides on matters which did not impact on Trading Standards. This is in contrast to the views of the Institute (or Society) in the early days, when it was the keenest and most active supporter of metrication.

To round off a long-running story, gas meter examiners in 2012 were employed by a private company named SGS (UK) Ltd under a contract to the National Measurement Office to provide an independent meter examination service.

The Protection of Freedoms Act 2012 was intended to prevent abuse of powers by enforcers, but it could hamper investigations in relation to powers of entry. Consultation took place on a uniform set of powers for enforcement of legislation within the remit of BIS.

Consultations were also taking place on permitting hallmarking overseas, a Consumer Law Consolidation to replace 60 pieces of legislation and an Enterprise and Regulatory Reform Bill to further reduce red tape. There was consultation in June 2012 on proposals from the EU for a system of Alternative Dispute Resolution.

Court Cases: The long-running problem of 'toxic sofas' ended in 2010 when around 2,000 people who had suffered burns received payouts of between £1,200 and £9,000 each. Two PhD students in Leicestershire were sent to prison for clocking offences in February 2010.

Unfortunately, in 2011, the convictions for the Lapland New Forest Theme Park scam were overturned because a juror had texted a friend during the judge's summing up. In 2012, there was a report about a Birmingham family which had been defrauded when booking a pilgrimage to Mecca; the offender received a custodial sentence. In 2010, there were reports about unjust baggage scales and incorrect luggage size gauges at many airports. In 2011, it was confirmed that five of the largest retailers of energy were to stop selling by cold-calling.

Many Trading Standards departments used the Proceeds of Crime Act (POCA) to good effect. In February 2010, a POCA order for £3.23 million was made in a case in Kent involving counterfeit bags and shoes. West Berkshire used part of the proceeds of confiscation orders to fund assistance to the service by a police support officer.

A loan shark in Manchester had to pay £1.2 million. Money confiscated from loan sharks in Hampshire was used to give a bonus of £20 to people who had joined a credit union. These were all trumped by a counterfeiting case in Enfield where an order for £11,182,609.52 was made under POCA in May 2010.

Training: In the period 2007-2010, the Institute provided training for the Consumer Focus programmes and OFT's Consumer Direct. In March 2012, the Institute launched a new training package called Telephone Tutorial. The first module was about digital surveillance and lasted 60 minutes.

At the end of 2011, the TSI Academy was launched as an aid to making progress through the TSQF. It contained nine elements based around tailored online training. There were five courses available at the start. TSI also had a Competency Framework that contributed to Continuing Personal and Professional Development and this should not be confused with the Qualifications Framework.

Since 2006, over 1700 students had developed their competency and qualifications via the TSQF

Trading Standards Practitioner: It was also necessary to cope with the various ways in which the title of Trading Standards Officer was used. At one time it meant a person who held the DTS or equivalent, but in the mind of the public and the media it had come to mean many different posts in a Trading Standards department. The Institute produced a report in February 2010 that included a definition of a Trading Standards Practitioner involving high academic status, qualification in trading standards, evidence of professional development and TSI membership. The TSI Council hoped that in the future all those working within trading standards would aspire to achieve the top level status of a Trading Standards Practitioner.

TSI Income: TSI continued to receive income from ECC-UK, NIS (National Information Service), Training courses, Qualifications, NTSB (National Trading Standards Board) and Codes of Practice, in addition to subscriptions but at a reduced level because of economic conditions. In June 2011, TSI was accredited for its ISO 9001 quality management system.

Royal Charter: In 2010, TSI was again discussing whether to apply for a Royal Charter, and in the following year the Council was optimistic about negotiations with the representatives of the Privy Council. The advantages of achieving a Charter include recognition of the status of the Institute and enhancing the influence TSI could have in talking to Government and trade and professional organisations. TSI also considered seeking charitable status, but this idea was deferred in 2011 in favour of focusing resources on achieving Royal Charter status.

Executive Board: The Institute added a further seven members to the Executive Board in September 2011, making a total of 13 members.

Information Technology: A facility to create a microsite in TS Interlink was launched by TSI in 2010, and an updated product was launched in March 2011. The improvements that had been made in response to feedback from users included improved visual design, navigation and search facilities. It was also available on most smart-phones.
In 2010, there was an article about the Local Authority Assured Trader Scheme Network (LAATSN) that had been developed by the OFT. At that time there were 44 members with 17 schemes in place. TSI was considering taking over the network.
In 2011, the Fair Trading Award was extended to include a module called 'Do You Pass?' This module was to be delivered by a TSI-accredited trainer to business delegates.
Also, in 2012, it was announced that the Air Transport Operators
Licence Scheme (ATOL) was to be reformed to provide more assistance to holidaymakers when things go wrong.

171

College of Fellows: In 2011, a report from the College of Fellows confirmed that 242 people had been chosen as Fellows since the College was formed in 1951. A full list of names is included in Appendix 1. In 2013 there were 117 Fellows.

In addition to a regular portfolio of welfare activities, the College has promoted development and education. In the last decade around a dozen scholarships have been completed, ranging through package travel, systems mapping, age-restricted sales, consumer protection and product safety.

The College has also helped sponsor shorter punchier travelling bursaries for younger members to study specific consumer problems in other countries. The countries visited include France, Germany, Netherlands, Spain, Italy and as far away as South Africa, California and St Kitts and Nevis. The series of reports were published in *TS Today* and are held in the College's LIbrary. They include reports on rogue traders, counterfeit controls, metrological problems, and the different legal and consumer protection systems worldwide.

Chief Executive: In 2010, the Chief Executive, Ron Gainsford, was awarded the OBE for services to consumers and business. He later announced his retirement from April 2013. He and his motorbike at the leadership helm are sorely missed. Ron has been well known for his vision and foresight and not looking back: "Today is already history, think about tomorrow."

TS People: In the preparation of this book, colleagues have spoken to a number of members who can recall working in the profession as far back as 80 years. In May 2010, an interview was published in *TS Today* with Norman Naish at the age of 96. Norman was Chief Inspector for Folkestone Borough until he retired in 1974. He clearly remembered seeing Earl Haig at the unveiling of the Cenotaph in 1919.

Henry Gray celebrated his centenary on the last day of 2011. Henry worked for 62 years in Oxfordshire, Kent and Hampshire and enjoyed the variety of his working life. In an interview, published in the *Monthly Review* in January 2012, he related a number of anecdotes about milk and spirit sampling.

On the Lighter Side...

The history of measurement is put into context by a small item in the press, which showed that the size of shuttle booster rockets was determined by the size of railway tunnels through which they had to pass. In turn, the size of the tunnels had been determined in the time of horse-drawn railway wagons by the width necessary for the backsides of two horses to pass.

Also on the subject of measurement, it was noted that the metric

System, which is based on the convenience of the number ten, actually uses subdivisions of the kilogram equal to x2, x4, x8 etc, and also the very peculiar units of 150 grams and 75 grams.

Epilogue

Of course the start of the Institute is lost to living memories but in publishing this book we earnestly hope that the history will come alive to those who read it.

Perhaps in closing a history it is appropriate to look to the future. In 2013, the Institute and its members are surrounded by challenging scenarios, but their history shows they will respond with energy, innovation and good humour to whatever minor and major obstacles arise.

Despite all the trials and tribulations, the Institute and its members will continue their mission because, in the words of Alexander McCall Smith (Emeritus Professor of Medical Law at the University of Edinburgh), taken from his *No 1 Ladies' Detective Agency* series:

"There is a world beneath the world inhabited by ordinary, law-abiding people; a world of selfishness and mistrust occupied by scheming and manipulative people."

Those people are unlikely to go away.

Humour through the ages

LIBRA — Striking the Balance.

The Leet Jury, or Ward Inquest.—By GEORGE CRUIKSHANK.

JOHN BULL: Thank you, Joseph, but if it is all the same to you, I will have my crisis weighed without the paper.

The Morning Leader 1899

Tipping the Scales
Leslie Thrasher 1936

THE WAY THEY DO IT IN CARDIFF.

Cardiff Evening Express, 1896

Member of Markets Committee: "Understand Inspector, your instructions are to examine scales and traders, and if any are defective, give one warning and then prosecute." "Yes sir."

Another Member: "Inspector what do you mean by summonsing my friend Mr Lightweight, the most respected and esteemed trader in town? It's simply disgraceful that such people can be prosecuted."

THE GOOD SOLDIER CARRIES ON : 1945

The Western Daily Press, 1965

"THERE THEY GO - TWO MORE UNDERCOVER MEN FROM THE WEIGHTS AND MEASURES DEPARTMENT, TESTING THE FROTH ON GLASSES OF GUINNESS"

Flantoons, 2009

The Grocer Magazine, 1964

"Just show me where the Act expressly forbids a sign like that!"

The Weekly News, 1955

"Repeat after me—'I swear to tell the truth, the whole truth and nothing but the truth!'"

The Coal Merchant and Shipper, 1956

"STOP COMPLAINING HENRY, AND KEEP COUNTING!"

APPENDIX ONE

FELLOWS elected by the Institute since 1952

NOTE TO APPENDICES.
In compiling these appendices the College of Fellows has encountered difficulties in ensuring that every detail is correct. We apologise for any errors or omissions. Please notify the College of mistakes, if any.

Name	Authority	Date, Place Elected
Adams, Jeremy Hugh	Cambridgeshire CC	2010, Edinburgh
Adams, W B (deceased)	Borough of Swindon	1973, Aberdeen
Aldridge, Bryn	City of London	1993, Edinburgh
Alexander, W (deceased)	Fife Council	1952, Cheltenham
Allen, Anthony Paul OBE	East Sussex CC	1980, Edinburgh
Anthony, Brian John	Birmingham MBC	2002, Birmingham
Armstrong, Christopher L	Newham LB	1996, Bournemouth
Arneil, Gavin (deceased)	Midlothian CC	1972, Bournemouth
Bainbridge, Clive George	Kent CC	2011, Bournemouth
Baker, Leslie [deceased]	Birmingham MBC	1991, London
Barnes, C S [deceased]	Cardiff City	1958, Scarborough
Barnes, Oswald Weston	Cardiff City	1967, Aberdeen
Beckett, Bryan W (deceased)	Avon CC	1977, Blackpool
Beer, J (deceased)	Worcester CC	1968, Brighton
Bennett, John [deceased]	West Yorkshire CC	1985, Inverness
Bentley, S E (deceased)	West Midlands CC	1978, Cardiff
Birkett, Frederick L. [dec.]	Warley CB	1975, Scarborough
Blyth, Alan D (deceased)	Tayside RC	1992, Torquay
Bolchover, Stephen	Strathclyde RC	1989, Glasgow
Bottomley, Philip	Hackney LB	1993, Edinburgh
Brady, Carol	Local Better Regulation Office	2009, Brighton
Breed, W R (deceased)	Council Member	1954, Margate
Brewer, Raymond James	Enfield LB	2000, Brighton
Brookhouse, David Thomas	Stoke on Trent	2001, Cardiff
Brown, R S (deceased)	Argyl & Bute CC	1972, Bournemouth
Brown, W (deceased)	Paisley Council	1958, Scarborough
Brudenell, C W (deceased)	Humberside CC	1978, Cardiff
Buckley, Michael J. [dec]	South Yorkshire Standards Unit	1999, Edinburgh
Bucknall, Frank M [dec]	Council Member	1954, Margate
Burleigh, David Malcolm	East Sussex CC	1988, Scarborough
Burnett, Howard James	Somerset CC	2001, Cardiff
Burrell, L W (deceased)	Angus CC	1967, Aberdeen
Burton, P (deceased)	Middlesex CC	1957, London
Burton, Timothy Alec	Corporation of London	2001, Cardiff
Butt, Gordon John	Somerset CC	1984, Blackpool
Butterworth, Stephen S	Staffordshire CC	2005, Brighton
Cain, Kenneth William	West Sussex CC	1984, Blackpool
Cairns, Thomas [deceased]	Glasgow City	1970, Plymouth
Card, Charles C (deceased)	Essex CC	1955, Llandudno
Carroll, John Ronald	Newham LB	1983, Eastbourne
Cartwright, F W [deceased]	Cambridge City	1963, Blackpool
Cassie, William James MBE	Aberdeen Council	2007, Manchester
Chapman, M A (deceased)	Wiltshire CC	1967, Aberdeen
Chicken, Edward Robert	Middlesbrough	1998, London
Clark, J Goldie [deceased]	Southend-on-Sea DC	1977, Blackpool
Clark, Paul Adrian	North Lincolnshire	1999, Edinburgh
Clifford, Brian	West Yorkshire CC	1977, Blackpool
Collier, Harry Bruce	South Ayrshire	2000, Brighton
Constantine, Roger Robert	Staffordshire CC	1998, London

Corfield, John James	Greater Manchester	1980, Edinburgh
Cottee, G E C (deceased)	Somerset CC	1971, Southport
Cull, Nicholas Ivor	LACOTS	2000, Brighton
Cunningham, Sean Patrick	Central Regional Council	1990, Bournemouth
Dale, K B (deceased)	Kingston-upon-Thames	1974, Eastbourne
Daly, Kenneth Stephen	Dundee City	2011, Bournemouth
Davenport, W A (deceased)	Buckinghamshire CC	1953, Scarborough
Davies, T A T (deceased)	Cambridgeshire CC	1969, Scarborough
Davis, G L (deceased)	Buckinghamshire CC	1972, Bournemouth
Davys, Ivan (deceased)	Northamptonshire CC	1986, Torquay
Deering, Ronald G (dec)	Havering LB	1971, Southport
Delahaye, Stephen James	Mid Glamorgan CC	1990, Bournemouth
Denard, Christopher P MBE	Surrey CC	1991, London
Dixon, Bryan (deceased)	Kent CC	1983, Eastbourne
Drewry, James Michael	Durham CC	1986, Torquay
Edmunds, W E (deceased)	Past Institute Chairman	1952, Cheltenham
Edwards, Neil	Fife County Council	2005, Brighton
Edwards, R T [deceased]	Institute in Wales	1955, Llandudno
Elliott, Timothy Richard	Cheshire CC	1988, Scarborough
Emberson, Colin Thomas	Leicestershire CC	1987, Blackpool
Evans, Frank J (deceased)	Northamptonshire CC	1974, Eastbourne
Evans, John Gregory	Hounslow LB	1994, Brighton
Forrow, Elizabeth Joy	Hampshire CC	2010, Edinburgh
Fox, Neville Stanford	Warwickshire CC	1991, London
Fryer, John Stewart	Somerset CC	1997, Antwerp
Gainsford, Ronald F OBE	LACOTS	1999, Edinburgh
Gale, Robert OBE	Cumbria CC	1984, Blackpool
Galland, Paul Richard	Gloucestershire CC	1998, London
Gascoigne, Stanley (dec]	Sheffield City	1966, Torquay
Gass, Alan Ewert	Dumfries & Galoway	2003, Edinburgh
Gay, Harold	Alliance Boots	2011, Bournemouth
Gaywood, Peter Leonard	Essex County	2002, Birmingham
Gethin, Janet	Mid Glamorgan CC	1993, Edinburgh
Girdwood, John Millar	Grampion Regional Council	1988, Scarborough
Golbey, Julian	Croydon LB	2010, Edinburgh
Gordon, G T [deceased]	Hereford & Worcester CC	1976, Birmingham
Graham, J T R B (deceased)	Cheshire CC	1959, Cardiff
Gray, W (deceased)	Institute Secretary	1952, Cheltenham
Green, Peter Bernard	West Sussex CC	1982, Plymouth
Greenhill, L G (deceased)	Surrey CC	1959, Cardiff
Gregory, T L E (deceased)	Institute Treasurer	1952, Cheltenham
Gresty, Gordon Sidney	North Yorkshire CC	1988, Scarborough
Grice, Robert	Doncaster MBC	2010, Edinburgh
Griffiths, E H [deceased]	Hertfordshire CC	1961, Lowestoft
Griffiths, L M (deceased)	Editor of the Journal	1952, Cheltenham
Grigg, F J (deceased)	Stockport MBC	1958, Scarborough
Grimes, Derek Arthur	Dorset CC	1990, Bournemouth
Gutowski, Michael Joseph	Birmingham MBC	2009, Brighton
Halliday, J M 'Ian' [dec.]	Ipswich County Borough	1973, Aberdeen
Hammond, F V (deceased)	Leicester	1956, Bournemouth
Hannibal, F [deceased]	Smethwick	1955, Llandudno
Hanson, Michael Graham	Barnsley MBC	1999, Edinburgh
Hargreaves, Steven [dec]	West Midlands CC	1979, Brighton
Harvey, Michael John	West Sussex CC	2006, London
Heafield, Peter John	Lincolnshire CC	2004, Manchester
Hill, Roy Douglas	Oxfordshire CC	1993, Edinburgh
Hillier, John	ELSPA	2006, London
Holder, Jack (deceased)	Cheshire CC	1983, Eastbourne
Hopkinson, J W (dec)	West Riding of Yorkshire	1956, Bournemouth
Howard-Luck, Clive (dec)	Strathclyde RC	1980, Edinburgh
Howell, Gerard C (deceased)	Dudley MBC	1989, Glasgow

178

Hudson, Stephanie Maria	Liverpool City	2012, Manchester
Hughes, David John Sprake	Hampshire CC	1989, Glasgow
Hullah, Haydn James [dec.]	South Glamorgan CC	1977, Blackpool
Humble, James Kenneth OBE	Office of Fair Trading	1975, Scarborough
Hunter, Noel Campbell OBE	Warwickshire CC	1986, Torquay
Hurley, Keith	West Yorkshire TS Service	1992, Torquay
Ingham, David	North Yorkshire CC	1987, Blackpool
James, Kenneth Thomas	Southend-on-Sea DC	1991, London
James, Lionel K (deceased)	Glamorgan County Council	1973, Aberdeen
Jarvis, Marshall Steven	Nottinghamshire CC	2009, Brighton
Jenkins, David (deceased)	West Midlands CC	1985, Inverness
Jenkins, G C (deceased)	Staffordshire CC	1968, Brighton
Johnson, D W (deceased)	Slough Borough	1971, Southport
Jones, J D M (deceased)	Cardiganshire CC	1978, Cardiff
Jones, John Edward [dec.]	Devon CC	1985, Inverness
Keeley, H A [deceased]	Examiner for Testamur	1954, Margate
Kenyon, WH	Past Chair Incorporated Society	1952 Cheltenham
Keohane, Timothy	Caerphilly CBC	2013, Brighton
Kilsby, Robert E. [deceased]	Surrey CC	1972, Bournemouth
Knight, J R	Gwent Council	1984, Blackpool
Knight, Richard John	Leicester	1997, Antwerp
Ladds, W A (deceased)	Institute Chairman	1952, Cheltenham
Lewin, Bryan MBE	Northamptonshire CC	2005, Brighton
Livingstone, David	Northern Ireland	2012, Manchester
Malone, John Sebastion	Wirral MBC	1990, Bournemouth
Malone, Thomas (deceased)	Salford MBC	1966, Torquay
Manford, Elizabeth	Cheshire CC	2005, Brighton
Manley, Roger OBE	Warwickshire CC	1980, Edinburgh
Marshall, David Howard	East Sussex CC	1994, Brighton
Marshall, G W [deceased]	Bristol City	1965, Southport
Marshall, N [deceased]	Barnsley Council	1952, Cheltenham
Marston, F W (deceased)	Somerset CC	1963, Blackpool
Martin, Henry	Cambridgeshire CC	1981, Harrogate
Martin, K R C (deceased)	Council member, S W Branch	1954, Margate
Martin, Wendy Joan	Merton LB	2003, Edinburgh
Mason, Philip Roger	Cambridgeshire CC	1995, Scarborough
Matthew, James I A	Angus	2004, Manchester
May, Philip	Derbyshire CC	1988, Scarborough
McAuley, Anthony J P	East Lothian	2012, Manchester
McCruden, Jennifer Ann	Northamptonshire CC	2007, Manchester
McHugh, Leslie	West Midlands CC	1985, Inverness
McKellar, J.J (deceased)	Perth City	1967, Aberdeen
Meiehofer, Harold Lyndley F	North Lanarkshire Council	2009, Brighton
Melrose, Eric McIntosh	Aberdeen	1997, Antwerp
Mercer, E C (deceased)	Immediate Past Chairman	1952, Cheltenham
Metcalfe, T J (deceased)	Chairman Parliamentary Com	1952, Cheltenham
Middleton, Robin E V CBE	Waltham Forest LB	1994, Brighton
Miller, Harold Thomas	Western Isles Council	2008, Bournemouth
Milner, F S (deceased)	Council Member Midlands	1954, Margate
Mitchell, Archibald McKenzie	Tayside RC	1994, Brighton
Morgan, M Ellen	B&Q plc	2013, Brighton
Munday, Edgar H (deceased)	Somerset CC	1979, Brighton
Nattrass, WK MBE (dec.)	Cheshire CC	1974, Eastbourne
Nisbett, Eric A (deceased)	Hertfordshire CC	1967, Aberdeen
Nobbs, A (deceased)	Cumberland	1955, Llandudno
Norris, J A (deceased)	Chesterfield	2008, Bournemouth
Northcott, Anthony Peter	Haringey LB	1994, Brighton
O'Keefe, J A (deceased)	Public Control, Middlesex	1953, Scarborough
O'Neill, Helen Doreen	South Lanarkshire	2011, Bournemouth
Owen, W J [deceased]	Bradford City	1959, Cardiff
Parkinson, R E [deceased]	Devon CC	1971, Southport

179

Parton, John Michael	Doncaster MBC	1995, Scarborough
Peerless, John Colin	Brighton and Hove	2012, Manchester
Peters, Kathryn	Caerphilly	2012, Manchester
Pettit, H W (deceased)	Crewe Borough	1972, Bournemouth
Phillips, David John	Cornwall CC	1997, Antwerp
Philpott, Thomas	South Western Provincial Council	1986, Torquay
Playle, Steve	Surrey CC	2013, Brighton
Porter, L C (deceased)	Council Chief Corresponding	1954, Margate
Potts, Jim	Lancashire CC	2011, Bournemouth
Preston, J S	Hampshire CC	1975, Scarborough
Price, Geoffrey Kenneth	Consultant and Denbighshire	2006, London
Pudney, Stuart	North Yorkshire	2007, Manchester
Race, R (deceased)	Tunbridge Wells BC	1969, Scarborough
Reid, D [deceased]	Fife Council	1960, Rothesay
Richardson, F (deceased)	Nottingham City	1958, Scarborough
Roberts, David C. E.	Shropshire CC	1984, Blackpool
Roberts, G [deceased]	Peterborough	1963, Blackpool
Roberts, J R (deceased)	Manchester City	1952, Cheltenham
Robertson, J W (deceased)	Glasgow, Scottish Notes	1955, Llandudno
Robertson, R [deceased]	Fife Council	1952, Cheltenham
Robinson, Eric	Cleveland CC	1993, Edinburgh
Robinson, H (deceased)	Chief Corresponding /Orator	1952, Cheltenham
Roderick, David James	North Lanarkshire Council	2005, Brighton
Roderick, Margaret Rose	Fife County Council	2002, Birmingham
Rogers, Christopher Urban	Westminster Consortium	1982, Plymouth
Rose, Philip Anthony	Islington LB	1992, Torquay
Routledge, J H (deceased)	Durham CC	1969, Scarborough
Rowell, Dr Roland Arthur	Director Legal Eyes	2007, Manchester
Rushton, Martin	Lothian Regional Council	2002, Birmingham
Russell, Graham J MBE	Better Regulation Office BRDO	2013, Brighton
Sanders, David Charles	South Glamorgan CC	1996, Bournemouth
Sandys, Eldon Charles	Devon CC	1978, Cardiff
Sedgwick, G V (deceased)	Past Institute Chairman	1952, Cheltenham
Sharratt, John	Borders Council	2001, Cardiff
Shaw, K (deceased)	Buckinghamshire CC	1982, Plymouth
Sheret, Edward Nichol	Lothian RC	1983, Eastbourne
Sherratt, P (deceased)	Stoke on Trent CC	1970, Plymouth
Short, James	Lothian RC	1980, Edinburgh
Sibbert, David	Oxfordshire CC	1989, Glasgow
Simmonds, John Maurice	Kent CC	1996, Bournemouth
Simpson, L W	Nottinghamshire CC	1966, Torquay
Smith, G	South Yorkshire CC	1986, Torquay
Smith, H C [deceased]	Editor Monthly Review	1952 Cheltenham
Smith, Reginald John	Humberside CC	1981, Harrogate
Smith, William Frank	Herford & Wocs CC	1992, Torquay
Sopp, C C E [deceased]	Berkshire CC	1965, Southport
Speight, H W (deceased)	Past Institute Chairman	1952, Cheltenham
Spinks, James William	Croydon LB	1987, Blackpool
Stevenson, M (deceased)	Eastbourne	1960, Rothesay
Stewart, J (deceased)	Aberdeenshire	1957, London
Stone, Brian Frederick	West Sussex CC	2009, Brighton
Stone, Oswald J (deceased)	Surrey CC	1979, Brighton
Stratton, Peter John	Essex County Council	2003, Edinburgh
Street, Alan James	Greater Manchester	1983, Eastbourne
Strick, Nigel Neil	Oxfordshire CC	2008, Bournemouth
Strugnell, S (deceased)	Past Institute Chairman	1952, Cheltenham
Theobold, L G [deceased]	City of Westminster	1976, Birmingham
Thomas, H A (deceased)	Anglesey County Council	1973, Aberdeen
Thomas, J E (deceased)	Scarborough BC	1961, Lowestoft
Thomson, David	South Ayrshire Council	2010, Edinburgh
Thornley, John R [deceased]	Essex CC	1966, Torquay

Townend, Clive Richard	Coventry	2012, Manchester
Treloar, Bruce Richard	West Sussex	1998, London
Turier, A S (deceased)	Past Institute Chairman	1952, Cheltenham
Turner, B W	Clwyd CC	1981, Harrogate
Venn, Graham Ralph	North Yorkshire CC	2004, Manchester
Wade, Christine Hilary MBE	Northamptonshire CC	1990, Bournemouth
Walker, David	Shropshire CC	1984, Blackpool
Walker, S A (deceased)	Ayr Council	1960, Rothesay
Waller, A E (deceased)	Northamptonshire	1956, Bournemouth
Waller, E John (deceased)	Derbyshire CC	1979, Brighton
Walters, Gareth	Monmouthshire CC	2013, Brighton
Wankling, Roger Michael	East Sussex CC	1987, Blackpool
Warwick, Ian	Dorset CC	2004, Manchester
Welch, E L F 'Ian' [dec.]	Hertfordshire CC	1976, Birmingham
Wells, Charles R (deceased)	Sheffield City	1970, Plymouth
White, Alan (deceased)	Enfield LB	1981, Harrogate
Wiggins, S, Rev (deceased)	Chairman of the Institute	1954, Margate
Williams, Benjamin Anthony	Gloucestershire CC	1981, Harrogate
Wolfinden, A [deceased]	West Riding of Yorkshire	1957, London
Wood, Roger William	Avon CC	1982, Plymouth
Wright, R C	West Suffolk	1965, Southport
Wright, R G (deceased)	Coventry	1953, Scarborough
Wright, Robert Vincent	South Yorkshire	1983, Eastbourne
Wrighton, Brian Frederick	City of London	1973, Aberdeen
Writer, E C (deceased)	Ed of Monthly Review	1952, Cheltenham
Young, C G (deceased)	Past Institute Chairman	1952, Cheltenham

APPENDIX TWO

Officers of the Institute

PRESIDENTS

British Association of Inspectors of Weights and Measures
1881 - 1885	Cllr W. Scott Brown, Chairman of the W & M Committee of Manchester CC
1885 - 1887	Alderman Chandley, (Warrington)
1887 - 1893	Sir Joseph Terry, Lord Mayor of York

Incorporated Society of Inspectors of Weights and Measures.
NB-The President was always the Chairman of London County Council until 1948
1893 - 1895	Sir John Hutton, DL, JP.
1895 - 1897	Sir Arthur Arnold, JP, DL. Chairman of L.C.C.
1897 - 1898	Dr. Sir William J. Collins, KCVO, MD, DL, JP.
1898 - 1899	The Rt. Hon. T. McKinnon Wood, LLD, DL.
1899 - 1900	The Rt. Hon. Lord Welby, GCB.
1900 - 1901	The Rt. Hon. Sir Willoughby Hyatt Dickinson, KBE, DL, JP.
1901 - 1902	Sir Andrew Mitchell Torrance, JP, DL.
1902 - 1903	Sir John McDougall, JP.
1903 - 1904	The Rt. Hon. Lord Monkswell, DL, JP.
1904 - 1905	Sir John William Benn, Bart., DL, JP.
1905 - 1906	The Rt. Hon. Sir Edwin A. Cornwall, Bart., DL, JP, MP.
1906 - 1907	Sir Evan Spicer, DL, JP.
1907 - 1908	Sir Henry Percy Harris, KBE, DL, JP.
1908 - 1909	Sir Richard Atkinson Robinson, DL, JP.
1909 - 1910	Sir R. Melvill Beachcroft.
1910 - 1911	William Whitaker Thompson, Esq., JP.
1911 - 1912	Sir Edward White, JP.
1912 - 1913	Major-General the Rt. Hon. Lord Cheylesmore, GBE, KCVO, KCMG, DL, JP.
1913 - 1914	Sir Cyril S. Cobb, KBE, MVO, JP, MP.
1914 - 1915	The Rt. Hon. Viscount Peel, GCSI, GBE, DL, JP, DCL.
1915 - 1916	Sir Cyril Jackson, KBE, JP.
1916 - 1917	Alfred Fowell Buxton, Esq., JP.
1917 - 1918	The Most Hon. the Marquess of Crewe, KG, PC.
1918 - 1919	Ronald Collet Norman, Esq., JP.
1919 - 1920	The Rt. Hon. Lord Downham, PC.
1920 - 1921	Sir John William Gilbert, KBE, LLP, JP.
1921 - 1922	Major Sir Percy Coleman Simmons, KCVO, DL, JP.
1922 - 1923	Sir Francis Robert Anderton, MA, JP.
1923 - 1924	Sir Henry Cubitt Gooch, JP.
1924 - 1925	Sir J. Herbert Hunter, JP.
1925 - 1926	Capt. Sir Oscar Emanuel Warburg OBE. (Chair of LCC).
1926 - 1927	Sir George Hume, JP, MP. (Chair of LCC).
1927 - 1928	Sir John Maria Gatti, JP, (Chair of LCC).
1928 - 1929	Lt-Col Sir Cecil Bingham Levita, KCVO, CBE, DL, JP, MVO.
1929 - 1930	The Rt. Hon. Lord Monk Bretton, CB, DL, JP.
1930 - 1931	Sir Robert Inigo Tasker, DL, JP.
1931 - 1932	Sir Ernest Sanger, JP.
1932 - 1933	Sir Angus Newton Scott, FCA, DL, JP.
1933 - 1934	Ernest M. Dence, Esq., LLD, JP.
1934 - 1938	The Rt. Hon. Lord Snell, PC, CBE, LLD, JP.
1938 - 1939	Ewart G. Culpin, Esq.
1939 - 1940	Mrs. Eveline Mary Lowe, JP.
1940 - 1941	Albert Emil Davies, Esq., JP.
1941 - 1942	Charles George Ammon, Esq., JP, MP.

1942 - 1943	J. P. Blake, Esq.
1943 - 1943	Sir Alfred Baker
1943 - 1944	Richard Coppock, Esq.
1944 - 1945	Dr. Somerville Hastings, MS, FRCS.
1945 - 1946	Charles Robertson, Esq.
1946 - 1947	John Cliff, Esq.
1947 - 1948	The Lady Nathan, MA, JP.
1948 - 1949	Walter R. Owen, Esq.
1949 - 1952	John William Bowen, Esq., CBE, JP.
1952 - 1953	Edwyn Bayliss
1953 - 1953	Sir Arthur E. Middleton
1953 - 1954	Mrs. I. M. Bolton
1954 - 1955	Victor Misheon
1955 - 1956	Norman George Mollett Prichard
1956 - 1957	Helen C. Bentwich
1957 - 1958	Ronald McKinnon Wood
1958 - 1959	A. E. Samuels
1959 - 1960	Sidney J. Barton
1960 - 1961	Florence E Cayford
1961 - 1962	Harold H Shearman
1962 - 1963	Olive E G Deer
1963 - 1964	A Reginald
1964 - 1965	Lord Stoneham of Suffolk
1965 - 1974	Vacant /not recorded

Institute of Trading Standards Administration

1974 - 1983	The Rt Hon Lord Darling of Hillsbourough PC
1983 - 1986	The Rt Hon Lord Drumalbyn PC, KBE
1986 - 1994	The Rt Hon Lord Ezra
1994 - 1995	The Lord Gordon Borrie QC
1995 - 2006	The Baroness Wilcox

Trading Standards Institute

2005 - 2007	The Lord Garden KCB
2007 - 2009	Vacant
2009 to present	The Baroness Crawley

CHAIRMEN

British Association of Inspectors of Weights and Measures

1881 - 1882	Tom Wimhurst [Manchester]
1882 - 1883	James Johnson, (Salford)
1883 - 1884	E. Place, (Warrington)
1884 - 1885	E. Place, (Warrington)
1885 - 1893	Not recorded
1893 - 1895	J. E. Morris, (South Staffordshire)

Incorporated Society of Inspectors of Weights and Measures

1892 - 1898	Thomas Kyle, (Buckinghamshire C. C.)
1898 - 1900	J. A. Ridgeway, (Yorkshire East Riding)
1900 - 1902	G. F. Allwood, (Wolverhampton)
1902 - 1905	A. Granger, (Birmingham)
1905 - 1906	A. J. Street, (City of London)
1906 - 1908	C. MacDonald, (Glasgow)
1908 - 1910	Henry Wright, (Reading)
1910 - 1912	W. Crabtree, (Nottinghamshire)
1912 - 1914	Talbot Kyle, (Surrey)
1914 - 1918	G. W. Davis, (West Bromwich

1918 - 1920	S. Cooper, (Gateshead)
1920 - 1922	G. B. Cole, (Manchester)
1922 - 1924	J. Wright, (Berkshire)
1924 - 1926	A. H. Rutherford, (Leeds)
1926 - 1928	W. D. Laird, (Cheshire)
1928 - 1929	W. Kenyon, (Sheffield)
1929 - 1930	T. Latham, (Yorkshire)
1930 - 1931	W. Senior, (Edinburgh)
1931 - 1932	W. E. Allen, (Kent)
1932 - 1933	T. Allchin, (City of London)
1933 - 1934	A. W. H. Poole, (Bedfordshire)
1934 - 1935	J. W. Bache, (Durham)
1935 - 1936	E. Sloan, (Coventry)
1936 - 1937	T. H. Jenks, (Buckinghamshire)
1937 - 1938	R. Robertson, (Fife County)
1938 - 1940	G. A. Owen, (Smethwick)
1940 - 1942	E. Templeman, (Nottinghamshire)
1942 - 1944	A. S. Turier, (Somerset)
1944 - 1946	H. W. Speight, (Newcastle upon Tyne)
1946 - 1947	G. V. Sedgwick, (Yorkshire East Riding)
1947 - 1948	W. E. Edmunds, (City of London)
1948 - 1949	C. C. Young, (Stirling City)

Institute of Weights and Measures Administration

1949 - 1950	S. Strugnell, (Kent)
1950 - 1951	E. C. Mercer, (Wiltshire)
1951 - 1952	W. A. Ladds, (Blackpool)
1952 - 1953	R. G. White, (Coventry)
1953 - 1954	S. A. Wiggins, (London County Council)
1954 - 1955	W. Gray, (City of Leicester)
1955 - 1956	E. C. Writer, (Liverpool)
1956 - 1957	T. L. E. Gregory, (Nottinghamshire)
1957 - 1958	T. J. Metcalfe, (Smethwick)
1958 - 1959	K. R. C. Martin, (Cornwall)
1959 - 1960	A. A. Wallace, (Staffordshire)
1960 - 1961	J. Stewart, (Aberdeen)
1961 - 1962	H. Robinson, (Chester)
1962 - 1963	W. R. Breed, (Dorset)
1963 - 1964	L. M. Griffiths, (Westminster)
1964 - 1965	L. C. Porter, (Bootle)
1965 - 1966	J. R. Roberts, (Manchester)
1966 - 1967	J. A. Norris, (Chesterfield Borough)
1967 - 1968	F.W. Marston, (Somerset)
1968 - 1970	F. M. Bucknall, (Grimsby)
1970 - 1971	J. H. Routledge, (Durham)
1971 - 1972	G. Roberts, (Poole)

Institute of Trading Standards Administration

1972 - 1973	T. Cairns, (Glasgow)
1973 - 1974	D. W. Johnson, (Slough)
1974 - 1975	J. Beer, (Worcestershire)
1975 - 1976	W. K. Nattrass, (Cheshire)
1976 - 1977	F. J. Evans, M.B.E. (Northamptonshire)
1977 - 1978	L. K. James, (Mid-Glamorgan)
1978 - 1979	S. Gascoigne, (Sheffield)
1979 - 1980	J. Short, (Lothian)
1980 - 1981	E. L. F. Welch, (Hertfordshire)
1981 - 1982	E. C. Sandys, FITSA, (Devon)
1982 - 1983	A. P. Allen, FITSA, (East Sussex)
1983 - 1984	J. J. Corfield, (Southend on Sea)

184

1984 - 1985	R. J. Smith, (Humberside)
1985 - 1986	K. G. Shaw, (Buckinghamshire)
1986 - 1987	B. Dixon, (Kent)
1987 - 1988	C. W. Brudenell, (Humberside)
1988 - 1989	R.V. Wright, (Barnsley)
1989 - 1990	R. Gale, (Cumbria)
1990 - 1991	N. C. Hunter, (Warwickshire)
1991 - 1992	D. Hughes, (Hampshire)
1992 - 1993	J. M. Drewry, (Lothian Region)
1993 - 1994	A. P. Allen, FITSA (East Sussex)
1994 - 1995	G .Gresty, (North Yorkshire)
1995 - 1996	A.P. Northcott, (L. B. Haringey)
1996 - 1997	M. Wadsley, (Essex)
1997 - 1998	P. Galland, (Gloucestershire)
1998 - 1999	E. Robinson, (Edinburgh)
1999 - 2000	D. Sibbert, (Oxfordshire)

2000 - 2001	S. Delahaye, (Caerphilly County Borough)
2001 - 2002	E. R. Chicken, (Middlesbrough Borough Council)
2002 - 2003	M. Gibbons-Loveday, (Fife Council)
2003 - 2004	B. Aldridge, (City of London)
2004 - 2005	I. Warwick, (Dorset)
2005 - 2006	N. Strick, (Oxfordshire)
2006 - 2007	D. Roderick, (North Lanarkshire)
2007 - 2008	B. Lewin, (Northamptonshire)
2008 - 2009	P. Denard, (Surrey)
2009 - 2010	D. Sanders, (Vale of Glamorgan)
2010 - 2011	P. Heafield, (Lincolnshire)
2011 - 2012	L. Livermore, (Cambridgeshire)
2012 - 2013	C Heemskerk (Surrey)
2013 - 2014	J Peerless (Brighton and Hove)

CHAIRMEN AND REGISTRARS - COLLEGE OF FELLOWS

	Chairmen		**Registrars**
1951 - 1956	W A Ladds	1951-1955	E C Mercer
1957 - 1958	A S Turier	1956-1957	W Gray
1959 - 1965	H Robinson	1958-1968	G V Sedgewick
1966 - 1967	L M Griffiths	1969-1977	F S Milner
1967 - 1971	W Gray	1978-1983	J Beer
1972 - 1977	E C Writer	1984-1992	O W Barnes
1978 - 1985	G Roberts	1993-1999	J R Carroll
1986 - 1989	J Short	2000-2006	B Aldridge
1990 - 2002	J J Corfield	2007-present	P Bottomley
2003 - 2007	D Sibbert		
2008 - present	R V Wright		

HONORARY SECRETARIES

1881 - 1885	T Wimhurst, (Manchester)(d. 1885)
1885 - 1892	J. W. Robinson, (Manchester)
1892 - 1893	Mr. Massey
1893 - 1894	W. Crabtree (Nottinghamshire)

Incorporated Society of Inspectors of Weights and Measures

1891 - 1894	C.J. Martin, (Surrey C.C.)
1894 - 1899	Allan Granger, (Birmingham)
1899 - 1901	W. Crabtree, (Nottinghamshire)
1901 - 1908	H. Cunliffe, (Smethwick)
1908 - 1923	R. Robertson, (Hertfordshire)
1923 - 1926	George Alfred Owen, (Smethwick)
1926 - 1932	J. E. Sloan, (Coventry)
1933 - 1940	H. T. Fawkes, (West Bromwich)
1940 - 1941	A. C. Ashburner, (London C C)
1941 - 1945	J. W. Bache, (Co. Durham)
1945 - 1947	J. A. White, (Southport)
1947 - 1953	W. Gray, (Leicester)

Institute of Weights and Measures Administration

1953 - 1964	J. R. Roberts, (Manchester)
1965 - 1974	O. J. Barnes, (Cardiff)

Institute of Trading Standards Administration

1974 - 1974	L. G. Theobald, (Westminster)
1975 - 1978	J. Goldie Clark, (Southend-on-Sea)
1978 - 1983	H. Martin (Cambridgeshire)
1984 - 1989	R. Gale, (Cumbria)
1989 - 1999	A. Street (Nottinghamshire)
1999 - 2000	P. Bottomley (Hackney LB)

Trading Standards Institute

2000 - 2010	C. L. Armstrong (consultant)
2010 - 2013	N. Warren (Director TSI)
2013 to present	R. C. Martin (Director TSI)

EDITORS OF THE JOURNAL

Incorporated Society of Inspectors of Weights and Measures

1892 - 1893	F. Cliffe, (Surrey)
1894 - 1898	J. P. Stubbs, (London County Council)
1898 - 1900	C. McDonald, (Glasgow)
1900 - 1901	R. MacKinnon, (Govan)
1901 - 1929	H.C. Smith, (Hastings)
1929 - 1938	G. A. Owen, (Smethwick)
1938 - 1940	A. C. Ashburner, (London C C)
1940 - 1941	L. M. Griffiths, (London C C)
1941 - 1949	E. C. Writer, (Liverpool)

Institute of Weights and Measures Administration

1949 - 1959	L. M. Griffiths, (London C C)
1959 - 1967	J. T. Graham, (Stockport)
1967 - 1975	D. W. Johnson, (Slough & Manchester)

Institute of Trading Standards Administration

1975 - 1979	R. Manley, (Warwickshire)
1979 - 1984	K. G. Shaw, (Buckinghamshire)
1984 - 1986	A. J. Street, (Greater Manchester)
1986 - 1990	H. Holding, (Birmingham)
1990 - 1999	A.J. Street, (Nottinghamshire)
1999 - 2000	A. Northcott (Haringey LB)

2000 - 2010   A. Northcott (Haringey LB)
2010 - present   S. Kuyser (Service Director TSI)

TITLES OF THE MONTHLY MAGAZINES

1881 to 1893   The Record of the British Association
1892 to 1986   The Monthly Review of Incorporated Society
1987 to 1987   Fair Trader
1988 to 2001   The Trading Standards Review
2001   TS Today

TREASURERS and FINANCE DIRECTORS

British Association of Inspectors of Weights and Measures
1881 - 1892   W. H. Hopkins, (Henry Pooley and Sons)

Incorporated Society of Inspectors of Weights and Measures
1892 - 1894   T.H. Morgan, (Kent)
1894 - 1897   J. Webb, (London)
1897 - 1898   J. A. Ridgway, (Yorkshire: East Riding)
1898 - 1918   O. J. Kirby, (Batley)
1918 - 1930   T. Kyle, (Surrey)
1930 - 1943   G. B. Cole, (Manchester)
1943 - 1949   E. C. Mercer, (Wiltshire)

Institute of Weights and Measures Administration
1949 - 1955   T. L. E. Gregory, (Nottinghamshire)
1955 - 1967   F. S. Milner, (Wolverhampton)
1967 - 1973   W. B. Adams, (Swindon)

Institute of Trading Standards Administration
1973 - 1977   B. F. Wrighton, (City of London)
1977 - 1990   J. R. Carroll (Newham LB)
1991 - 2001   P. Bottomley, (L.B. Hackney)

Trading Standards Institute
2001 - 2008   J. Evans, Treasurer (Hounslow)
2001 - 2009   P. Bottomley (Finance Manager/Director)
2009 - 2013   N. Warren (Finance Director)
2013 to present R. C. Martin (Finance Director)

CHIEF EXECUTIVES

Institute of Trading Standards Administration
Apr 1993 - Apr 1999   A.J. Street
May 1999 - Aug 2001   A. Charlesworth

Trading Standards Institute
Jan 2002 - Mar 2013   R. F. Gainsford
Apr 2013 to present   L. Livermore

187

APPENDIX THREE

Honours awarded to Members and Vice-Presidents

Members

Paul Allen, OBE, 1997, Chief Trading Standards Officer, East Sussex

Peter Astley, MBE, 2011, Head of Public Protection, Warrington/Halton

Brian Beckett, OBE, Chief Trading Standards Officer, Avon

Ann Beer, MBE, 2010, Staffordshire

Barrington Bezant, MBE, 1984, Chief Consumer Protection, W Glamorgan.

D W S Brown, MBE, 1935, Jedburgh Council

Frank Bucknall, MBE, 1972, Chief Inspector of Grimsby

Frederick Bullions, MBE, 2006, Senior Technical Officer, Hampshire CC.

Beverley Burns, MBE, 2012, Northern Ireland Trading Standards Service

Bill Cassie, MBE, Head of Consumer Protection, Aberdeenshire Council.

H E Chapman, Major, OBE, 1920, Deputy Chief Constable and Chief WM Insp Kent

William Cormack, OBE, Chief Constable and Chief WM Insp Caithness

Christopher P. Denard, MBE, 2011, Head of Trading Standards, Surrey C C

Frank Evans, MBE, 1974, Chief Inspector of Northamptonshire CC

Terry Everett, MBE, 2008, TSO at Thurrock

Ronald Gainsford, OBE, 2010, Chief Executive Trading Standards Institute

Robert Gale, OBE, 1998, Cumbria, ITSA Honorary Secretary

J W Georgeson, OBE, 1963, Chief Constable and Chief WM Inspector Caithness

William Gray, MBE, 1956, Chief Insp Leicester CC, IWMA Secretary

Tom Gregory, MBE, 1969, Nottinghamshire CC

Edward Holmes, OBE, Chief Constable and Chief WM Inspector Leicestershire CC

James K Humble, OBE, 1996, Chief Executive, LACOTS

Noel Hunter, OBE, 2002, Director Libraries, Heritage, Trading Standards Warwickshire

Fullerton James Capt. CBE, OBE, Chief Constable/ Chief WM Insp. Northumberland

T H Jenks, MBE, 1941, Chief WM Inspector Buckinghamshire CC

David W Johnson, MBE, 1980, Greater Manchester, Editor Monthly Review

Jacqui Kennedy, OBE, 2009, Director Birmingham Regulatory Services

Bryan Lewin, MBE, 2010, Chief Trading Standards Officer, Northamptonshire CC

T.W. Lowes, OBE, Newcastle, 1921, Food Department during the War

John B. Mair, MVO, OBE, 1920 Chief Constable and Chief WM Inspector Morayshire

Roger Manley, OBE, 1994, Chief TSO Cheshire CC

A G Martin, OBE, Chief Constable and Chief WM Inspector Gravesend

Robin Middleton, CBE, 2008, Secretary of State's Representative for Marine Salvage.

Kenneth Nattrass, MBE, 1976, Cheshire CC

John A O'Keefe, OBE, 1959, Chief WM Officer Middlesex CC

Henry Palmer, MBE, 1957, Senior Inspector, London County Council

Davinder Pangli, MBE, 2006, Head, Consumer Advice Unit, Warwickshire CC

Nichola Louise Pasek, MBE, 2010, Cambridgeshire. ' Ask Cedric'

David Reed, MBE, 1977, Director of Consumer Protection, Fife Regional Council

R A Richey MBE, 1963, Council Member for Northern Ireland

Mary Risso, MBE, JP, 2011, Director Office of Consumer Affairs, Gibraltar

J. Reg. Roberts, MBE, 1965, Chief Inspector of Manchester City Council

Peter S. Roberts, MBE, 1988, Director of Trading Standards – Leicestershire CC

James R Robertson, OBE, 1938, Chief Inspector of Weights and Measures, Glasgow

Graham J Russell, MBE, 2011, Chief Executive, Local Better Regulation Office

Christine Wade, MBE, 2002, Chief TSO, Essex CC

S A Walker, MBE, 1958, Chief Inspector Weights and Measures, Ayr County

Reginald John Wilkinson, OBE, 1943, City of London Weights and Measures

Martin Woodley, MBE, 2011, Oxfordshire CC

Vice Presidents

Sidney I Dennett, OBE, JP, Vice President, Chair of SWPC/SWPE Dorset

Shashikant D.i Dholakia, MBE, 2005, TSO and Councillor, Wellingborough BC

W. Emerson, OBE, 1994, TSI Vice President and Councillor

Alma Williams, OBE, 2003, TSI Vice President

APPENDIX FOUR

In memory of Institute Members who gave their lives on active service

The First World War

James William BLACK, d. 28th April 1915, age 31 – Inspector of Weights and Measures, Edinburgh. Private, Royal Scots. 5th Battalion.

Horace Milton BUDDERY, d. 18th August 1917, age 29 – Inspector of Weights and Measures, Yarmouth. Private, Manchester Regiment, 2nd/6th Battalion

William M. FINDLAY, d. 25th September 1915, age 33. Inspector of Weights and Measures, East Riding of Yorkshire. Private, Gordon Highlanders, 8th Battalion.

James GLEN, d. 20th April 1917, age 29 - Inspector of Weights and Measures, Glasgow. Sergeant, Royal Army Medical Corps, 1st/1st Lowland Field Ambulance.

Thomas Michael KETTLE, d. 9th September 1916, age 36 - Professor of Economics Dublin. Vice President of Incorporated Society. Lieutenant, 9th Royal Dublin Fusiliers.

Sinclair Munroe MACKAY, d. 2nd July 1916, age 33 - Inspector of Weights and Measures, Lancashire, (Bolton). Co. Sgt. Major, The Loyal North Lancashire Regiment, 10th Battalion.

Arthur ORMEROD, d. 20th September 1917, age 33 - Inspector of Weights and Measures, Buckinghamshire. Lance Corporal, Wiltshire Regiment, 6th Battalion.

John Wells WELFARE, d. 19th October 1917, age 30 - Inspector of Weights and Measures, Burnley. Gunner, Royal Garrison Artillery, 115th Siege Battery.

The Second World War

Alan Charles ASHBURNER, d. 11th. May 1941, age 38 - Inspector of Weights and Measures, County of London. Civilian, Secretary Society of Inspectors of Weights and Measures.

Will AVISON, d. 2nd November 1943, age 39 - Inspector of Weights and Measures, County of Huntingdon. Lieutenant, RNVR, H.M.S. Hannibal.

Leonard Samuel BARKER, d. 28th February 1942, age 27 - Inspector of Weights and Measures, County of Hampshire. Sergeant, (W.Op/Obs), RAFVR, 255 Squadron.

Herbert Ernest BLACK, d. 9th November 1940, age26 - Inspector of Weights and Measures, County of Leicester. Sergeant (pilot), RAFVR, 46 Squadron.

Herbert Denham BROTHERIDGE, d. 6th June 1944, age 29 - Inspector of Weights and Measures, Buckinghamshire. Lieutenant, Oxfordshire and BucksLight Infantry, 2nd (Airborne)

Thomas Maughan CARTER, d. 2nd June 1942, age 28 - Inspector of Weights and Measures, City of Newcastle-upon-Tyne. Pilot Officer (Obs), RAFVR, 102 Squadron.

Ernest James FLETCHER, d. 26th December 1944, age 28 - Inspector of Weights and Measures, West Riding of Yorkshire. Flying Officer, RAFVR, 235 Squadron.

Thomas NAYLOR, d. 18th October 1944, age 32 - Inspector of Weights and Measures, West Riding of Yorkshire. Aircraftman 1st Class, RAFVR.

Walter PHILLIPSON, d. 1st November 1943 - Inspector of Weights and Measures, County of Middlesex. Private, RAOC.

Eric Leonard STOODLEY, d. 13th May 1941 - Inspector of Weights and Measures, County of Essex. Sergeant, RAFVR, 234 Squadron.

Edmund Fitzwalter TURTON, d. 6th December 1942 - Inspector of Weights and Measures, City of Sheffield. Sergeant, RAFVR

Arthur Wilfred WATKINS, d. 15th December 1941, age 25 - Inspector of Weights and Measures, City of Canterbury. Lance Corporal, The Buffs (1st Royal East Kent Regiment)

Ronald WILDMAN, d. 21st December 1941, age 28 - Inspector of Weights and Measures, County Borough of Barnsley. Ordinary Coder, R.N, H.M.S. Audacity.

Ralph Edward WILSHIRE, d. 15th August 1941, age 24 - Inspector of Weights and Measures, Huntingdonshire. 2nd Lieutenant, Bedfordshire and Herts, 70th Battalion.

John Philip WINFIELD, d. 25th October 1942, age 27 - Inspector of Weights and Measures, City of Sheffield. Squadron Leader, RAFVR, 151 Squadron and No. 1 RAF Depot, Uxbridge.

Ernest WALTERS, d. 14th August 1944, age 31 - Inspector of Weights and Measures, County of Surrey. Lieutenant, Royal Armoured Corps,141st (7th Bn. The Buffs [Royal E. Kent Reg.]

APPENDIX FIVE

Sources & General History

Sources

The periodicals of the Institute under various names including –
The Record, 1881 to 1893, (some copies not seen), British Association of WM Inspectors
The Monthly Review (monthly except in wartime), 1893 to 1949, Incorporated Society WM
The Monthly Review (monthly), 1950 to 1971, Institute of Weights and Measures Admin.
The Monthly Review (monthly), 1972 to 1986, Institute of Weights and Measures Admin.
Fair Trader (monthly), 1987, Institute of Weights and Measures Administration
Trading Standards Review (monthly), 1988 to 2000, Institute of Weights and Measures
Trading Standards Review (monthly), 2001, Trading Standards Institute
TS Today (monthly), 2002 to 2012, Trading Standards Institute
Confidential Bulletins, Graffito and Communiqué,

Minutes of Institute meetings
Conference Reports of the Institute
Occasional Papers of the Institute
Website of TSI including "Members Only" material

General History

Airy, Wilfrid on Weighing Apparatus Institution of Engineers 1891

Cook, Chris & Stevenson, John, Modern British History

Moor, Nigel, The Look & Shape of England, 2010

Borrie, Gordon and Diamond, Aubrey, Consumer, Society and the Law, Penguin, 1968

Booker and North, Castle of Lies Duckworth and Co 1996

Brauer, E, Construction of the Balance, 1909

Breed, W Roger, Weights and Measures Act 1963, Chas Knight

Butterworths Law of Food and Drugs, 2011

Butterworths Stone's Justices' Manual, 2012

Butterworths Trading and Consumer Law, 2011

Cairns, Warwick, About the Size of It

Goode, Roy, Editor, Consumer Credit Law and Practice, Butterworths

Graham, John, Scales and Balances, Guide to Collection, Shire Publications, 1981

Graham, John Thomas and Stevenson Weights and Measures, Shire Books

Gresty and Rowell, Sweet and Maxwell Practical Food Law, edit **Philpott and Pickering**

Grice, Robert, Metrological Miscellanea and Muddle, TSI, 2010

Humble Jim, A Grandad's Life Cockasnook Books 2008

Institute, Inspector of Weights and Measures Handbook, Institute, Various dates

Johnson and Stevenson Centenary Review, ITSA, 1981

McGreevy, Thomas, Basis of Measurement Volume 1, Historical Aspects

McCance, Robert A and Widdowson, Elsie M, Chemical Composition of Foods, HMS

Mawrey and Riley-Smith, Butterworths Commercial and Consumer Law Handbook, 2011

Mitchell Jeremy, Marketing and the Consumer McGraw Hill 1978

O'Keefe, John Alfred, Weights and Measures Act 1963, Butterworths, 2011

Owen George , Law Relating to Weights and Measures, Chas Griffin, 1930

Philpott, Tom and Pickering, David, Sweet and Maxwell Practical Food Law

Poole A W H, Owen's Law Relating to Weights and Measures, Chas Griffin, 1948

Porter, L C, 75 Years History (of the Institute), IWMA, 1969

Rhodes Gerald, Central-Local Relationships RIPA 1986

Rhodes Gerald, Trading Standards and Uniformity RIPA 1986

Rush, Philip and O'Keeffe, on Weights and Measures

Treatise on Measuring Equipment, Institute

Treatise on Weighing Machines, Institute

Trollope Anthony, The Three Clerks, Oxford University Press 1858

Turner, ES, Shocking History of Advertising, Penguin Books, 1965

Trading Standards publications and CD-rom in the TSI Library
Legislation published by the Government
Reports and White Papers published by the Government
Other Websites - too numerous to name

INDEX

194